THE STORY OF
DUDLEY

THE STORY OF
DUDLEY

EDWARD CHITHAM

The
History
Press

First published 2014

The History Press
The Mill, Brimscombe Port
Stroud, Gloucestershire, GL5 2QG
www.thehistorypress.co.uk

British Library Cataloguing in Publication Data.
A catalogue record for this book is available from the British Library.

ISBN 978 0 7509 5569 0

Typesetting and origination by The History Press
Printed in Great Britain

CONTENTS

INTRODUCTION AND ACKNOWLEDGEMENTS

Anyone working on the history of Dudley is aware of the great deal of work previously done by historians of all kinds. Early commentators, such as Payton and Twamley, concentrated on the castle, while Clark recorded nineteenth-century politics. Arthur Rollason collected data which he published in the *Dudley Herald*. E.Blocksidge, the Dudley printer, collected details about the castle and town. In the twentieth century J.S. Roper lightened the load of research with his enormous energy in transcribing documents, and in the transcript series published by the borough he sketched out the story of Dudley from the Middle Ages to the eighteenth century. In the mid-twentieth century Batsford published a volume by Chandler and Hannah, with chronological tables. The book is enhanced with drawings by Mrs Hannah. The authors relied on material in the town library, much of which is now in Dudley Archives.

More recently, archaeologist John Hemingway has produced his trilogy of books on Dudley history, expertly illustrated and containing much primary material in transcription. He has unearthed a great deal of evidence, and I am indebted to many leads he has given in tracing books and documents. Trevor Raybould has concentrated on the development of mining, and the history of the grammar school. Mention must also be made of the splendid research by Jason Ellis on glassmaking. Ned Williams has produced a fine series of books on Dudley, and I am extremely grateful to him for permission to use some of his information which has been gathered meticulously. I owe considerable debt to all these sources and more, which will be acknowledged in the notes and bibliography.

Thanks must be extended to the friendly and efficient staff at Dudley Archives, whose collection is first rate and includes much material from the Dudley Lordship. I also wish to thank the staff at Worcester Record Office and Worcester History Centre for their efficiency and helpfulness. There are many deeds and other documents in Worcester, with useful microfilm copies, which will be detailed in the bibliography. As always, staff at Birmingham Reference Library have responded to my frequent requests. Thanks are also due to staff at the William Salt Library at Stafford.

Details of picture sources are at the end of the book.

one

PREHISTORY AND EARLY HISTORY

Saxons and Normans

The modern Metropolitan Borough of Dudley embraces the old parishes of Kingswinford, Oldswinford, much of Halesowen, large parts of Sedgley and fragments of other parishes, but at its heart is the old manor of Dudley (including the district of Netherton, arguably at one time a manor or sub-manor), with its two old parish churches of St Edmund and St Thomas. This was a borough in the thirteenth century, and it is this core Dudley with which we shall be concerned. Any view of Dudley town is dominated by the medieval castle, yet amazingly this ancient building and the hill on which it stands were not even in the same county as the rest of the town, being historically (so far as we have documentation) in the parish of Sedgley in Staffordshire, while the rest of Dudley was in Worcestershire. Castle Hill was a Staffordshire peninsula protruding into Worcestershire, but Dudley itself is an island of Worcestershire protruding into Staffordshire. These confusing boundaries will not be totally observed in this book, and we shall cross them occasionally in mentioning Wren's Nest (actually in Sedgley) and Pensnett Chase (divided between the two counties, to the confusion of at least one late map maker).

The old manor of Dudley, including Netherton, was bounded on the north-east by Tipton, itself part of the super-manor of Longdon; on the east by Rowley, divided into Regis and Somery; the wild area of Pensnett Chase, stretching in an arc from the south of Netherton to Barrow Hill (Kingswinford parish) and Holly Hall; and Sedgley to the north, which parish included fringe areas of land that was geographically part of Dudley, and was sometimes in contention with Dudley over these areas. The boundary on the north-east, east and south was marked by watercourses, but on the south-west could be more easily blurred. These brooks are often unnamed in documents, but the north-western one is sometimes Holbeache, the north-eastern one Stockwell, while the brook dividing Pensnett Chase (Dudley portion) from Rowley parish is mysteriously

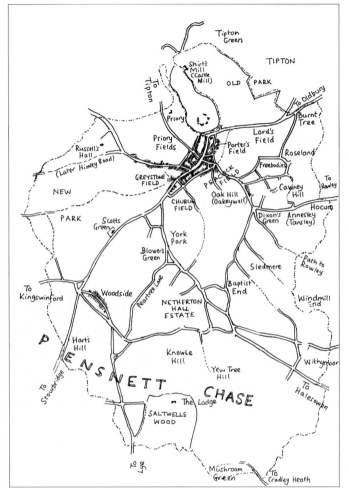

Left 1 Outline map of the parish and manor of Dudley

Below 2 Dudley MBC flyer: 'The Wren's Nest'

The Geology of the
WREN'S NEST
National Nature Reserve

Dudley
www.dudley.gov.uk

called Mousesweet at times, though also more simply the Bourne brook. These boundary brooks are by now insignificant, mostly mere runnels behind houses or factories, or even piped underground.

There is no doubt that Dudley boundaries, which probably date from about the tenth century, relate to different tribes claiming possession of tracts of land. Worcestershire was part of the lands of the Hwicce, with a principal settlement at Worcester, eventually defined and sanctified as a diocese. These men were racially Saxons, whereas the Staffordshire parishes were developed by men who are thought to be Angles and whose chief towns were Tamworth and Lichfield. Dudley, so far from the sea, and with its unproductive land, forms part of an area developed late, cut off from centres of civilisation by the wild waste of

3 The view westwards from Cawney Hill.

4 A steep pathway down Cawney Hill.

Pensnett Chase. But unknown to its early inhabitants, the ground beneath their feet held potential riches in the shape of minerals – coal, ironstone and limestone – which would one day make their descendants rich, but the countryside polluted. Today, little sign of mining remains, but there is still plenty of industry and a flourishing town, out of which the castle on its high hill rises anomalously. Both Castle Hill and Cawney Hill, the two separated by a valley, provide views for many miles over the countryside, and it is surprising that no Iron Age activity has been found on either of them. Cawney Hill, at least, has never attracted the archaeologists, so such habitation cannot be ruled in or out.

Prehistory of Dudley

Just outside the area which would one day become Dudley, 300 million years before these early inhabitants began to clear the forests, the sea covered

Wren's Nest, eventually causing fossils to be created in the limestone: these sea creatures, called trilobites, made Wren's Nest famous. There were hundreds of species of these corals and gastropods, but they remained unrecognised until the seventeenth-century author Dr Robert Plot, keeper of the Ashmolean Museum at Oxford, mentioned them in his book *The Natural History of Staffordshire* in 1686.[1] Similar fossils were found in the limestone caverns under Castle Hill, and a different kind of fossil occurs in coal measures, set down some 100 million years after the sea creatures lived. These geological phenomena were exploited in the mid-nineteenth century, after the visit of the Duc de Bordeaux in 1844 was featured in the *London Illustrated News*.

Early Topography

Dudley has no Anglo-Saxon charters and the early historical period has left little record except changes to the landscape and place names. Early eleventh-century Dudley was owned by an Anglo-Saxon lord called Earl Edwin. We know nothing further for certain about this landowner, and his land was confiscated after the Norman Conquest. At this time, Dudley was a village rather than a town, a state in which it would remain until the foundation of the borough by Roger de Somery III, apparently in the 1260s. Despite our lack of knowledge about this period, some clues from later times help us to reconstruct the nature of the manor which Earl Edwin owned and the barons descended from FitzAnsculf could survey from their castle on Castle Hill. (It is worth mentioning that Sedgley, where Dudley Castle was to be built, was owned by Leofric, a Mercian lord whose wife is the much more famous Godiva of Coventry.)

At this time, Coventry was the principal town in the West Midlands, and several Coventry residents owned land in Dudley during medieval times. In a rent roll of 1541 the Throckmorton family are in possession of a messuage (house) named 'ye Hall-house', and with this we may link the very ancient name of Hall Street (sometimes Hall Lane).[2] The hall can be located where eventually the Phoenix glassworks stood, approximately at the south side of the present junction of Trindle Road, Hall Street and King Street. Near this for many years was the pinfold or pound, where stray animals would be kept until their owners could fetch them after paying a fine. In the dip in the road to the south was Waddams Pool, located just where we might expect a medieval fishpond to be. An ancient track, frequently referred to in court rolls, ran from the south side of the glassworks (which were not built until the eighteenth century) to what is now Birmingham Road through the Lord's Fields. This track crosses Hall Street and becomes what we now know as King Street.

Hall Street, still without any known name, divided just beyond this point, with one branch continuing through present-day Churchill Precinct, becoming New Street and leading past the priory (which was still to be built at the period we are considering) and forming the route to Tipton by means of a low-lying, muddy valley. The other branch was long known as Back Lane but is now King Street. This turns north near St Thomas' Church and leads to Wolverhampton. Very slight traces of this route remained on maps until it eventually became Stafford Street. In the other direction, Hall Street was part of an ancient track, even to this day known further east as Portway. This old market road provided a route via Dixon's Green, across the hills to Whiteheath and Rowley, eventually to Birmingham (probably to Coventry). It can be seen that the likely site of the medieval Hall House was the centre of the system of tracks, and that this area, with St Edmund's Church, formed the nucleus of the village which must have existed before the foundation of the borough.

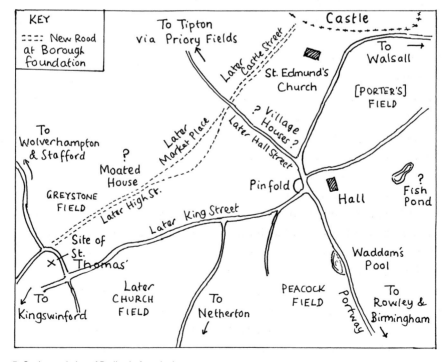

5 Conjectural plan of Dudley before the burgages.

There is one more interesting point which may support this suggestion. Between what is now Priory Street (earlier called Sheep Fair and The Horsepool) and modern High Street, the eighteenth century recognised as Moat Close. This can only mean that a moated house occupied a position between The Horsepool (on the site of the former 58 trolley-bus terminus) and what is now High Street. Once the market had arrived, with the burgages lining it and its extension beyond Stoney Lane (Stone Street), there would have been no room for a moated house. The moated house must have been part of 'village Dudley' before the present High Street was driven through fields from the castle to Queens Cross.

No doubt this small village already had its open field system. One of the fields must have been Porters Field, which in one late document is written as Potters Field, suggesting a possibility that this may have been where the local ceramicists obtained their clay. Pottery making was very necessary in medieval times, but was a considerable fire risk and was often banished to the edge of settlements, as it was in this instance. To the south of the old manor was a field which later appears in documents as Peaks Field; this seems to be a name later extended to Peacocks. We have no written evidence about whether there was another field to the north, but the matter will recur when we deal with the foundation of the borough. The manorial mill was presumably the one which eventually became Castle Mill, reached by the track already mentioned which led to Tipton. If these geographical suggestions are correct the site of the present market place may well have been part of the open field eventually called Greystone, or land attached to the moated house already mentioned. All these features existed before the lords of Dudley Castle laid out their planned borough.

Dudley is built on a ridge, which caused a difficulty: water supplies, though not far away, were meagre, and this was to prove a severe hazard in later times. What sufficed for a small village was little use to a developing industrial town. In the Middle Ages, watercourses flowed to the south of what became King Street and through fields towards Netherton, while on the other side of the ridge, a few hundred

6 Greystone Street preserves the name of the northern open field.

yards away, small streams ran down towards the present Birmingham Road, where there was another moated house, then across a rabbit warren towards Tipton. This water would eventually reach the North Sea via the Tame and Trent, while the water from the south-west of the Dudley ridge ended up in the Severn. There were wells dotted throughout the early settlement, but not nearly enough to supply the large town that would eventually grow here.

St Edmund's Church

We can be sure of only one building being erected in Anglo-Saxon Dudley: the church of St Edmund, King and Martyr. This was not, of course, the present-day brick building, and we have no exact knowledge of the appearance of the first church – it may well have been wooden.

St Edmund was an East Anglian saint, connected with Bury St Edmund's, but there were a few dedications to him in the rest of England, notably at Exeter. After the Norman Conquest, dedications to St Edmund ceased. Very shortly, the dynasty of William I would bring a governing elite of Norman nobles to England, including one Ansculf and his son, William Fitz-Ansculf, to Dudley.

Dudley in Norman Times

The Domesday Survey, written in 1086, tells us that after Earl Edwin, William Fitz-Ansculf holds 'Dudley, and there is his castle'. As he also held Sedgley, there could be no hindrance to his founding Dudley Castle in the next parish and county. During the previous twenty years, a motte was built overlooking St Edmund's Church. This was an enormous mound of earth, excavated from surrounding fields by Anglo-Saxon labour, and it was on this that Dudley's earliest castle was built. The mound still exists, with all later castle buildings being set on it also. No record of the nature of the first buildings has survived, though later Normans built with stone and some of their work does remain. The earliest parts of Fitz-Ansculf's building could have been constructed of wood, and there are marks of walls within the bailey (the courtyard adjoining the motte, also marked out and fortified during Fitz-Ansculf's rule) which have not been excavated.

Fitz-Ansculf's baronial territory stretched through vast tracts of the Midlands; he also held other swathes in Buckinghamshire, Berkshire and beyond.

The whole group of manors was called 'The Barony of Dudley'.[3] These links across many parishes, even to the home counties, became important when subsequent lords decided to make Dudley into a town. It is at this point where a glimpse of Fitz-Ansculf's character comes to light: he was in dispute over the manor of Selly (also called Weoley), and this manor was bought before 1066 by one Wulfwin, a Saxon lord. On his deathbed, Wulfwin wished to pass the manor to his wife, and after her death back to the church. Anyone who tried to take it should be excommunicated. Fitz-Ansculf didn't care, and took it.

The family of Ansculf originated in Picquigny near Amiens, and were not therefore true Normans but Picards. It is said that the name Picquigny was a test word for Anglo-Saxons, because they could not pronounce it, and this was still the case up to the sixteenth century. Historians are not sure why the next generation to hold Dudley Castle and manor were the Paganels (variously spelt); it is thought possible that Fulke Paganel married a daughter of Fitz-Ansculf, but there is no precise record that he even had a daughter. Fulke held all Fitz-Ansculf's former possessions, including Newport Pagnell in Buckinghamshire.

The Domesday Book further states that Dudley had one hide, and in demesne one carucate, and there were three villeins, ten bordars and one smith with three carucates. There were two bondmen and two miles of woodland. Both hide and carucate are measurements of ploughland, while bordars are small farmers of land on the periphery of the estate. It is quite impossible to locate any of these features in eleventh-century Dudley, and hard to guess exactly which woodlands are meant. Within the next centuries many trees, especially oaks, were cut down for building within the area, but these were all from Pensnett Chase or, as it is more frequently known, Penniak (though this description includes Woodside, much of Netherton and Dudley Wood).

Either Fulke or possibly his son Ralph is thought to be responsible for rebuilding Dudley Castle in stone. Norman work remains in the gateway, with the inner and outer arches both exhibiting architecture recognisable as Norman.[4] An arch of Norman type in the buttery has been partially unblocked. It is clear, however, that Dudley never had a square donjon tower like a number of other Norman castles. After 1106, castles were being demolished rather than reinforced, and we must therefore guess that the new building at Dudley came twenty or so years later, when civil war engulfed England and parts of France. In 1138 the castle was besieged by an army of King Stephen, against a garrison holding it for Empress Matilda. By this time Ralph Paganel had married a daughter of Earl Ferrars of Tutbury and succeeded his father. The siege failed, which suggests that the gateway and other fortifications not now remaining had been built by Ralph as he saw wartime returning. A later document states that Ralph also wished to found a monastery, but did not live long enough. This pious task was left to his son, Gervase.

Dudley Priory

The precise date of the foundation of Dudley Priory is not known, but is thought to be in the 1150s, certainly no later than 1160. The priory site is low-lying, well watered by streams which rise on the north side of the ridge, near what is now Dudley town centre. These were needed both to provide a source of water for cooking, washing and sanitation, but also to dam for a moat and fishpond. An area round the priory site, as well as a tranche of other lands away from Dudley, was given to the monks by Paganel. It is clear that this Cluniac foundation depended on St Milburga's at Much Wenlock (though not necessarily from its beginning), and the endowment included the churches at Sedgley and Northfield, as well as other churches far from the Midlands. Both Sedgley and Northfield were to have close relations with Dudley in the future; a main road out of Netherton is still called Northfield Road. Most importantly, the priory, dedicated to St James, was also given the churches of St Edmund's and newly founded St Thomas', in 1182. At some point Wombourne was added

7 General view of the priory from the south in the 1950s

to the endowment, with its chapel at Trysull, also including Seisdon. There was also a not very clear link with Sandwell Priory, which was founded at about the same time. Sandwell Priory continued to hold land in Dudley until 1526.[5]

Gervase Paganel reaped the reward of his father's support of Matilda. Her son Henry, who was later to become King Henry II, visited Dudley Castle in 1153–4, the year before his coronation. Among his actions there was the signing of a deed, describing him as Duke of Normandy and Aquitaine and Earl of Anjou, and granting to the church of Wolverhampton the same liberty that was held in the time of his grandfather, King Henry I. Gervase Paganel signed the deed as one of the witnesses. There is so little left of the Norman parts of the castle that we cannot know what Henry saw as he looked round the rebuilt bailey, but in any case it did not last long. Gervase eventually turned against Henry, joining his rebel sons, and twenty years after Henry's visit, by royal edict the castle was slighted, that is demolished, apparently to the ground. Weeds, bushes and rubble remained on the desolate site for almost 100 years.

St Thomas' Church

The next part of the story is conjecture, based on a suggestion by I.C. Hannah.[6]

Dudley's 'Top Church', St Thomas', is dedicated to St Thomas Becket, who was murdered (some would say in mysterious circumstances) on 29 December 1170. He was recognised as a saint in 1173, the year of the rebellion against King Henry II. Gervase Paganel's castle was torn stone from stone in retaliation for his support of the revolt. Almost immediately after this a new church was dedicated to St Thomas at the opposite end of the village, its tower clearly visible from the castle motte and perhaps even built of stone from the castle. Unfortunately there is now very little trace of this medieval building. On payment of a large fine (500 marks), Gervase was restored to favour by the king. St Thomas' may have been so called in defiance of the king, but despite this it can probably be seen as a

8 St Thomas's Church – 'Top church'.

9 Old St Thomas's Church from the south.

thank you offering for Gervase's restoration. The king later endowed Dudley
Priory with the two churches of St Edmund and St Thomas, the precedence of
St Edmund being shown by this word order.

There was confirmation of the status and possessions of Dudley Priory in
1182, when the pope produced a document naming 'the church of St James',
with its 'chapels', St Edmund and St Thomas, as owner of churches in
Northfield, Cofton Hackett (also called Coston), Wombourne and other
places. He provided for the monks to bury their dead in the priory grounds,
and the use of a chapel bell is mentioned. However, St Edmund and St Thomas
were not 'chapels', they were parish churches, operating separate parishes with
their own churchwardens and geographical areas, though only one vicar, before
1646. How exactly such an arrangement came about is unknown, and it is possible that it was not originally the case, but it seems the Vatican authorities
made a mistake in calling the two churches 'chapels'.

Layout of the Priory

Some parts of the original twelfth-century priory buildings still remain: the footings of the apsidal chancel and the lower part of a pillar, between the apse and the south transept, with other small fragments.[7] A Norman tympanum was discovered in excavations, depicting St Michael fighting a dragon. It is hard to know which doorway it was placed over. In Cluniac fashion, there were two other apses, one in the south and one in the north transept. Nothing remains above ground of the southern apse. As at Sandwell Priory, the living and administrative quarters were on the north side of the church. It is not clear why this was so, though at both places there may have been problems of flooding. Part of this range may have been built in the twelfth century, but the church was certainly not finished at this time.

The quarrels between King Henry II and his sons prevented him from joining the crusade to the east, and by 1189, worn out, he died. Gervase Paganel attended the coronation of his successor, King Richard I, but also died soon after this (probably in 1194), leaving no heir. Gervase's sister Hawise had married John de Somery, a baron with family in East Anglia. On the death of Gervase, her son Ralph paid to inherit the Dudley lands. It is doubtful whether these events had much effect in Dudley, though in the course of time the de Somery family would change the place for ever. During all this time the castle ruins mouldered, and the manor was in the hands of a steward.

At the priory there was more building in the late twelfth century, extending the church (north wall), and early in the thirteenth century the administrative buildings continuing the line of the north transept were extended. This work seems to have progressed, with more work on the nave of the church and the west side of the cloister during the next decades. The west door of the priory church, still standing, dates from this period, and above the door can be seen triangular stonework which seems to indicate a porch later removed. The west window as currently visible replaced higher windows, perhaps typical thirteenth-century lancets.

There is no record of the number of monks at Dudley during this period. It seems that there were never many, perhaps generally about four, with support from laypeople. How they affected the economy of the area is conjecture. They seem to have organised the rural husbandry of the priory lands, stretching from the edge of modern Wolverhampton Street to the ruined castle, and from the priory buildings to the brook dividing Dudley from Sedgley. The lay workers may have been chosen from among the villagers, but there is no proof of this. The continuing development of the priory buildings would mean that local quarries (perhaps very local) required men to mine the limestone, a trade that would last for centuries.

There was a dispute in the 1230s which led to a prior being excommunicated. The argument involved jurisdiction over the priory and its possessions, and turned on the question of whether the Cluniac priory was extra-diocesan or not. Both the Bishop of Worcester and the Cluniac order apparently claimed authority over the priory. This was, in general, a Cluniac principle, to retain very tight control over the daughter monasteries. We have little clue as to the exact settlement, but the current prior was excommunicated in 1237 after a decision was made in favour of the bishop. The extension and rebuilding of the priory continued, resulting in the currently visible south wall of the church and some work in the southern apse which was later refaced. Finances for this expansion presumably came from the priory's land in Dudley and part of the tithes of the priory's possessions in Sedgley, Wombourne and Northfield.

Thirteenth-Century Dudley

In trying to reconstruct thirteenth-century Dudley we must imagine away all industry apart, perhaps, from quarrying. It is possible that coal was gathered, but not mined, from outcrops in the manor, since coal pits are recorded in Sedgley in 1272. There is still no town and almost certainly no market, and Dudley does not yet stand out from its neighbours Rowley, Tipton and Sedgley. Roads as we know them do not exist; mere tracks lead from hamlet to hamlet. The arable fields are farmed in strips (there will be much evidence of their location later). Meadows frequently flood and provide the best grazing. There are probably no stone buildings apart from the priory and churches; the castle lies derelict. Peasant houses are of wood and thatch. Beyond the present-day centre of Netherton and west of Woodside the woodlands flourish with their oaks, birches, alders and, here and there by the streams, willows. Deer and foxes live among them and are hunted with bows and arrows. Castle Mill, in the far north, grinds corn, and on the banks of the Bourne brook, at Withymoor, another mill serves Dudley and Rowley. However, a change is coming. More than halfway through the century the lords will return to Dudley and transform it from a small village to a prosperous town.

two

THE LATER MIDDLE AGES

The last half of the thirteenth century was crucial for Dudley's development, but unfortunately the evidence for it is confused. Local events in the 1260s are the direct results of national events, but no eyewitness wrote down for us exactly what happened. We have no option but to work partly from circumstantial evidence.

The three major developments which appear to date from the 1260s are (1) the rebuilding of the castle; (2) the foundation of the borough, and (3) the granting of a market charter.

Members of the de Somery family were, for a long time, engaged in foreign wars and in fighting lawsuits at home. One intermittent 'foreign' war was in Wales, whose border with Shropshire may have seemed perilously close to Dudley. After a long period of physical absence, the lords of Dudley now returned to the centre of their barony. In 1262, Roger de Somery II decided to rebuild the castle, but this was a time when the king could not trust his subordinates: the barons had been seething with revolt. He ordered de Somery to stop refortifying. But Roger was able to show proof of his loyalty to King Henry III in his war in Wales; in fact, it was just because of this loyalty that he wished to refortify Dudley. In 1265 he was granted a licence to 'crenellate', rebuild the castle with fortifications; this proved to be enormously significant for the ridge-top settlement at Dudley and for the area as a whole. (At the same time, Roger was allowed to crenellate Weoley Castle.) He planned, but did not live to execute, a strong curtain wall along the top of the bailey overlooking Dudley, which would guard the new buildings he proposed for the castle. However, in 1272 he died and was buried in the priory.

A Market Granted to Dudley

The grant of a market was a royal prerogative. Clearly, to provide a market would involve a physical location for it. Market places needed to be wide enough to accommodate stalls and crowds. It seems certain that providing such a space in Dudley would need to go hand-in-hand with making the small town into a borough, with burgess plots lining the market. The problem for historians is that there is no direct reference to the foundation of Dudley Borough. Roger de Somery would gain from having a borough at the foot of his castle, with its prosperous market and inhabitants who would rally to his cause if needed. But there was already a market at Wolverhampton, evidenced in a deed of 1204, where the dean of the church was a force to be reckoned with.[1] This dean, Giles de Erdington, was a holder of a number of manors, who fought successfully to retain some local power for Wolverhampton against the diocese of Lichfield. A medieval charter forbade markets to be less than 7 miles apart (though this dates from 1327), but there are only 6 miles between Dudley and Wolverhampton. In 1261 there was a law case between Giles de Erdington and Roger de Somery concerning markets, in which it was maintained that Dudley had a market before Wolverhampton: this seems unlikely. However, we cannot rule out the possibility that Dudley already did have a small market, or that de Somery was trying to establish the right to hold one.

It may have seemed to the king that Giles de Erdington was gaining too much power. In addition, Roger de Somery supported the king against Simon de Montfort's rebellion in 1264–5. He was taken prisoner at the Battle of Lewes, and in 1265 fought at the Battle of Evesham. The following year Roger was one of eight high-ranking nobles to draw up the 'Dictum of Kenilworth', which restored the barons to their customary duties. It might seem likely that he could be rewarded by the grant of a market to Dudley, whatever the distance to Wolverhampton. There is also a piece of mysterious documentary evidence that has proved almost impossible to interpret but which is the only written material we have relating to this process. Its defects and possible meaning require some discussion.

A Deed of Disputed Date

A report of this document (the original has never been found) first surfaced in the *Birmingham Archaeological Journal* for 1913.[2] A text was printed, in English, purporting to date from 1218. The text begins:

> Be it known by these p[re]sents that I, Roger ye son of Roger Somery, Knight, Lord of Dudley, have given and granted by these p[re]sents have confirmed to all Burgesses of ye Borrow of Dudley all liberties hereafter following.

This is seventeenth-century English; any medieval grant would have been in Latin, and this is not a contemporary medieval translation. The deed is signed by witnesses, the first of whom is Henry of Bushbury, who was keeper of Dudley castle as late as 1327, more than 100 years after the purported date. What is to be made of this confusing piece of evidence?

One possible suggestion is that the medieval date, in Roman numerals MIILVIII, was mistakenly written MIIVIII (1218 instead of 1268). If so, this must have been on the seventeenth-century copy, since medieval deeds did not make use of Roman numerals.

Another is that the deed as translated is a summary of two or more deeds, made in 1327 or later, a kind of confirmation of existing privileges. Perhaps both theories are true. The date 1218 must give some information, however muddled. The year 1268 is a time when Roger de Somery is known to be actively developing Dudley, and an inquisition post-mortem of 1273, when he died, confirms that the market was producing revenue by that time. Though we cannot rule out an earlier foundation of the borough, and some kind of market may have existed before this, 1268 seems likely enough.

The borough at Dudley belonged to a group called seigneurial boroughs, that is, they were created by the lord of the manor. It seems probable that de Somery ordained a new street almost parallel to the supposed original road (now King Street), lining the market place with burgage plots, in which he placed loyal burgesses. Burgage plots in every town were long, thin plots, with a frontage, often narrow, to the main street. The dimensions of these plots lasted through history, influencing modern times. At Dudley, the plots on the south of the market seem to be exactly opposite those on the north (except where amalgamations and purchases have taken place). They extend north from King Street across the market to Tower Street in a number of cases. This suggests that each plot may have occupied the width of a pre-existing arable strip in the open fields. Such development would avoid the need for new surveying. Evidence from a much larger Midland borough, founded in 1196, is that of Stratford-on-Avon, where the burgage plots also follow the lines of pre-existing arable strips.[3]

We might wonder what these new burgage houses were like. Very few domestic buildings of the thirteenth century exist in the whole of the British Isles, and indeed it has been established that up to the end of the twelfth-century houses were usually of wood, not expected to last beyond the life of the inhabitant or his son. In other parts of the country some stone houses exist from this date, but it seems to have been much later that any houses were built out of stone in Dudley. We might suppose that some burgage houses were of cruck construction, that is, the basic frame was of two large wooden beams meeting at an apex, with walls partly of wooden frame infilled with mud or clay. The use of clay is in fact confirmed by the document we have mentioned, rendered in the seventeenth-century English as 'ye same Burgesses shall have clay to make their walls'. It is unlikely that these early burgages would have had more than one storey, or any partly floored-over high area being reached by a ladder.

The document made other provisions. No one was to be made a burgess except on the authority of the other burgesses; the burgesses would not have to pay toll in Wolverhampton or Birmingham and would have the right to grant permission to build houses on the lord's wasteland. They could pasture their cattle and pigs in the lord's woods, and could have any dead wood freely. These rights could be exercised both in the town and in the foreign, that is the 'foreign' parts of the manor beyond the town limits. This is the first occasion in Dudley when this term is used. The same word is used in Walsall and Birmingham for the outlying parts of the manor. In the case of Dudley, the town limits were drawn quite tightly round the main inhabited area. Small 'rescue' digs have shown traces of medieval buildings in the town centre, including some substantial foundations in what became New Street.[4] Precise dating of these small pieces of evidence is hazardous.

Dudley Castle Rebuilding

An authoritative statement of the condition of Dudley, not long after the disputed date of 1268, comes from the inquisition post-mortem of Roger de Somery, who died in 1272. Here his rebuilding of the castle is said to be 'newly commenced' and still not finished, so that it cannot yet be valued. Figures are given for the rent of the burgages, for the pasture of the castle, and for the market tolls. The assessors also listed Penniak wood, that is to say part of Pensnett Chase. They say that this is in Sedgley and Kingswinford manors, and they may be correct, but Dudley Wood was also part of the Chase, and they may or may not be including it. It is, they say, a mile and a half long and three-quarters of a mile wide.[5]

A lay subsidy (a tax document) lists the tax-paying inhabitants of Dudley at some point between 1276 and 1282, certainly after the foundation of the borough and market. Most of them would be burgesses. In the thirteenth century surnames were indicative of trade or origin, and so by examining their surnames we can tell a little about the make-up of the Dudley population. It seems that de Somery had planted burgesses from some of his other manors. There were, for instance, Galfridus (Geoffrey) de Rowley, Robertus de Bermyngham, Petrus Bulston, Walterus de Saltley, Johannus de Russel (Rushall) and Radulphus de Bannebur[y]. There is no reason to suppose that these surnames do not reflect the birthplace of the individuals concerned. Some inhabitants came from nearby; for example, Johannus de Wrosne (Wren's Nest). Others are distinguished by the name of their parent, including Adamus filius Ricardi and, perhaps surprisingly, Benedictus filius Alicie (his father's name not given). There were two Pistors (fishermen) who were to give their name to countless Dudley residents, and after whom Fisher Street is ultimately named. Willielmus Frebodi must have been an early free tenant, whose descendants gave their name to the area round Kate's Hill, long called Freebodies.

Roger de Somery was followed as lord by his son, also named Roger, who occupied the position for nineteen years and continued to rebuild the castle. He probably completed the curtain wall round the bailey which his father had begun. The two other major works of this period were the huge donjon towers, originally four, and the rebuilt gatehouse. It may be that these were finished in the next generation by Roger's son. We have to remember that the castle was not only a huge fortification towering over Dudley, but the centre of a barony much of the land of which was in the Midlands, but which included parts of Buckinghamshire and other areas as well.

Roger de Somery's Estate

By the time Roger de Somery died in 1291, the assessors at his inquisition were able to put a value on the castle (26s 8d, with accessories). This document mentions the rabbit warren which was probably on the hill itself and Conigre park, the area to the north-west of Castle Hill now covered by Tipton Road, hotels, and the A4123. It also included land in Tipton and two water mills, Castle Mill at the north end of Castle Hill and Withymoor at Netherton, are also mentioned in the list of possessions. Mines of carbo maris (sea coal) were mentioned in the 1272 account (in Sedgley) and are mentioned again in 1291. (Sea coal simply means 'coal' as opposed to charcoal, as it was usually transported by sea to London from the mines in the north-east of England.) The value of these mines had declined during the nineteen years from nearly £4 to 26s 8d. Iron mines are also mentioned. Much of the mining is likely to have been opencast, the 'pits' being literally pits in a field, not tunnels below ground.

At the same time an account of the manor was produced, describing the main features of Dudley as seen by the king's 'escheator'.[6] Here the burgesses are specifically mentioned (their rent was £6 10d per annum), as are free tenants who paid on aggregate just over £4 per annum. The ordinary peasants owed plough service, hoeing, reaping, providing pannage for pigs and sending oats to the castle, as well as carrying hay from the meadow. It is possible that the 'meadow' in question was Lord's Field, though the term usually applies to land near a brook or river.

The Prior of Dudley Against Northfield Church

Meanwhile the other source of authority in Dudley was the priory. In 1293 there was a tussle between the church authorities at Northfield and the prior; it is clear from the course of the argument that both were concerned about income and possessions. The Bishop of Worcester was involved, and eventually the prior was excommunicated by the Archbishop of Canterbury. Though it is hard to establish anything about the monks or priors at Dudley, many monks in general seem to be members of the same families as the temporal lords, and it is likely that their motives and manners were similar to these men. The battle of excommunications was waged as determinedly as the battle for Scotland.

Whenever money was available, it seems that additions or improvements were made to the priory. About the beginning of the fourteenth century the porch of which traces remain at the west end of the nave seems to have been demolished and the door repaired. Wider windows were inserted. The priory had become the natural burial place for the lords of Dudley and their families, and now Agnes de Somery, who had been head of the family since 1291 and attended the coronation of King Edward II in 1308, died and was buried at the priory. It is not clear whether the alterations to the priory were for her burial, or done during her lifetime.[7]

Roger de Somery's son was John. He probably completed the castle in the early fourteenth century. John de Somery, a fierce fighter, had been born at Weoley Castle in 1280. Wars and revolts among the nobility during this period were so pervasive and so crippling that it is almost impossible to imagine the Dudley burgesses having a quiet time. Of John de Somery it was said that he 'domineered more than a king'. No one could live in his domains unless he provided a bribe to de Somery, or else helped to build the new castle. He is also charged with setting siege to houses to murder the owners, or else extort money from them. Such was the builder of Dudley Castle, dreaming now as a romantic ruin, but once a savage symbol of tyranny. Luckily, John de Somery was often abroad, or unsuccessfully pursuing Scottish clansmen. As with previous

west elevation

east elevation

10 Elevations of Dudley Priory.

members of his family, he was often found to be loyal
to the king, while other barons in Staffordshire took
a very different stance. It is important not to intro-
duce modern notions of statecraft into this period:
there were almost always wars, deliberately sought
and often fought far from the Midlands.[8]

11 Shields of the Lords of Dudley.
The right-hand shield is that of the
Wards, 'goldsmiths'.

The Effect of War with France

Yet another conflict broke out in 1327: war with France. This was, however, the
reason for a new lay subsidy, which gives us a revised list of the chief inhabitants of Dudley.

There are forty-two names on the list, contributing in all 76s 8d to the war
effort. Some of these citizens are descendants of those taxed in the previous century. Nicolas de Bannebury has succeeded his father and Ricardus de Rushale
reverted to a topographical spelling (though his namesake Ricardus Russel has
not). Ricardus Frebody has inherited the family holding, probably on Kate's
Hill. There are still Pistors (Fishers), now joined by Petrus le Fleshewar, whose
name suggests that the borough was already concerned with the quality of
meat sold in the market. New names include William and Elia Bondy, with
their kinsman Johannes Bendy (names which will play an important part in
Dudley history), Stephanus de Holie, whose name indicates the existence of a
primitive Holly Hall, and the slightly sinister Henricus le Fox. Another father-
less inhabitant is Adam filius Emmae. Unfortunately there is little information
about the exact dwelling places of any of these men. A possible exception is
the home of the Russel/Rushale clan, who almost certainly lived on the site of
Russell's Hall.[9]

In the meantime, while Dudley was increasing in trade and prosperity, the
owners of the castle and manor were suffering. John de Somery died in 1321
and was succeeded by Margaret, his daughter, who had become the wife of
John de Sutton (on-Trent, Nottinghamshire). Her sister, Joan Botetort, took
Weoley and West Bromwich.

John de Sutton apparently supported the rebellion of the Earl of Lancaster,
and was arrested. His lands were taken by a usurper, Hugh Despenser, who had
been a favourite of King Edward II. John de Sutton was chained and thrown
into prison. It is almost impossible to assess the characters of these childish

and combative medieval noblemen, but quite unlikely that any real effects were felt in Dudley. It was years before the Suttons were restored to their castle, meanwhile the most catastrophic event of the fourteenth century took place: the arrival and spread in England of the Black Death.

Black Death

Unfortunately there are no records relating to the progress of the plague through Dudley town, but there is careful analysis for the neighbouring parish of Halesowen, now divided, but partly in Dudley Metropolitan borough.[10] Halesowen Abbey was larger and more powerful than Dudley Priory; one of its patron saints was St Barbara, a mythical saint of Turkish origin. Before and during the Black Death, St Barbara lost her popularity; so much so that pilgrims, some of whom would almost certainly be from Dudley proper, failed to visit her shrine. The Abbot of Halesowen complained to the Bishop of Worcester about this, and about the costs that the abbey suffered in entertaining pilgrims from a distance. As the Black Death advanced, processions were held in the villages in Halesowen parish, but an estimated 40 per cent of the abbey's tenants died, leaving farms temporarily untenanted. It can be assumed that the percentage of tenantry dying in Dudley Castle territory would be about the same. It is quite clear that population levels dropped catastrophically, and the graveyards at St Edmund's and St Thomas' would be in heavy use.

While plague raged in England, the barons were involved in war with France. We should not imagine the Suttons resting quietly in the castle, which often seems to be in the hands of stewards. Nevertheless, action was taken in 1338 to add more farming land claimed from the wastes in Dudley, Sedgley and Rowley Somery, suggesting that in the years between the famine of the first part of the century and the onset of the plague, population had been growing. It is probable that John de Sutton II, who became baron in 1327, added the barbican and the chapel block to the castle, but by 1346 he was fighting at the Battle of Crécy, and after a recall to Parliament he was again in France during 1350.

Relief at surviving the plague did not prevent lawlessness by Dudley residents. In 1391 Richard Frebody and Richard Marshal of 'Duddeley', with Matilda Dymmok, were sued by one Robert Burgylon for allegedly dispossessing him of lands in Sedgley.[11] The case was initially proved, and a fine was awarded. In a counter-plea, Richard Frebody exonerated himself and was awarded damages

12 Canal basin on the eastern side of Tipton Crossroads, on the site of a medieval pool.

against Robert Burgylon. The case rumbled on in the way of medieval law cases: in 1396 Richard Marchal of Duddeley was summoned by an inhabitant of Tipton for stealing twelve oxen and a cow. Richard produced a deed stating that he was entitled to the rent from land in Tipton owned by the plaintiff, Thomas Neuport, but Neuport replied that in the previous case it had been agreed that if Richard did not lose lands or tenements formerly belonging to Matilda Dymmok, the rent of the Tipton lands would be annulled. He claimed that the lands had not been lost, and therefore there was no rent to be paid. It appears that Frebody and Marchal had taken the law into their own hands, as so often seems to have happened during this period.

While motives are hard to judge, it is certain that there was rivalry and even violence in the relationship between the monks and the castle authorities. For whatever reason, following the Black Death, raids were made on the priory by a significant group of Dudley residents (apparently backed by the castle authorities), and horses, oxen and armour, among other things, were removed. It is recorded that in 1349 there was no prior in charge, and perhaps the monks or lay brothers and servants had been killed or weakened to such an extent that the townsfolk and lords thought the priory was finished. In any case, it can be inferred that the priory was not rich; work on the building had been slow indeed, and no major development was to take place for 100 years.

In 1343, John Sutton II married Isabella, the daughter of the Lord of Powis. She survived her husband's death in 1359 and remarried. Her new husband's first name was certainly Richard, apparently with the surname 'le Fissher'. He is also called Richard de Dudleye, Seigneur de Dudley, in a charter. It is likely that he was one of the Fisher family of the fourteenth-century lists, and after whom Fisher Street (now the bus station) takes its name. The family was not noble, and it seems that Isabella may have married wealth rather than nobility. The couple did reside here, presumably at the castle, though they also spent time at Halesowen Abbey. Isabella lived to be 90, dying at the start of the new century and having kept several generations out of their inheritance.

John de Sutton V is mentioned in the Dudley estates in 1401 and there is a document probably from 1404 from Ricardus de Bello Campo (Richard Beauchamp) to the Dudley constable ordering that he should levy '*omnes homines deffensabiles*' to go to resist the Welsh raiders who were burning and destroying Herefordshire.[12] This was the Owain Glyndwr rebellion, which continued until 1410, outstaying John Sutton V by four years. John Sutton had married Constance, daughter of Sir William Blount, a Derbyshire baron. Their son, John Sutton VI, inherited from Constance in 1422, and became a great figure on the national stage. He was Lord Lieutenant of Ireland in 1428 and is unlikely to have spent much time in Dudley. At some time before 1459 he was honoured as a knight of the garter. Constance had lived for some periods at Himley, which was developing as an alternative residence to the castle.

Castle Property

The mention of a constable in the previous document suggests that the borough administration was functioning in the same way as later. Records relating to the borough or inhabitants surviving from this period are very sparse. An inquisition post-mortem on the death of John Sutton V lists some of his property, including Lord's Field, le Parkfield (near Russells Hall) and Yorke Park (to the east of Blowers Green). Another piece of land, unidentifiable, was called 'tordeffeld'. On the jury were William Freebody and Nicholas Russell. A deed from 1416 records a property transfer from William Antony of Dudley to John Scheldon of Rowley, William Corbyn of Kyngesswynfford and John Clerk of Tybindon (Tipton). The property, including land, is described as being in 'smytheslane' between two other properties belonging to Richard Hegens and

Agnes Bloxwych.[13] This is the first time a name for the lane leading from the market towards Wolverhampton is recorded, and it may be presumed that the label 'smythes' means that this is the area where the metalworkers congregated. It is also worth noting that property is owned by people who no longer live in Dudley itself, but in neighbouring parishes. Though this property is not stated to be a burgage, and may be beyond the area originally designated for allocation in burgages, this is not just a land transfer, but one involving buildings, suggesting that the route to Wolverhampton is being colonised as an overflow to the town centre.

In 1441, William Clerk of Dudley transferred to John Sutton, lord of the manor, lands and a tenement (perhaps just a holding, though a building may be implied) which he had as a gift from a former vicar, William Loudun.[14] The transfer excluded six selions of land and a parcel of meadow lying in Greyston field and one shop lying next to (iuxta) the high cross (altam crucem) in Dudley town. This reveals some of the topography of the centre of Dudley in the mid-fifteenth century. Greyston (Greystone) field stretched from the present Stafford Street towards Eve Hill. Later maps show some meadow land but not a great deal. The high cross was at or near to the place of the present statue of Duncan Edwards, at the west end of the market – it had already appeared in a deed of 1339. Such crosses in medieval England had the function of protecting traders and purchasers against malpractice, but it is quite likely that the borough officials had already put in place a surveillance system of which we see plenty of evidence in later documents. A deed of 1446 transfers a manorial burgage and curtilage to John Holyns of Bewdley. Evidently, burgages were saleable commodities and did not pass automatically from father to son (see Appendix).

More topography is revealed in a deed of 1473, in which John Sheynton of Trysull transfers property to John Asshurste of Dudley. This is a messuage (house) cottage and garden. Its position is precisely described, one of the indicators being Greystone field.[15] A little family history surfaces, when it is mentioned that the current owner, Eleanor, is the daughter of Elizabeth, late wife of William Fissher the elder. Another plot of land, a croft, is between a lane extending towards Porters Field and the field itself. It is not sure where this is located, since we cannot precisely identify the lane: it could perhaps be Fisher Street, but it might be the lane which later became Birmingham Street. William Fyscher the younger makes his appearance in the deed as a holder of land in this area.

The Great Fire of Dudley

Three years later, a fire swept through the town, but whether it should be known as 'the great fire of Dudley' is not a given, since there are no details of how far it spread. Most, if not all, of the houses were wooden, and there might be little left of them. However, it is known that the fire destroyed the chancel of St Edmund's Church. The antiquarian Elias Ashmole (1617–1692) apparently visited Dudley before St Edmund's was again destroyed in the Civil War and saw the church which had been rebuilt after the fire. He recorded a great east window depicting William Dudley (second son of John Sutton VI), who had become Bishop of Durham, kneeling before Our Lady. A scroll issued from his mouth recording his help in the building of 'huius capille' ('this chapel') and installing the window. There is, unfortunately, a little ambiguity in Ashmole's account, since it is not known whether his reference to the 'chapel' means the 'church' of St Edmund's or a chantry chapel to Our Lady, which had been endowed with Dudley lands at some previous time.[16] There certainly was such a chapel, and the lands were later used to finance the grammar school.

Some years after the fire, in 1485, the chancel was rebuilt. For this purpose sixty oaks from the forest of Kinver were given by the king. How this rebuilding relates to the east window mentioned is not clear. Attempts have been made to guess the layout of the church in the fifteenth century, but it is not certain whether the chantry chapel was a protruding addition on the north side of the nave or an eastern addition to the chancel. Sixty oaks seems a large number to account for roof beams etc., unless the whole new chancel was to be of wood. After such a devastating fire, it seems more likely that the church would have been rebuilt in stone.

John Sutton VI died in 1487 after a scintillating career on the national stage. He had been Royal Treasurer, constable of the Tower of London and had been given many manors in the Midlands and elsewhere by a grateful royal household. He left £20 to be used on a memorial in the priory, where his ancestors had been buried, in preference to one of the parish churches. His will provided for a fine funeral, with twenty-four torches to be lighted during its course and a feast of music, for which each singing clerk was to be paid 3d. It can reasonably be assumed that the requiem was by a successor of John Dunstable and echoed through the valley delightfully. The singers would not be local people, but imported, and staying at the castle.[17]

John Sutton had earlier spent some expense renovating and altering the lady chapel at the south-east end of the priory church. New vaulting was added, and

a splendid new east window inserted, of
which enough remains to judge its scope.
It is not clear that John Sutton's tomb was
in the chapel, though there is a strong suggestion that he had intended this. An effigy
with the decoration of the Order of the
Garter was moved to St Edmund's after the
priory church was abandoned. Here it was
seen by at least three antiquarians, whose
descriptions leave little doubt that it was
John Sutton VI's tomb being described.
The effigy must have been crushed at the
destruction of St Edmund's in the seventeenth century. Other effigies did survive,
though, with sculpture from a tympanum
and decorated floor tiles.[18]

13 The priory: south-east end of the Lady Chapel.

Seven children had been born to John
Sutton, of whom the third, John, became
the ancestor of the Duke of Northumberland, who played a great part in the
reign of Queen Elizabeth. Eleanor Dudley married first Henry Beaumont
of Wednesbury, then George Stanley of West Bromwich. John's first son was
Edmund, who died before him; Edmund's son, Edward Sutton, became baron
in 1487. A junior branch of the family descended from him and occupied
Russell's Hall. Edward Sutton had an intermittent and unpredictable time at
court, at times in favour with King Henry VII and at times out of favour. He
had been knighted in 1486 as part of the settlement which ended the Wars
of the Roses but like many barons in these years he was dragged through the
courts despite being a member of Parliament. There is little evidence that he
paid much attention to his borough of Dudley.

Netherton

During all this time there was a minor settlement in Dudley parish of which
there is little trace: the supposed manor of Netherton. This centred on
Netherton Hall (not necessarily so-called). None of the medieval lists which
we have quoted make any distinction between Dudley proper and Netherton,

and this continues to be the case with most of the documents from the sixteenth century.

It is by no means clear that Netherton was a manor at all. In a similar situation at West Bromwich, a dispute arose as to whether Sandwell was a manor. The judgement was that if there were no court rolls it was not a manor. Court rolls for Netherton have never surfaced, and Netherton property appears in the Dudley court rolls, though these are mostly later than the time when Netherton could conceivably have held its own court.

It must be remembered that much of what we now think of as Netherton was simply considered as part of Pensnett Chase, and had no inhabitants other than deer and foxes. On the other hand, the Foley family certainly did have a geographically discrete estate at the beginning of the eighteenth century, based on Netherton Hall.

It is possible that there was a small hamlet at Netherton in medieval times, but there is no real evidence for this. There certainly were some individual holdings at Blowers Green, Baptist End, Cinderbank and Lodge Farm (none of these names would necessarily be in use at the time; Cinderbank may be a corruption of sunder-bank, i.e. a hillock sundered – parted – from the main settlement). There seems to be no trace of strip farming in Netherton, though some fields, such as Austin Barbers, were held in separate parcels during later centuries. It could also be argued that the name 'field', as in Broadfield and Brookfields, both on the north-east side of Netherton, is a word normally used of medieval open fields. A narrow strip of Netherton, near the brook at Windmill End and Withymoor, was later counted as part of Dudley manor. This essential source of water must surely have been one of Dudley's early resources, and it is hard to see ownership contested between a powerful town and a small hamlet being resolved in the hamlet's favour.

three

TUDOR DUDLEY

Edward Sutton was the owner of Dudley Castle as the new century dawned in 1501. He did little to enhance the fabric of the castle, and was mainly away on various national business. In 1492 he was summoned to Parliament, and attended from time to time for the next forty years until his death in 1532. By that time crucial events were brewing in England: King Henry VIII was beginning a process in order to change the religious slant of the country away from its traditional allegiance to the Roman hierarchy in Italy. This was to affect Dudley Priory, and in time the whole economy and balance of power in the town.

Lawlessness continued to plague the lives of ordinary people. In 1528 Edward Sutton wrote to Cardinal Wolsey complaining about an attack on a tenant, one John Moseley, who had been beaten and robbed by two 'servants' of Edward Byrmyngham, Robert Sutton and Henry Fox. They stole £4 8*d* from Moseley, and left him for dead. So the letter claims, but the surname Sutton for one of the servants makes one wonder if this was some family feud in which Edward Sutton wished to involve Wolsey. In Tudor times, 'servants' was a term including bailiffs and other members of the elite retinue; we should not think of these attackers as unprincipled or uninfluential 'working-class' men (there was no such thing as a working class in Tudor times).[1]

Edward Sutton's castle staff continued the regular work of administering the property, as appears from a number of deeds dating from the early sixteenth century. For example, a tenement in Smythelane (later Wolverhampton Street) was leased to Henry Astley in 1528. It was said to adjoin land of John Mowklowe (Mucklow) on three sides, while the lane made up the other side.[2] Deeds of the period begin to show us how the town was developing; two years later there is evidence of open butts (short farming strips) in Porter's Field and the same short strips in Pecoke Fyld. This deed also mentions Cawnell Hill, a first reference to a geographical feature whose etymology is uncertain.

Burgages and Other Houses

The burgage system continued to operate, with burgages bought and sold. One such was transferred back to the Suttons in 1530. Its land extended from Peyse Lane (Tower Street) to Horsfeyr Strete (later Priory Street). With this burgage went land in Greystone Field, bounded by Diglake, near the junction of what became Stafford Street and Wolverhampton Street. Meanwhile, enterprising citizens of Dudley were betaking themselves to London, where, for example, John Mucklow had become a citizen and scrivener by 1530.

Taxes for a French War

Europe's disturbed history continued to exert major influence on policy in England. A complicated set of alliances and feuds meant that King Henry VIII was determined to conquer northern France, and no male citizen in Dudley or anywhere else could be left untouched by taxes (even a few women had to pay). In 1522 there was a military survey, checking on the value of lands and property and what resources could be put to the service of the warring English.[3] Twenty-five landholders were registered, ranging in wealth from Elyzabeth Colborne and the absentee John Mucklow (written Moklow in the document), whose lands could be taxed for 26s 8d and 13s 4d respectively, to the 2s tax on William Gran [ner?]. Mrs Colborne's land is likely to have been at Shaver's End.[4]

Fifteen men were taxed on their goods, each at 20s. Some could be relied on to provide weapons, either a bow and arrows or a bill. One bill man was William Smallman, who seems to have lived to 1572, and whose will is more concerned with the distribution of farm animals than weapons of war. He gave sheep and lambs to his grandchildren, and 12d to 'the poor men's boxe'.[5] He also owned at the time of his death a black cow, a mare and a pied cow. After the priory had been dissolved, William occupied the priory croft. A friend of William Smallman, John Cooke, was also taxed 20s and owned a bow and arrow to provide for the armoury. John Moosley, who was attacked by Edward Byrmyngham's two henchmen, is also mentioned in the taxation list, but he had no weapon to contribute. Mention must also be made of John Bekensale (his family name variously spelt), whose relative Thomas became the vicar of Dudley and is prominent in any work where fluent writing is required.

Disputes with Much Wenlock

Meanwhile there was, as perhaps happened often, dissension between other ecclesiastics at Dudley, the monks of the priory, and their mother house. In 1521 the Prior of Wenlock, Richard Singer, died. There was an election to which the monks of Sandwell and Dudley should have had access, but this was denied. The election was, of course, a matter of personal attendance in the chapter house at Wenlock, and it is most likely that the Dudley and Sandwell monks were at least represented despite the ban. One Roland Gosnell was elected, but almost immediately William Corvill, the sacrist, snatched up the convent seal and took it to Dudley. Without it, the election could not be valid. The Dudley prior travelled up to London to put the monks' case to Cardinal Wolsey, but he came down on Gosnell's side and his election was ratified by the Bishop of Hereford, called in by Wolsey to enforce the matter.

The European ferment of the early part of the sixteenth century was heightened by religious disagreements. King Henry's resolution to acquire more power from the Catholic Church involved a plan to get rid of monasteries, of which locally Halesowen, Dudley priory and the small priory at Sandwell were examples. Work began with the small institutions. Sandwell was dissolved in 1526 and the lands given to Cardinal Wolsey. The monastery owned some small properties in Dudley, the extent of which are recorded in an Exchequer document.[6] Robert Hall of Alcester held a small plot adjoining Porter's Field. There was a little croft located by 'pestlan', whose boundaries extended to glebe land belonging to the vicar Sir Hugh Tailor. 'Pestlan' may be Pease Lane (Tower Street). Mucklow makes his appearance yet again as the owner of a plot of land near Churchfield, beside which was another Sandwell holding. Margaret Paston (written Patson) was the tenant of Sandwell land in Smythie Lane, which already had the alternative name of Hampton Street, such were the Main Sandwell Possessions

There was a further taxation document just before Sandwell was dissolved, a lay subsidy charging up to 5s on the richest citizens, though most ordinary inhabitants seem to have paid only 4d.[7] Up to 103 names appear on the list, though unfortunately their houses cannot be loacted. Among the richest were James Colborne, Richard Jones, John a Parke (his descendants usually have the alternative name Pershouse or Parkhouse),Thomas Watte and Edmonde Stevyns. Those who paid only 4d include Roger Ruston, Roger Dauks (Danks), Rycherde Moseley, Thomas Homer and Roger Darbye. These names have still not died out among the modern population of Dudley. In all, £4 16s 8d was levied, though whether it was actually paid is doubtful.

John Sutton VI died in January 1532, and was succeeded by his son John Sutton VII. This gentleman acquired a poor reputation based on the fact that he sold parts of the Dudley barony, and mortgaged others. He seemed feckless and inept to his contemporaries, who gave him the nickname of Lord Quondam (the has-been lord). However, the process of mortgaging was in part designed to regain money which had been spent by his father. John Sutton VII certainly angered some of his relatives. His brother Arthur, a clerk at Lichfield Cathedral, was accused in the Court of Chancery, of breaking into the castle and smashing his way into the oak chests where important documents were kept: these are listed as charters, court rolls, rentals, terriers, etc., and would have constituted very useful material for Dudley historians. Arthur is alleged to have refused to return these documents 'at all times'. Lord Quondam could do very little about it. Yet he may have been maligned; this ill-repute was gained at a time when a much more powerful member of the Dudley family was enthusiastically trying to regain control of the castle and lands. This was the Earl of Warwick, afterwards Duke of Northumberland.

The End of Dudley Priory

While this scheming was afoot, in Dudley itself the priory was in danger. Henry VIII's plan to dissolve the monasteries had not stopped short at the smaller ones like Sandwell. Soon he cast his eyes on the larger establishments, seats of power antithetical to his own; among them were the priory at Much Wenlock and its dependent house at Dudley. During the late 1530s preparations for dissolution were being made, and the final act took place in 1539. Priory land was confiscated and in due course became part of the castle estates. Much of the territory was round the priory itself, and at the crucial period was tenanted by the richer Dudley inhabitants.[8] Among them were William Pattyngham, tenant of Tutbury Croft; Alice Colbarn, tenant of *unam clausam voc.* Horsepole; William Hyll, a messuage and field called Barkhouse Croft, and George Throckmorton *miles* (knight), Eveshill. Barkhouse Croft was opposite the end of modern Priory Street. Sir George Throckmorton was the owner of Coughton Court in Warwickshire.

In the vicinity of the priory buildings were two pools used for raising fish, and an orchard (*pomario diversis veteribus arboribus*: with various old fruit trees

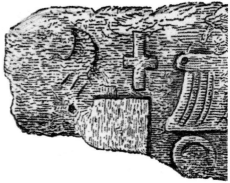

14 & 15 Carved stones from the priory (*left* 3ft x 20ft and *right* 34ft x 19ft).

in decay). More fields stretched towards Wolverhampton Street: Barne Close, Buskey Field with a close, Colpytt Close, Whete Croft and several other closes and crofts. The priory also owned some land on the high ground above what is now the A4123, at Rowse Land. It is not clear precisely how much land belonged to the priory here. A croft of 3 acres and a meadow of 1.5 acres are mentioned, but the document also talks of 20 acres, a considerable part of what became Rose Land Farm. Nor can we obtain an idea of how many monks were affected by this dispossession, or how many retainers were out of work. For a while the priory buildings decayed, and we must wait some time before gaining an insight into what became of them.

Priory Buildings

At the time of the dissolution the priory buildings consisted of the church, the living accommodation and the service areas. The church, of which significant parts remain, had a long chancel, a nave of about the same length and two transepts. From the south transept the Sutton chapel was reached, its fabric renewed during the fifteenth century in superior style. Its east wall and window remain. Much of the west wall of the nave is also still standing. All or part of the church was floored with encaustic tiles. It is not certain whether there was a tower over the crossing of the church, but the general view is that it could only have been a low one (it is thought that lower walls, parts of which remain, would not have sustained a high tower).

The living accommodation for the monks surrounded a cloister, which originally had an arcade so that they could exercise in poor weather. This began to deteriorate soon after the priory was abandoned, and there is little beyond the footings of walls left to be seen today. This group of buildings contained a kitchen and dormitories, which were connected to the church by a night stair, the final few steps of which are still to be seen. Little is known about the stables and other service buildings in which the monks kept husbandry tools for their farming enterprise in the valley below the castle wood.

16 Encaustic tile from the priory, featuring 'Vanity' holding a mirror.

Local Preparations for War

Threat of war did not recede in the late 1530s, and another check on military preparedness among the chief inhabitants of Dudley took place in 1539.[9] Among those listed as archers were John Coke (Cook), whom we met seventeen years before as an archer, and William Gallwey or Galloway, who had also been named as a tenant of priory lands. His name is interesting as it suggests that there may have been Scottish or Irish immigration into Dudley at this or an earlier time. The list of billmen included Richard Jones, whose inventory on his death in 1572 mentions hens and geese, a mare and a colt, twenty-four sheep and three pigs, but no weapons of war.[10] However, it is possible that this was the earlier Richard's son or another relative.

Two years after the muster roll, a Dudley revenue list gives details of people charged for their holdings in cottages, burgages,etc.[11] The Richard Jones featured must surely be the billman. He rented two tenements, three burgages and a bark-house. This may be adjacent to Barkhouse Close. Richard also had a horse mill, a grinding mechanism in which horses would walk round and round, supplying power to the process, and also known as a treadmill. One of Richard's burgages was previously W. Colbarn's. This family had a house near Shaver's End, and together with the bark-house this may suggest that Richard Jones' holdings were in Wolverhampton Street beyond the immediate town limits.

A major landholder was Sir George Throckmorton, paying 10s 5d for his yearly fee. William Smallman was one of his tenants. The Hall House, mentioned in Chapter 1, was in his portfolio, and there are a number of tantalising names of premises belonging to him. A burgage at Peselane End could be on Stone Street, or could be at the castle end. The Stony House is an intriguing name, perhaps also in Stone Street. Since the fire of 1476 it must have seemed useful to build houses of stone, yet to judge by more recent evidence that was not very often done. Most of the houses must still have been of wood, or this label would not have distinguished Throckmorton's house. There is mention of a smithy 'next the Drapry'. We may guess that this was in High Street, but there is no confirmation. Throckmorton paid 1s 6d for 'the Signe of ye Cow', possibly a public house, but in the days when there were no street numbers, houses other than pubs could be adorned with pictorial signs. A croft in Viccars Lane may have been on the east of what became Birmingham Street, but could have been near the Hall House on Hall Street. Viccars Yate, on the other hand, was near St Thomas' and constituted the vicar's route into Church Field. There were, of course, no helpful maps in those days, to show us the exact location of these properties.

A few more place names occur in this document. Yerns Wall, occupied by William Sheldon, can be identified with Trindle Croft, approximately on the site of the present Railway Hotel. Priory Croft, tenanted by William Smallman, was adjacent to the newly dissolved priory. The prior still makes his appearance on the list, as the tenant of 'Morleees ground' (unidentifiable). Another place name which remained for centuries was Parsons Fields, near the site of present Parkhead Locks. A burgage and another two tenements belonged to 'our lady', i.e. they were part of the endowment for the chapel in St Edmund's, soon to be used to found Dudley Grammar School. The vicar, Thomas Bekynsall, held a burgage, and personally wrote and signed the document itself.

Rebuilding of the Castle

John Dudley, later Duke of Northumberland, outwitted the allegedly slow and thoughtless Lord Quondam. Making use of a financial agent and legal experts he pressed his claim to the Dudley barony, with its centre on the hill overlooking the town. He achieved this by a purchase, probably in 1537, of the mortgaged inheritance of the Sutton family. In 1540 his hand was strengthened

17 & 18 Dudley Castle: the watchtower (*left*) and the triple gateway (*right*).

by receiving the lands of the dissolved priory and other ecclesiastical land in the Midlands and elsewhere. He arrived in Dudley to find a castle whose most recent major buildings were 200 years old and in sore need of repair. Hoping to live there himself at such times when he was not in London, he found an architect in Sir William Sharington who could add new elements to the old castle in a style, and using building materials, harmonising with the medieval work.[12]

Sharington's rebuilding was on a vast scale. Repairing the medieval chapel block and the great hall, he added a whole range of new buildings to the north of these, close against the eastern curtain wall which overlooked the valley on the Tipton side. The change of direction in this curtain wall forced Sharington to compromise on the overall effect of the range, and at the point where the direction changes he placed a bay, originally three storeys. The first-storey windows are round-headed in traditional style, as are the windows of the first-storey windows in the rooms to the south. The block enhanced by the bay contained a buttery, pantry and bedrooms above. Next to the north are the kitchens, again with bedrooms above, the outward profile being varied from the more southerly block by the tall gables with their bedroom windows. On the north side of the courtyard, Sharington placed a further range including a postern gate. This looks directly across the courtyard to the old turrets of the keep.

In addition to the domestic accommodation provided by these new buildings, Sharington changed the course of the curtain wall in the south-east corner of the castle, strengthening the access through the old gatehouse. All this new work involved demolition of some existing premises, a few traces of which remain, such as the serving door between the kitchen and buttery, dating from the twelfth century. The new buildings have obscured the medieval work in this part of the castle, and information about the previous layout is impossible to find. However, the whole of his design shows Sharington as a traditionalist, adapting medieval styles and building techniques to his new architecture rather than taking up new Italianate styles. He could have made the castle a Classical edifice in the Renaissance mode but chose instead to harmonise his new ranges with the existing thirteenth- and fourteenth-century building. Nevertheless, he did modernise, adding little in the way of gargoyles and buttresses.

Precisely when these developments took place at Dudley is not clear. They may have begun as early as 1540, but Sir William Sharington suffered a period of imprisonment after 1548 and may have been unable to carry forward the Dudley project for a time. It does seem likely, however, that the work was finished by about 1552, when John Dudley became Lord Protector, with the duty of guarding King Edward VI, the new young monarch.[13] He was very positive towards the new Protestant (or English Nationalist) movement and

19 & 20 Dudley Castle: the kitchen block (*left*) and the postern gate (*right*).

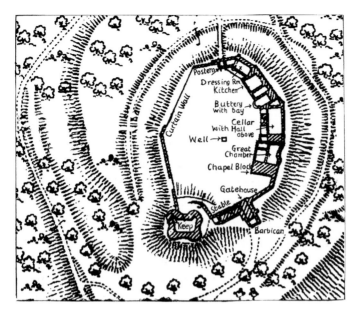

it is suggested that floor tiles removed from the Dudley Castle chapel were found in 1982, implying that the chapel was stripped of decoration during Sharington's alterations in accordance with the new Protestant emphasis on simplicity.[14] Meanwhile, Sir John Dudley had become Earl Marshal and Duke of Northumberland. It is doubtful whether he had much time to visit Dudley or deal with local matters, though in 1542 he had written to his 'Cosen Wrotisley', asking him to look into the finances of Sedgley Manor. Mentioned in the letter is George Willoughby, who is recorded as owning an estate at Netherton in the time of Edward VI. This must presumably have been the Netherton Hall estate.

Netherton in 1562

Another small light is shone on Netherton in 1562, when the new lord of the manor, Edward Sutton, leased to William Atkys 'of Dudley' a pasture or close already in Atkys' tenure, called Monks Field. This is described as being in the foreign. The foreign included Netherton, and this land can be identified as the area now thought of as central Netherton, between Simms Lane and Sweet Turf. Apart from buildings at the north end of the pasture, there were no other houses on this stretch of land at this time. The name suggests that this could once have been part of the priory territory, but since none of the land described in the documents relating to the priory can be identified with Monks Field, it may be that this belonged to Halesowen.

Our Lady's Lands

In the same year, 'Our Lady's Lands' were granted to Cecilia Pickerell as payment for a debt owed to her by the Duke of Northumberland.[15] They were described as 'now or late in the tenure of the wardens of the parish church of Dudley'. There were fourteen of these properties, the rents of which were to be used to establish a school in the borough 'and for other charitable uses'. Some consisted of open land, but there were a number of messuages or houses, including some small cottages in Hall Street.

The notional owners of these properties were the vicar, Thomas Beckensall, John Oswen, William Atkes, Thomas Persehouse, Richard Harrison, John Persehouse,Thomas Patyngham, Arthur Dixon, Henry Finch, William Harrison (farmer), Henry Tomens, Humphry Jukes, Humphrey Wright, William Harrison ('parcar', i.e. official in charge of the lord's deer parks), Thomas Fisher, Thomas Bradeley, Richard Persehouse, Christopher Owen, Richard Atkes, William Patyngham, Oliver Dixon, Adam Persehouse, Richard Harrison, son of Arthur Harrison, Robert Lane and Richard Shaw the younger. Thus most of the prominent Dudley inhabitants were involved in the charity, but it is not clear how far the proceeds of the rents were actually applied to children's schooling, as some seventy years later a major enquiry took place suggesting that this had not happened.

The Suttons Restored

The new lord of Dudley was Edward Sutton II, who had been fighting in Ireland, but returned to England in 1553, the first year of the reign of Queen Mary. That he did so suggests that he favoured the cause of 'the old religion' and could be relied upon to reverse the decisions of King Henry VIII. Many of these could not be reversed; it was too late to return their rights to the monks of Dudley Priory, or restore the tiles to the castle chapel. Nevertheless, Edward Sutton was granted land which had been taken over by the Duke of Northumberland, including the castle, its surrounding territory, the Conigree,

Old Park (land between the castle and Burnt Tree) and the manor of Rowley Regis. A whole series of manors that had once been Dudley possessions followed, including Sedgley, Kingswinford, Wombourne and Harborne, as well as the tithes of Northfield. A deed of 1563 describes land leased by Edward Sutton to William Grove as part of the lord's 'domaynes' and specifies butts in Peacocks 'Filde' and Greystone, the latter near Church Croft,with two 'lands' (strips of land) between land previously of William Colborne on both sides.

Queen Mary died in 1558 and was replaced by the new queen, Elizabeth. Edward Sutton found himself fighting on the continent at this time, and since he had favoured Queen Mary, seems to have been always regarded with suspicion by the new queen and her court. During his absence his wife Katherine presumably dealt with affairs in the local manor and barony. In 1564 a lease was made notionally by Edward Sutton, but perhaps authorised by Katherine, transferring the 'Olde Parke' to Hugh Liddiatt of Halesowen and William Harrison of Dudley.[16] The park was 'inclosed with palle heggings', and provided pasture for deer (for hunting), cattle and horses. The 'palle heggings' would be of stakes, thousands of which would have been needed to fence off such a large area. Katherine was in Dudley at the time of her own death, in 1566, being buried in St Edmund's, thought of as the castle church. Edward Sutton remarried, but his second wife lived only two years and was likewise buried at St Edmund's. Meanwhile, another lease bears testimony to the extraction of coal; 'Colepitt Leasow' was leased by Sir Edward Sutton to William Smythe, clerk (the vicar of Dudley).[17] Several fields with this name emerge over time, and this particular one was probably off Wolverhampton Street.

Queen Elizabeth at Dudley

In 1575, Queen Elizabeth was entertained at Dudley Castle. She had intended to go to Worcester on one of her peregrinations through the land, but smallpox broke out in the county town. Hasty preparations for her entertainment were made, perhaps including conversion of the original great chamber into a drawing room which certainly took place about this time. Some of the alterations to the castle seem rather rough, suggesting haste. It is probable that the queen's arrival was heralded by a pageant, but no record of such an event has survived. Halesowen church register does, however, mention a 'trayne' and candles 'when the queen was at Dudley'. St Edmund's parish register contains a surprisingly

accomplished drawing of the queen, said to have been drawn by the vicar of the time. She stayed at Dudley on 12 August 1575 and continued to Hartlebury, where the Bishop of Worcester had his palace, the following day.

Mary Queen of Scots

During the sixteenth century the relations between England and Scotland were turbulent, and an attempt to marry the then Scottish queen to King Edward VI failed.

This was Mary, Queen of Scots who had been constantly feared by the English throne and courtiers throughout most of Queen Elizabeth's reign. Though she never went to Dudley, her name is always associated with the castle, as it was carefully vetted to see whether it could provide a suitable prison in which to hold her – Edward Sutton would have been happy to provide the necessary imprisonment facilities. Sir Amyas Paulet, or Powlett, who was in charge of discovering a likely prison, paid a visit to Dudley in 1585 to survey the ground. He was not impressed by the state of the town. It was, he said, 'One of the poorest towns I have seen in my life.' Since Lord Edward Dudley was not in the castle at the time, Sir Amyas was put up at an inn in the town itself, though unfortunately it is not known which one.

Lord Dudley sent him the keys to the castle from Warwick. Sir Amyas used them to 'take a full view' of it. He was not pleased. Other than the lodgings set aside for Queen Mary herself, the accommodation was 'little and straight'. Heating might be difficult: 'There is great plenty of sea cole, charke-coale and fire woodd at hand', but it would have to be paid for by the providers, whereas at the present location of the queen, Tutbury Castle, the royal estates could provide the firewood. As he walked round the castle, Sir Amyas discovered it to be utterly destitute of tables, cupboards, forms, stools, etc., showing that the family had removed all they needed to Himley or elsewhere, and were letting Dudley remain an empty shell.[18]

There was a barn on Castle Hill which could easily be converted to a stable, but the royal servants would not like their rooms, which had no inner chambers. A major problem was the water supply, which consisted of water from the ditches round the castle – presumably the part-silted remains of the medieval moat. There was a well in the centre of the castle courtyard, and Sir Amyas was told this would supply enough for the purpose 'yf yt were clensed'. The lodgings proposed for the queen looked out over Old Park, as we can see from later plans, and this did cause some doubt: the regime was very much afraid Queen Mary would escape. The high bank on the east side of the castle might have prevented this, but the surveyor was finding reasons to turn Dudley down as a likely site. The queen, however, was not healthy enough to run away 'on her feet'. At the age of 43 she had already had enough adventures and troubles to seriously damage her health.

Dudley Castle, Sir Amyas agreed, did have strength, and there was a good supply of all kinds of victuals in the surrounding counties of Worcester and Warwick, but, he noted, corn 'groweth to be deere in all these parts'. Whether Mary could have escaped by jumping out of a window and engaging supporters to spirit her away one night is unsure, but in the event the castle was not chosen for her prison. One interesting point in the report is the prominence given to 'brewing vessels', which were said to be decayed. It must be remembered that water quality was so bad in Dudley as well as the rest of England that beer was the staple drink.

Setting aside the bias of Sir Amyas, it does appear that the castle was in a poor state despite Sharington's new building. The comments in the report about the poor condition of the town are worth pondering. Not a great deal of development had taken place since the borough had been founded. Many of the houses would still have been largely made of wood, their roofs thatched. The market had, by now, acquired its Middle Row, a common situation in market towns where the market had been planned as a wide area, but where stalls were gradually replaced by more permanent buildings.

From the inventories of Dudley men and women dying in the 1580s, we can see that the usual town trades were being followed. George Attwood was a 'shumaker', John Munday a mercer, Humfrey Jukes a blacksmith. But metal industry was more prominent here than elsewhere. Several men of the late sixteenth centuries reveal themselves as nailers (nail masters), and there would undoubtedly have been much noise in Dudley, with dust and dirt everywhere in the main streets. Sir Amyas Powlett may well have been unused to this kind of town.

Nailers and Ironworkers

Nailers' and ironworkers' equipment is found in a number of inventories. Thomas Shaw the younger had 'Smythie towles' and 'Ballies' (bellows); he also had over £10 worth of ready-made nails. Thomas Lowe, the town bailiff, died in 1586 with a 'pere of ballis' for the smith valued at 6s 8d, suggesting that he employed a blacksmith to work for him.[19] Humfrey Jukes had 'Smythie belleyes with stydie and other tooles'. Thomas Bradley had smithy tools. Most of the inhabitants also kept farm animals, whatever the size of their holdings. Humfrey Jukes had four ewes, four lambs and one ram; Lewis Pryse had eleven sheep, while George Attwood possessed a mare, two swine and '7 Stoore Swine' at his death. Thomas Shaw the younger had corn growing in his fields at Freebodies as well as twenty-two 'shipe', four cows, two calves, a mare and a store pig. There were a few luxury items in Dudley houses, such as 'painted cloths'. The best sheets for the beds were of linen, while pewter pots and dishes were somewhat better than the wooden or pottery vessels often in use.

Thomas Shaw was unfortunate in dying young. His father, Richard, witnessed his will along with friend, and probably a relative, Robert Smyth from Wombourne. Two thirds of his fortune was left to his wife Katherine, and the other third to his two sons John and Richard. Some wills were very specific about the property to be willed to individual legatees, while others, like Thomas Shaw, simply divided material mathematically. Joyce Wheeler left land in Church Field with various household equipment to her son Humfrey. She left a flock bed among other things to her son Thomas and a flock bed to another son James. Her three daughters each received pewter dishes and linen sheets, and her grandchildren also had a pewter dish each, while her grandchildren by Alis, her eldest daughter, each had 2s. This daughter was probably Alis (Alice) Mason or Robinson. The Mason/Robinson family kept their dual surname for generations, sometimes appearing in documents as Robinsons and sometimes as Masons. When John Robinson the elder died in 1580, James Wheeler was one of the appraisers of his property. He owned a number of closes, tenements and burgages both in the borough and foreign, which he left specifically to pay for his children's education.[20]

Land transfer deeds at the end of Elizabeth's reign give some further details of the topography of the town. Just before Edward Sutton II died in August 1586 his steward leased out for thitry-one years a pasture near Castle Hill Foot between the street leading to the castle, the lane leading to Old Park, and other land recognised by its owners. The same deed describes land in Porter's Field – 'six days' work' – between Peacock Field, Rushie Croft, the lane leading from Dudley to Birmingham, and the land of Adam Waddams. Rushie Croft has now disappeared under the eastern bypass, while the lane leading to Birmingham is the old Portway going via Turner's Hill. Adam Waddams was remembered for many years by the name of the pool, Waddams' Pool, situated on the north-east side of this track.

The Last of the Suttons

Edward Sutton II was buried in London, bequeathing his iron works and woods in Dudley to his wife Mary, with others including Henry Carey, whose family had Midland connections, and occupied a hunting lodge on Pensnett Chase (this turns out to be Lodge Farm). Edward's daughter Ann married for a second time, to a Thomas Wilmore or Wilmer, who also lived for a time in Dudley. The castle was inherited by Edward Sutton III, an Oxford graduate, notable for disputing the sale of Prestwood to the Lyttletons, taking the law into his own hands and driving off from Prestwood 'fourteen kyne, one bull and eight fat oxen'. The kine were driven to Dudley Castle, where they fed rather poorly on the grass in the castle courtyard. They were intended to be sold at Coventry market, but instead perished in the courtyard at Dudley. It is possible that Edward helped to fight the Spanish Armada in 1588, though it seems no record has survived. He married one Theodosia Harrington, but she did not accompany him to Dudley, living in straightened circumstances and selling her jewellery to pay her debts. Nevertheless in 1588 they had a son, Ferdinando. Three other children followed, but despite this Edward Sutton 'took to his home [in Dudley] a lewd and infamous women, a base collier's daughter'. This was Elizabeth Tomlinson, with whom Sutton had eleven children, including the entrepreneur 'Dud' Dudley.

We know the name of one of Edward's servants at Dudley, William Goddarde, who had the profits from land rented by Robert Hodgetts of Nether (Lower) Gornal. The lease has a detailed terrier attached, mentioning Battell Meadow, Evehill Leasow, Wigge Field, The Worthings, Scotts (Green), as well as the open fields at Peacock Field, Church Field and Porter's Field. Battell Meadow, near the site later occupied by Jesson's Junior School, presents an interesting question. Had an old medieval or even Saxon battle taken place there, or was this the site of mock battle, jousting perhaps, as a regular entertainment? Part of the meadow was glebe land belonging to St Thomas' Church. Wigge Field was on the south-east side of the road 'leading from Dudley to Stourbridge', next to Scotts Green.

There is a further record of Dudley's wealthier inhabitants in the Lay Subsidy of 1603. William Goddard, 'gen.' (gentleman), paid 20s in tax. Thomas Duddeley of Russell's Hall paid £3 and Richard Colborne, with property at what became Shaver's End, Oliver Dixon and William Pattengeam 40s each (the original uses Latin versions of their names). The rest of the gentry paid 20s each. Their names represent the main landowners and town officials of Dudley for the next two centuries: Richard Shawe, John Sowthall, Geoffrey Fynch, John Payton, Richard Hamlet, Hugh Dixon, and Laurence Tomson (was he any relation to the lewd collier's daughter? – despite the apparent difference in the name, scribes can be vague at the time, for example constantly varying between Watson and Watkins). John Shawe, Margaret Perks, Geoffrey Mason (or Robinson?), Henry Engley and Thomas Darbie made up the rest of the landholders, and Richard Holmer was taxed £3 for his goods.

Russell's Hall

The most prestigious house in Dudley, apart from the castle, remained Russell's Hall. This historic house occupied a position near the top of what became Himley Road, on the north side of the road, which was only a track in Tudor times. It had been owned by the Burnell family, and had more than 30 acres of territory by 1293. By 1485 the estate had passed to the Lovels, and was considered part of Dudley foreign in 1490.

It is not clear how it returned again to the lords of Dudley, but in or just before 1532, Edward Sutton conveyed the whole 'pasture' land to his son Geoffrey. This gentleman also leased 'Nethertown', which we can assume to be Netherton Hall, and was a rider of the chases and parks of Pensnett.[22]

Geoffrey died in 1572, leaving his hall and land to his wife Eleanor. The will is unfortunately damaged, but his inventory is in better shape and gives a list of the rooms in Russell's Hall, namely a 'hall', 'parler', 'buttrye', and 'ketchyn' on the ground floor and six chambers above. Geoffrey had six oxen, twelve 'kyne', two bulls, two heifers and seven yearlings, with 120 sheep and seven pigs. The Netherton property passed to Thomas, Geoffrey's son, who was to pay a share to his sister Bridget. Eleanor Dudley, Geoffrey's wife, provides an inventory at her death in 1583, which is somewhat more specific, listing in fair detail the table cloths, sheets, towels and napkins classed as 'howshowld stuffe', with pewter of all sorts, brass pots and pans and the precise location of all the beds and chests in the house. Eleanor also had 'peces of a broken Cope of satten and gold' and some silk 'quishins'. She was the daughter of Sir Gilbert Talbot of Grafton in Worcestershire, who bequeathed fine clothing to her when he died in 1542.

The hall itself cannot be entirely reconstructed from these details. Later pictures show a classical frontage, but it is quite likely that a timber-framed building still lurked behind this. The inventory seems to make no account of outhouses or single-storey extensions, though there surely were some. At the demolition of the hall it is said that some stones were used for repairing other local properties; this mention of stone suggests that even in the sixteenth century there may have been some stone building as well as those using a timber frame.

four

THE SEVENTEENTH CENTURY

A t the start of the seventeenth century, Edward Sutton III still had many years to live, though he does not seem to have spent much of his time in Dudley. He was called to Parliament in 1595 and put in regular appearances there until 1639. Meanwhile he continued to spend more than he could afford, and was continually mortgaging his estates in and out of the West Midlands. He was, however, in Dudley some of the time, during which he took Elizabeth Tomlinson, the 'lewd and infamous' collier's daughter already mentioned, as a mistress. The surname Tomlinson occurs in Tipton, and in 1611 we have an early proof of Sutton's relationship with her in a deed. Dated 16 April it conveys to Elizabeth Tomlinson of Tipton, 'spinster', with 'Dudde Tomlinson' and Martha Tomlinson, her son and daughter, 9 acres of arable land in Porter's Field. The four witnesses included the celebrated Simon Ryder of West Bromwich. Elizabeth was to pay 9s a year rent for this land.

Under the name of Dudley, Dud produced in 1665 a pamphlet called *Metallum Martis*. Part of the aim of the pamphlet seems to have been ingratiation with the newly restored monarchy. It rehearses the details of a patent issued to him by Charles I for 'the making of Iron, and Melting, Smelting, Extracting, Refining and Reducing all Mines and Metals with Pit-cole, Sea-cole, Peat and Turf …' He says he was 'at 20 years Old … fetched from Oxford … Anno 1619, to look and manage 3 Iron Works of my Fathers, 1 Furnace, and 2 Forges, in the Chase of Pensnet, in Worcester-shire.' The chief claim of the pamphlet was that Dud had discovered a way to smelt iron using 'sea-cole' or 'pit-cole' instead of charcoal. He certainly had been placed in charge of these iron works, and was an extremely strong agent. There was a good deal of rivalry in the field of iron production and at least two rivals claimed to have invented such a process at a time when patents were issued at royal command and were much disputed. In his pamphlet, Dud does not describe exactly how he had achieved the feat he claimed. Scholars have concluded that he was not in fact the inventor of the processes. His Latin memorial in St Helen's, Worcester, makes no industrial claims, merely restating his loyalty to the king and his father, and mentioning his capture in the turmoil of the 1640s. The same memorial also commemorates his wife Eleanor, daughter of Francis Heaton of Lincolnshire. Clearly Dud Dudley, despite his illegitimate origin, was regarded as part of the aristocracy.

Edward Sutton continued on his road to ruin, mortgaging further estates. At this point in his story there entered a London goldsmith, William Ward, who took up many of the mortgages. Edward Sutton's one legitimate offspring, Ferdinando, had married Honora Seymour, and they had a child, Frances Sutton, baptised at St Thomas' Church on 23 July 1611. Her mother, Honora, was buried in St Thomas' on 23 March 1620, and the following record was made in the register: 'Honor Ladie Duddeley wife to the honourable Sir Ferdinando Duddeley Knight was buried in the Parish Church of St Edmundes at Duddeley within the chancel upon Fryday night the 23rd of March 1620 about eleven of he clocke in the presence of diverse gentlemen and other inhabitinge neighboures within the townshippe of Duddeley.' A black plaque remains in the church recording her burial and adding Honor's (or Honora's) pedigree – daughter of Edward Lord Beauchamp, himself the son of Edward, Earl of Hartford and his wife Katherine, daughter of Henry, Lord Grey Duke of Suffolk. Somehow this plaque was not destroyed on the demolition of the medieval church during the Civil War.

William Ward's eldest son, Humble, was married to Frances Sutton and gained noble rank as Baron Ward of Birmingham. In 1613 Thomas Sutton of Russell's Hall transferred to his son, also Thomas, a burgageship adjoining a lane called Crumpton's Lane or the Gouldsmythes Row.[1] This looks as if it may be a reference to William Ward, who could perhaps be identified jocularly as 'the goldsmith'. Unfortunately there does not seem to be another occurrence of the name, and Crumpton's Lane is hard to identify. It seems most likely to be the lane leading from Hall Street towards Oldbury and West Bromwich, which has had a large number of names, including Vicar's Lane, Bannister's Lane and most recently Birmingham Street. It is possible, but very unlikely, that Dudley harboured a working goldsmith.

Contemporary leases continue to record the transfer of land in Dudley, and in doing so, help us to understand more about the inhabitants and local topography. In 1614, Christopher Chambers als Ireland of Hales Owen leased

22 Blackbrook Road: the old lane from Netherton.

to John Lowe of Netherton the house where Lowe was living, with its barn, smithy, foldyards, garden and backside.[2] The lease excepted part of the fold-yard which was needed for access to another house standing nearby called the Shingles House. Shingles were slates, tiles or stone roofing, a safer alternative to thatch, and their use clearly marked out this Netherton property. The location of the houses is said to be adjacent to lanes leading from Netherton Hall into Pensnett Chase ('chase, common or wood'), and on another side to a field called Colepitt Leasow. 'Pensnett Chase' might mean the area between Netherton and the Mousesweet brook, or else one of the lanes in question could be the lane now leading to Blackbrook canal bridge. The inclusion of the word 'wood' in the description reminds us that Pensnett Chase included land which later became Dudley Wood and Dudley Woodside.

Richard Foley and the Introduction of Slitting Mills

Richard Foley, whose father was also Richard, was christened in St Thomas' Church on 28 March 1580 and, like his father, was a nailer. He married twice, once to Margery Willetts of Rowley Regis, secondly to Alice Brindley of

Willenhall, daughter of an ironmaster.[3] His crucial discovery was how to make a nail rod by using slitting mills, a use already known in Sweden and thus producing nails more cheaply, so that they could undercut British producers. It is hard to evaluate the legend about him, which maintains that he went to Sweden in disguise as a travelling musician, introduced himself at the Denemara works and memorised details of the slitting mill. Two journeys were apparently necessary, but when he returned he was able to set up a mill at The Hyde in Kinver. The way in which he had gained the know-how became common knowledge and he was nicknamed Fiddler Foley. How exactly Foley learned the secrets of this method can never be proved. Roy Peacock discusses the legend in *The 17th Century Foleys*, but however fictional it is so vivid that it is unlikely to die. The Hyde slitting mill is certainly a fact. The Foleys began to make money and acquire influence. Richard Foley was Mayor of Dudley in 1616, but by 1630 he had moved to Stourbridge. However, the interest of his family in Dudley did not vanish.

Our Lady's Lands (Grammar School Property)

In many other towns in England, ecclesiastical land had been recycled in the mid-sixteenth century to provide capital for educational establishments. This had been the intention in Dudley in 1562, with the founding of the grammar school. The 'Lady Lands' had been vested in a trust to make such a provision. But the trust had not fulfilled its function. In September 1638 an inquisition was held in front of Lord Edward Dudley and other prominent aristocrats to find out what had happened to the Lady Land property.[4] It seems that the holders of the lands, identifiable as descendants of the original 1562 trustees, had in many cases not paid the rents for the maintenance of the school. It is worth examining the properties and their 'owners' in some detail, since this gives an insight into the early seventeenth-century topography of Dudley.

There were twelve properties or groups of properties itemised in the schedule accompanying the judgement. Here is a simplified list, with current owners and their records:

(i) John Juks held a messuage and land stretching from High Street into Peacocks Field. He paid no rent for four years.

(ii) John Atkys held a cottage with a garden next to St Edmund's Church. He paid no rent for two years.

(iii) Edward Baylyes and William Burder held a croft on the north-west of the High Street beyond what became Stafford Street. Baylyes, or Burder, had paid rent to the Mayor of Dudley.

(iv) John and Thomas Persehouse held land in Stoney Lane and had also paid rent to the mayor.

(v) Thomas Roades held a croft in Hall Street and had paid rent to the mayor for the previous six years.

(vi) Arthur Dixon held two cottages 'between the horsefayre and the sheep-fayre' and other land described, near the site of the present art gallery, and two acres in Peacocks Field, but he had paid no rent.

(vii) Roger Hill and Thomas Brooke held a garden in Stoney Lane. They had paid no rent.

(viii) Thomas Finch held a house of two bays in High Street, and had paid rent to the mayor for six years.

(ix) Oliver Shaw held land bordering Fishers Lane but had paid no rent for six years.

(x) Anne Henley held The Schoolhouse, adjoining St Edmund's churchyard, but had paid no rent.

(xi) John Roades and Abiathar his son held a garden near The Horsepool and had paid rent for the last six years.

(xii) Katherine Roades held land measuring about an acre in Peacocks Field, and a further plot of half an acre in the same field, and had paid rent to the mayor.

Although 3s per year had been paid to the mayor and bailiffs of Dudley, the jury agreed that rents which had been paid over to them had not been used as intended in the original 1562 document. They ordered that the properties should be made over to a new set of trustees headed by Richard Foley, whose family would play an increasingly important role in the town.

Besides the provisions of the 1562 settlement, the jury examined other charities, the funds of which had been misappropriated. The most significant was a legacy of Elizabeth Tomlinson, who had left between £40 and £50 (the sum was not exactly known as it was actually a debt owed to her). This money was to be for the benefit of the poor; the executors appointed at Elizabeth's death in 1629 decided to sell a horse to provide the money but apparently did not do so, since nine years later the horse was still in the hands of Thomas Dudley (one of the executors) and if any money had actually been raised, it had not been put to the use of the poor. There were other smaller legacies which had not paid any money to the poor. It seems clear that some of the more powerful citizens had disregarded their duties. Dudley's status as a borough was not being enhanced.

Richard Baxter and Dudley Grammar School

As a result of the enquiry about the grammar school lands, Richard Foley, now living in Stourbridge, was able to rebuild a schoolhouse and make an appointment to the post of master. His choice fell on Richard Baxter, son of another Richard from Eaton Constantine near Shrewsbury.[5] Baxter later wrote an autobiography in which he described his days at Dudley in the year 1638. He was ordained by the Bishop of Worcester in that year, and began teaching, aged 23, in the newly furnished schoolroom. As a clergyman, he also regarded it as part of his duties to take the pulpit at local churches, beginning with a sermon at St Thomas', his first ever. His feelings and opinions were strongly Protestant, just as were those of his patron, Richard Foley.

Baxter was not impressed by the previous behaviour of Dudley inhabitants, but he found them 'tractable' and 'more ready to hear God's Word with submission and reformation' than most other places he had lived. The neighbourhood was very populous, and he found woods and commons 'planted' with 'Nailers, Scithe-smiths, and other Iron- labourers, like a continued Village'. Doubtless he was thinking of Cawney Hill, parts of Netherton, and locations further afield in Rowley, Sedgley, Tipton and Kingswinford. However, he did not stay long in Dudley, feeling himself called to Bridgnorth within a year. His successor was a man named William Bradley. For many years Baxter's hymn 'Ye holy angels bright' was sung regularly at the start and finish of grammar school terms.

Dudley on the Verge of War

The lord of the manor, Edward Sutton, was nearing his end, as indeed was Dudley's peace. Sutton was to die within a few years, and the whole nation entered a period of civil war even before that. For a short while matters continued as normal. In 1637 Edward Sutton granted to John Payton a right of way through Rooes Land (Roseland Farm) by which he could reach an outlying field in his tenure, called Riddings. Ominously the document adds 'Let not this be shewed out to any one for it might do more harme than good.' We cannot know what mysterious dispute lies behind the caveat. By 1641, William Ward was acting as manorial lord, living at Himley and leasing land in Peacocks Field to a member of the Roades family, and near Dixon's Green to Henry and John Thornes, whose surname would be used later to identify this field. Finally, before war broke out, Edward Sutton leased to William Ward all the parts of Pensnett Chase which lay in Dudley manor, together with Roseland and Lord's Field.

It was the duty of the churchwardens to assess inhabitants for poor relief, and if possible to see that they pay the money. At no time was this easy. As we can see from the lack of support for the grammar school, the richer citizens did not always see it as in their interest to subsidise those less fortunate. Among others, the levy for 1640 has been preserved.[6] This gives us more information on who were the better off and how much they were expected to pay. Richard Foley of Netherton Hall led the field by a long length, being assessed at £1 6s 10d. The only other inhabitant paying more than £1 was Robert Dudley 'esquire', who paid £1 2s 11d for this property at Saltwater Mill (identifiable with Saltwells). Part of Russell's Hall was owned by Jeffrey Dudley or Sutton, and more by Selmon Wilcks. Other Netherton residents were Joseph Finch, Arthur Dixon, Henry and Edward Dixon and Edward Shaw (spelling modernised). Those who held small cottages were assessed at between 4d and 9d each.

Both the foreign and borough courts continued to be held as war threatened. The term 'foreign' was applied to the whole of the parish area outside the built-up portions of Dudley town: it included Netherton (including a large area simply thought of as Pensnett Chase), Windmill End, Dixon's Green, Cawney Hill, Sledmere, Freebody's, Eve Hill, Blowers Green, Woodside and Saltwells (not all these names were then in use). The borough covered only the main streets in the town, not including some parts of what became Wolverhampton Street or Hall Street. We see here the guarding of privileges related to the market and the original burgage properties, which had, however, by now been alienated from the families of their original owners. Later courts sometimes use the term 'manor' instead of foreign. It is not clear whether there was any legal distinction. The Dudley manor in fact did include the town area. It seems that the distinction between manorial government, in the hands of the manorial lords, and the borough government, in the hands of the burgesses, had become blurred.

In 1641, the borough jury, clearly chosen from those whose residence was in the town, consisted of (with the Latinised first names translated into English): William Bendie, John Baggley, Humphrey Bradney, Gilbert Gillians, John Payton senior, William Mansell, Edward Robinson, John Smart,

Thomas Holmer, Thomas Lowe, John Gillians, John Jewkes, Thomas Ascowe, John Hodgetts, John Dunton and John Marsh (surnames as original).[7] Names of those absent, who should have attended, are given; 16 appear to be burgesses and 67 other citizens. They were fined 1d or 2d according to status (the burgesses less than the others). The jury chose John Gillians as bailiff, Thomas Payton and Richard Parkes as constables, and Thomas Lacye and Edward Gillians as sergeants. Apart from these, officials were chosen to inspect various commodities coming up for sale in the market or in general in the parish. Their titles and tasks seem to have been varied in different years, at least at this period. Later, the titles and jurisdiction seem to have been more rigorously codified: in 1642 two officers were chosen to taste meat and fish, and two to check the quality of leather goods. Checking the weight of the butter and bread on sale in the market was the task of the bailiff and sergeant. A frequent problem seems to have been poor behaviour at alehouses, since the bailiff and sergeant were also to walk through the town twice a month on Saturday or Sunday nights to catch and punish offenders.

The 1641 jury were told that there were seven bakers producing bread which did not come up to standard (probably in weight, though the exact defect is not given). Fifteen ale sellers were fined 2d each for faulty beer, perhaps again deficient in quantity. These men didn't seem to care, as there are constant records of fines for infringements. Possibly the fines were too small to offset the profits made, and in any case, members of a jury might very easily find themselves charged the following year, suggesting that these were token fines administered by fellow tradesmen. The borough jury in 1641 was able to fine people for leaving pigs ('swine') unleashed, and for ineffective hedges, either too small or broken. These swine and hedges would be in the town itself.

The jury for the foreign held on 21 October 1641 consisted of Thomas Duddeley, Thomas Whitehouse, Richard Shaw, John Payton, Richard Parkes, John Cartwright, Thomas Feredie, Roger Hawkes, Thomas Billingsley, John Robinson, John Smith, William Turner and John English (Christian names de-Latinised, surnames as original). These men did not choose officers, and were clearly expected to accept the jurisdiction of the officers chosen for the borough. The jury ordered that Greystone Field should be better fenced, and that John Bagley (one of the borough jurors) should build a fence in Peacocks Field. A long-standing problem concerned 'inmates', presumably relatives or servants, coming to live with a householder and providing no security against the possibility of the parish having to sustain that person if he or she became ill.

The dominance of the borough court is emphasised in the 1642 roll, which rules on areas certainly outside the precise confines of the borough. Henry Fynch and George Bagley are to scour the ditch which leads from Woddams [sic] Hill to George Bagley's barn. The bailiff and mayor are to drive the wood four times a year, with help from reputable citizens ('paterfamilias' or 'aldermen'). Recalcitrant people could incur fines: Richard Hollies misbehaved and used *mala verba* ('bad words') against the bailiff. He was fined 2s. Edward Shord kept a *mordacissimum* ('very bitey') dog. This annoyed his neighbours and so he too was fined. Quarrels leading to bloodshed were penalised at 20d each: there were three in 1642. Many of these delinquencies continue through the years. They may even happen in Dudley today.

Dudley Castle becomes a Royalist Garrison[8]

The English Civil War affected Dudley greatly. The castle was one of three Midland centres fortified by the Royalists; parts of Dudley town were deliberately fired; St Edmund's Church was destroyed, and there were a number of smaller battles within sight of the castle. Little is recorded of the townsfolk, but the local presence of two warring forces must have caused great upset. Institutions such as the borough court continued, but under the shadow of disruption and the ruin of people's livelihoods. On the other hand, metal objects were in demand, and those involved in manufacture might make considerable profits. Richard Foley, now of Stourbridge, provided money for the king's horse, and Dud Dudley, illegitimate offspring of the manorial lords, provided resources. As the war began, troops of Welshmen arrived in Dudley to garrison the castle for the king. They are said to have been supported by nailers and colliers from Pensnett Chase. Once in the castle, they terrified the neighbourhood with drums and the random firing of musketry.

As commander of the garrison, the king chose Colonel Thomas Leveson of Wolverhampton, while a protagonist on the Parliamentary side was Sir William Brereton. There were no clear geographical boundaries in this war; some local towns, such as Birmingham, were more inclined to the Parliament, but the major landowners divided according to their own personal loyalties. Within a family, some could favour the king and some the Parliament. Doubtless this was the case also with the local inhabitants, though their main aim must have been to keep their property safe and to stay alive. In any case, they had to pay taxes to both sides and sometimes have their houses or goods requisitioned. Leveson was unhappy shut up in the castle, and in 1643 he led his motley men on raids throughout the northern parts of the Midlands, without achieving a great deal. Parliamentary organisation was in the hands of county committees, including in 1644 such men as William Bendy of Kingswinford and William Foxall of Trysull. It is possible that Dudley town gained from being in a different county from the castle, since the Staffordshire Committee did not have a mandate in Worcestershire. The maintenance of the garrison fell to the lot of inhabitants of the Seisdon hundred of Staffordshire. By May 1644 some of the members of the garrison were sloping off home towards Wales and had to be sought throughout the neighbourhood. No doubt many lurked in Pensnett Chase and were never found.

In June 1644, after successfully taking Rushall Hall near Walsall, the Parliamentary leader, the Earl of Denbigh, moved south-west to the Dudley area, appearing first near Stourbridge. He arrived at Dudley and camped at the foot of the castle, but different accounts of the skirmishes which took place make it hard to know what really happened. Denbigh mounted his only cannon in sight of the castle. It seems likely that this was on Kate's Hill, the most natural site from which to attack. During the excavations of 1980 a number of cannon balls were found, including one in the castle keep; this would be consistent with a Kate's Hill emplacement. The king's forces, under Lord Wilmot, were advancing from the south and Denbigh sent some of his men to oppose them. A fight took place somewhere in Dudley, perhaps at Battle Meadow, and Denbigh's men retreated. Wilmot advanced to the foot of the castle. Denbigh's men escaped in the direction of Tipton, either via the lane past the priory or along the Wednesbury road. A dispatch claimed that the Parliament soldiers were pursued to Tipton Green and routed, while Denbigh also claimed a victory. He had certainly besieged the castle, though it is not sure whether this was for a few days or three weeks as was later suggested. However, the siege was evidently not a success, since the Royalists continued to hold the castle despite a certain amount of damage which had to be repaired with 'lime … wood, timber and stone'. The departure of Denbigh's men was celebrated with music and, apparently, a feast.

For a while, Royalist and Parliamentary forces were occupied elsewhere, but the three Staffordshire fortresses of Tutbury, Lichfield and Dudley had to be attended to and Tutbury fell first, in spring 1646. Sir William Brereton led his troops to the castle on 5 May, having received a report about the strength of the garrison (265 soldiers, some with horses). His informant, Captain Seale, recommended that the area behind the gateway must be taken first: 'They have great store of Corne and a Corne mill and a powder mill but cannot make powder,' he wrote. There was a well in the 'Towre' which could be choked by battering the tower, and the gatehouse was very weak. There may have been some defects in Captain Seale's report, details of which are contradicted by an inventory taken later.

For his part, Leveson had tried to bolster the castle defences by clearing buildings close to the castle, such as demolishing St Edmund's Church. The stone lay about in piles and was now used by Brereton to make a wall from the end of Castle Street to the priory ruins. Houses had been set on fire, causing destruction at the east end of the town, but no townsmen moved to put the fires out, and the market was full of roving cattle, which Sir William Brereton tried to calm and return to their owners. Meanwhile men from Shropshire were wandering about and had arrived at the Priory pools, where they began fishing. Those in the castle saw this and ran out to the attack. Though sources do not mention it, the priory must have suffered damage at this point.

In any case, the buildings could not be defended and the Royalist soldiers were soon driven back inside the castle walls.

Dud Dudley Fights Again

For a while there was a lull in the fighting, not only in Dudley but through-out England. However, the Royalists were not yet finished, and in north Worcestershire Colonel Dud Dudley was foremost among the leaders of dissi-dents who were being drilled to fight on. A small force of 200 men was formed, and were trained at Boscobel. A surprise attack caught them, and Dud was taken to Hartlebury Castle and imprisoned. Showing enormous self-confi-dence, he tried to escape, failed and was taken to Worcester, but tried again and this time succeeded. One account says that, upon arriving in London, he was captured and condemned to death by firing squad, but escaped yet again and returned to the Midlands, though wounded in the leg, hoping to ensure the survival of his furnaces in Pensnett Chase.[9] An alternative story is that he was actually captured in a skirmish in early July 1648, among a group of gentry who were planning to drill soldiers in Shropshire. The skirmish is alleged to have occurred at Wolverley. The memorial previously quoted says he was 'saepe captus … *semel condemnatus et tamen non decollatus*', (often captured, once found guilty but not executed). Whichever version is correct, Dud Dudley did return to Worcestershire and lived throughout the Commonwealth period. Meanwhile, King Charles had escaped to France, returned to London, been tried and, on 30 January 1649, was executed.

Parochial Tidying

The Royalists had lost, perhaps it might have been thought for ever. Soon a Commonwealth was declared, with Oliver Cromwell at its head. During this period, churches were deprived of their functions: marriages took place before magistrates and much of the ornament left during the reforms of Henry VIII was removed; the Church of England prayer book was banned. Unfortunately we have no detailed account of how this affected St Thomas', by this time the only church left in central Dudley.

In Dudley the administrative system had to be rectified. With the castle damaged, the whole of the east end of the town in ruins, St Edmund's destroyed, along with many documents and files (the loss of which is still felt), it was necessary to begin taking stock and repairing information gaps. It seems likely that there was an intention to rebuild St Edmund's in the fairly near future, and parish boundaries were not abolished, since land transfer documents, etc., often state which of the two parishes the parties inhabit. However, there was only one set of churchwardens and parish officers, and only one vicar (after 1646, Mr John Taylor). Nothing could be done with the ruins, and nonconformist groups were arising to fill the gap formerly occupied by St Edmund's. Many years would go by before the church would be replaced, though the congregations of both Dudley churches repaired St Thomas' following a decision of 30 September 1648.[10]

A New and Thorough Survey[11]

Part of the clearing up after hostilities was the effort to discover who now owned or tenanted each piece of land, and the extent of that land. A survey was made in 1649 by the overseers of the poor, Jeffery Finch, John Finch, Thomas Shaw and William Price, to renew their records and evaluate the contribution

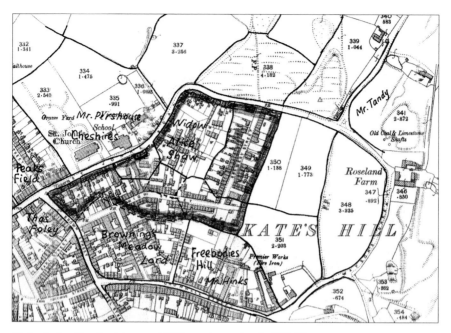

23 Freebodies: Shaw's estate around 1725, superimposed on the 1901 OS map.

to be demanded of each landholder. This survey gives a most detailed picture of Dudley in the mid-seventeenth century. It is impossible to give all the detail here, but it will be worth extracting some facts. Names of fields, approximate acreages, even some families holding land, remain the same for 250 years.

The surveyors began at the east end of Dudley town, walking down Castle Hill to Lord's Fields, the 48-acre estate on the south side of what is now Birmingham Road, a north-facing slope. Almost at the parish boundary they turned up Bunns Lane, noting Roseland (55 acres), and on to Freebodies (Kate's Hill), of which 3.5 acres belonged to Thomas Shaw. Proceeding across Cawney Hill, they noted Groves Land on the Rowley Regis side, then on the slope facing Sledmere, land at Tansley. They also took in part of Dixon's Green.

At Sledmere ('Sledmore' in the survey) they listed land belonging to Mr Foley of Netherton Hall, and walked down Buffery Road to Baptist End. They noted land at 'Cucks Tetnall' (where the gasworks would later be built) and then returned to the main Halesowen road at 'Orsonbarbas', soon to be the location for Cinder Bank Baptist Chapel. There were many small closes in the area where Netherton town would one day be built. Soon the surveyors were at Windmill End, noting Richard Parkes' (or 'Parkhouse') meadows by the side of the mill stream. Here also was Withey Croft, later Withymoor, and the edge of Pensnett Chase was reached. The chase still covered south-ern Netherton, and did not need to be surveyed. Returning northward, our surveyors passed Joseph Finch's property and arrived at Netherton Hall. On the north-east side of this, bordering the Halesowen Road on one side and stretching to the open fields surrounding the town, was Yoake Park, its name variously spelt over the years, and sometimes becoming Ox Park. To the west and south of the hall were fields called Cinderbanke, Peartree Leasow and five little fields called Silence. Near the hall itself was Motmeadow (Moat Meadow), showing that Netherton Hall once had a moat round it. Altogether, Mr Foley owned over 195 acres.

Walking towards Dudley town the surveyors next found The Farthings, next to modern Aston Road. On the hillside leading up to this was an estate belong-ing to a Mr Leader (elsewhere called Leather), nowadays the industrial area south-west of Blowers Green. This land was bounded by Eaves Brook. A field here was called Holes, presumably where coal was being dug out. On the other side of the Stourbridge Road was the strangely named Chilly Charles, men-tioned by the surveyors before they returned to the south side and looked at Parson's Fields, stretching to Woodside. 'Scots' indicated the place elsewhere called Scots Green, and on the north side of the road, Ashen Coppice. Entering the medieval New Park the surveyors found Gorstey Round Bank and other fields, then walked to the mill pool (it is not clear whether the ancient mill in the centre of Russell's Hall estate was still working at this time). They were now on the land of the Dudley family, owned by the Russell's Hall branch. Arbor Hill was the largest leasow here, at 14 acres.

Jeffery Finch and his companions (if they did the surveying themselves) were on the western edge of Dudley town, though still in the land called The Foreign. Near Eve Hill they noted Guns Croft, Battle Meadow and Tutbury Croft. Land which had belonged to the priory was listed and the acreages estimated. Among the ex-priory closes were Colpitt Leasow, Belman's Close, Long Meadow and Stockhall Field. A few fields lingered within the town itself, for example Safforne Croft, near modern Stafford Street, and a number of small crofts known only by the names of the current occupiers. The surveyors were principally interested in land, and so did not survey the small gardens attached to the houses in town, nor the houses themselves. However, there is a little more to be gained from their account of the valuations, where they do charge individual houses.

About 162 houses are mentioned in the evaluation for the levy, but there are many entries in which 'houses' are mentioned without a number being given.

A better indication of the number of houses in Dudley will be given some years later, on one of the Hearth Tax documents. A few locations in town appear in the levy. Sam Bagley has houses at Wadams Hill, Richard Bagley in Hall Street. Thomas Baylies' house is at Porter's Field, and the Dixons own Hill House, near Dixon's Green. Widow Idson's house is located 'by the Almeshouse' (in modern Tower Street), while one John Jewks has a dwelling at 'Cros'; another man of the same name lives at 'The Horspool'. The overseers of the poor avoided listing 'field land' on the ground that it 'passed almost as formerly …', but perhaps they found the listing and delineation of the complex small strips an intimidating task. The survey and evaluation contain other names, too many to detail here.

A Town Hall, Paved Streets and a Boundary Check

Clearing up after the war involved radical new building. A market hall, called the Town Hall, was built on the site of the present Dudley fountain in 1653.[12] It is possible that there was a previous market house, but no record of it seems to have survived. Old drawings of the 1653 building show an upper storey supported on pillars in the manner of Ludlow butter cross and many early market buildings. Construction was of brick with stone parapets and a clock tower, presumably added later. Records exist of a voluntary effort to pave 'ye St called Hampton Street or Hampton Lane', perhaps as far as the Horsefair (Priory Street).[13] The minister, John Taylor, may have been a dominant mover in this work, since he is recorded as giving stone from a glebe quarry, probably in the area beyond Shavers End.

In some cases the precise amount of help given is recorded: 'Captain' Dixon gave one day's work with a team of horses, William Parshouse one day's work for one man, Oliver Shaw and Henry Payton 'carriage', i.e. transport of stone and rubble. Henry Jewkes, limeman, contributed in a way not detailed, but presumably supplying lime for grouting the gaps between the large slabs of limestone. Two other members of the Jewkes family, given as 'of Horspoole', also gave assistance. A useful donor was William Price of Netherton Hall, and Thomas Oxford the schoolmaster is also mentioned.

Some church obligations were resumed despite the Puritan crackdown on forms of worship. It had been a custom in many churches to perambulate the bounds of the parish in Rogation week. This generally involved a number of parishioners leaving their work and taking young boys with them to imprint clearly on the minds of the boys exactly where their parish ended. The boys would grow up and in turn pass on their knowledge to future generations, at a time when written documents were accessible to few. Parish boundaries were most important, partly because anyone falling on hard times within a given parish would become a charge on that parish: immigration was not encouraged unless the immigrant could contribute wealth to the community. The Rogation-tide perambulation in Dudley in 1656 took place on 14 May.

The damaged report in the churchwardens' book laments the tiredness of the people walking.[14] Once again John Taylor led the enterprise, taking a group of elders such as Old John Edson, with small boys such as John Edson's grandson. They began on Pensnett Chase, with Saltwater Mill and the mill pool, and then up to Fensbanke and Fens Brook Side, probably the brook later called Ennis brook and Eaves brook (a very unstable name), to the east of the Pedmore Road. It is not clear that the identification of the boundaries was very accurate: 'some places in the Comon [Pensnett Chase, i.e. South Netherton] were not well known by som' and the writer admits that they were not perambulated. Not only were the parishioners dubious about the boundaries, but they were also 'weary'; their weariness was 'the greatest cause that hindered'. The defective book does tell us that eventually they reached the New Park, across the fields by what became Wapping Dock, identified by a house belonging to (Richard?) Wilkes. At this point the account breaks off, and altogether is not very satisfactory to anyone trying to trace Dudley boundaries after the Civil War.

It may be that the energetic Puritan minister, John Taylor, was a little too enthusiastic and organising for the natives of Dudley. Possibly their 'weariness' was in part reluctance.

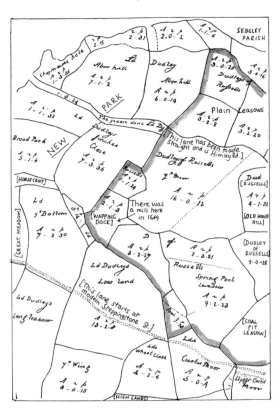

24 Plan of New Park: the fields, based on the Court Map.

Netherton Baptists

The site of Cinder Bank Baptist Chapel is still today partly free of building, and carries a memorial plaque. The congregation, now dispersed, could trace its origin to the year 1654, when a certain Edward Williams was baptised, though the exact location of this baptism is not known. Clearly the spirit of Protestantism was strong in the area, perhaps accentuated by the absence of any place of worship in Netherton. Church governance in the Baptist denomination was very different from the hierarchical structure which produced John Taylor, for all his Puritan leanings. Edward Williams was made an elder in 1665, and Hugh Davies was made deacon. The register book, though dating much later, records five or six baptisms in 1657, and three further in the following year.[15] The meeting house seems to have been built on the Cinderbank site from the first, though we can have no idea of its appearance. In all likelihood it was an offshoot from Cradley Baptist Chapel, as Edward Williams (if it was the same man) appears to have been a member there.

Land for the chapel was either given or leased by Hugh Dixon at Orsonbarbas or (later) Ashen Barbers, a mysterious name for the Netherton site, perhaps representing an earlier owner's name: Austin Barber (though no record of such a person has been found). Hugh Dixon seems to have been a committed member of the congregation. This was the first nonconformist congregation we hear of in Dudley, the first of many. Members seem to be drawn from a wide area, and since they do not seem to feature in land transfers, we may consider that they were small cottagers. Discipline seems to have been strict: for example 'Stevon Colle' was baptised in January 1672, but 'chast out' in August 1680 'offering the uctes of uncleanines'(acts?), but after being reproved and admonished he repented and returned to the fold. He later withdrew from the chapel, but rejoined after 'manifesting of sorrow'. In the 1670s Phebe Davis was cast out for 'mareying out the church … and giving to dancing.'

Hearth Tax[16]

After the monarchy was restored, King Charles II was in serious need of funds. He decided to tax hearths, on the grounds that the previous poll taxes failed to work because people could move about; hearths could not. Lists of taxpayers were drawn up by local constables, but these men were friends of some of the taxpayers. They often left their friends off the lists. There were various kinds of exemptions, the basic line being drawn at property worth 20s per annum. For these reasons the lists are defective. In addition, some lists have been nibbled by mice and stained by water.

For Dudley, there are lists from 1662, 1664 (two), 1671 and 1672–4. When it was discovered in 1664 that the local officials were cheating His Majesty, county collectors were brought in, so that the list for Michaelmas 1664 is much fuller than the earlier ones. It includes more detail about those exempted. In 1662 the constables failed to list them, merely noting that there were some 'poore peepell' from whom they could not collect. John Newcon junior and Richard Payton were in prison, and there were uninhabited houses whose owners lived outside the parish. Edward and Thomas Homer were two of them. Only a few of the 226 householders listed were identified by location. Thomas Payton was of 'Caney Hill', Henry Roods and John Smith of 'woods', Thomas Darby of 'lodge' (later Lodge Farm), one John Jukes of 'Horspoole' and another John Jukes of 'Cross'. One Thomas Shaw was of 'pinfold', while another of the same name was of the 'Cock'. These placings are an attempt to clarify when (as often in Dudley) there are more then one resident of the same name.

Another method is by trade, so that Henry Jukes is 'limeman', while one of the men called John Shaw is 'sithsmith'.

The list for Lady Day 1664 is badly damaged, but adds a few legible notes in the margin, such as 'no such person' and 'returned one too many', seemingly to try to diminish the numbers paying. This list also adds 'P' (for poor) by the side of many inhabitants, and lists over 240 houses (the exact number is dubious because of missing pieces). It was after this rather evasive listing that authority changed the system. The result was a much more comprehensive list, including 183 taxpayers and about 236 non-payers (there are possible gaps). The total would be about 419, which corresponds to a note apparently from 1663, giving a total of 432. Two other lists from the 1670s seem to have been based on pre-1664 records. They are not without interest, but the late 1664 register seems best.

These hearth tax returns give us some clue as to the total population of Dudley (including Netherton) in the 1660s. Researchers have calculated that the average household in the 1660s consisted of about 4.3 men, women and children. Using this as a multiplier, we get an approximate population for Dudley of just over 1,800. This is probably the most accurate estimate we can obtain before census figures begin in 1801.

Unfortunately it is impossible to identify many of the houses listed. Comparison with the 1649 levy suggests that many inhabitants have died or moved. Richard Bolton occupies the Priory (said in a marginal note to be 'in Staffordshire', though this is dubious). Gilbert Jelians or Gillians has five hearths and owns houses in 'town' as well as his own dwelling, probably near Dixon's Green (he is one of those who 'returned too many'); there are two Thomas Dudleys, one at Russells Hall and one at Netherton (1662). Henry Payton has five hearths and Henry Finch six, reduced to five on the plea of returning too many. Thomas Hawkes has a house called Bagley's Lodge with five hearths; the evidence for this comes from a contemporary deed, which situates the lodge in 'the Old Parke', i.e. near the castle.[17]

St Thomas' Church

Despite the rise of Netherton Baptists, most religious activity, and indeed social activity of any kind, focused on St Thomas'. Edward Mackerness was now vicar, but there were still signs of dissension. In 1674 the churchwardens, Edward Wells and John Worsley, named Richard Cartwright and the widow Margaret Payton for not paying a levy to the church, thirteen people for not paying their Easter dues, and five for complete non-attendance.[18] This revelation came at a bishop's 'visitation', during which the Bishop of Worcester and his subordinates made a detailed enquiry into the state of the church. The church itself and the churchyard walls were reported to be in good repair, but the issue of Nonconformity had become a serious concern, with the report of two 'houses' where 'strangers' meet, but who they are 'wee know not'. We may guess that one of these houses was the Cinder Bank Chapel already mentioned. It is not clear whether these chapels for 'strangers' are the same as the 'house newly built in his garden' by Robert Wall for a Nonconformist meeting place. There is also a note of 'presbiterians' meeting at a house provided by Margaret Milner, and a 'Turton of Rowley', probably the well-known clergyman William Turton, speaking there. Three members of St Thomas' had been excommunicated, and there were three Catholic recusants, Thomas Osborne, John Higgins and Henry Juckes.

Two years later, in 1676, the churchwardens listed forty-three people for 'dissenting'. Higgins, Osborne and Henry 'Jewkes' were among the list, and it is therefore not certain whether these dissenters were Catholic or Protestant. As well as the known Catholics, many holders of common Dudley names appear on this list: William Woodall, Roger Shakespeare, Thomas Darby, Henry Whitehouse, Francis Dudley and William Hancox are some examples (spelling modernised). A Hugh Dixon junior appears, suggesting that the Cinder Bank Chapel has been taken into account.[19]

In 1679 a Quaker meeting is mentioned. Its prominent figures are John Payton, Thomas Caddick and John Roades. The list of 'popish recusants' has grown. It still includes John Higgins, and the names of Thomas Osborne's wife (Elizabeth) and Henry Juckes' wife (Mary) are given. James Juckes, the son of Henry and Mary, is also named. To these are added John Baylies and Susanna, Robert Smith and Catherine, George Green and Mary. It does not seem that there is a Catholic church in Dudley, and we may think it likely that these popish recusants attended a church in Sedgley. Edward Mackerness was still the vicar in 1679, with Edward Elwell and William Finch as churchwardens. They kindly record that Mackerness is 'able and sufficient', and that the church and churchyard are in good repair.

Once again, in May 1682, there is a report from the churchwardens on the state of St Thomas' and religion in Dudley.[20] A problem has arisen about the state of the chancel at St Thomas', and the onus of repair is on the 'improprietor', Samuel While of Pedmore. In accordance with custom, the individual who bought the church tithes had a duty to repair that part of the church. Mr While had not done so, but promised to remedy the defects. The same Catholic recusants were reported as in 1679, and John Payton was again mentioned as the speaker at the Quaker meeting. There was an 'Anabaptist' meeting at which one William Pardoe 'of this City' had spoken. (We should not take the word 'city' too literally.)

Topography in the Late Seventeenth Century

Land transfers in this period continue to illuminate more about the landscape features of Dudley parish. Bagley's Lodge was 'situated in the Old Parke' and was bordered by a garden and part of the park. Its land projected into Sedgley, with the 'Wren's Nest Hill' on the west.[21] There was a hedge and ditch between it and the 'Great Poole Damms'. The lease to Thomas Hawkes, in 1663, excepted the Great Pool itself, the Castle Mill Pool, limestone quarries and the mill dam. Excavation of coal and ironstone is shown by a lease of 1667, which grants Robert Foley the minerals in 2 acres of land in Church Field, identifiable with an area below St Thomas' Church.[22] Queen's Cross bank features in a deed of 1668, with the road to Stourbridge and Kingswinford being called The Portway.[23]

In what became Wolverhampton Street, Gilbert Jelians bought a 'mansion house' in the occupation of John Lowe and Thomas Jewkes.[24] This area was still called The Horsepool. Further along the road on the north side, in 1674 a large house known as Colborne's House is described as a 'capital messuage or burgage'. It had barns, stables and other outbuildings attached. Gilbert Jelians' daughter, Alice, married Oliver Shaw in 1675, necessitating the drawing up of a detailed marriage settlement, which gives further details of the topography of late seventeenth-century Dudley. The items included land in Church Field and

25 Gilbert Gellians' (Jellians'; Gelians') house in Hampton Lane. Stones from the priory seem to have been incorporated in it.

a 'messuage, tenement and burgage' of Oliver Shaw the elder, with a dwelling house where John Wowen, gent, lived.[25]

The deed also mentions a close and burgages near Fishers Lane (Fisher Street), two closes called Swines Croft (in other deeds called Swaynes Croft) near Yoakes Park and a field called Peakes Field (near modern Dixon's Green). Between this field and the site of St Edmund's Church various fields were included, with a little croft by the churchyard which adjoined the 'head street' near the ruins of St Edmund's. Dixon's Green is named in a slightly later deed, with a field near Crookes Lane (at the beginning of the road now leading to Rowley via Knowle, which was not then built).

Dr Plot and Dudley Coal

It was in 1686 that a work was printed which throws light on the early days of Dudley's trade in coal. This was Dr Robert Plot's *The Natural History of Staffordshire*, intended to be part of a series of what we might call county histories.[26] Dealing with an incident of fire in a coal mine reported by the historian Camden, Plot corrects his authority by pointing out that fire can occur below ground spontaneously, and implies that this could be the case with Camden's example, which is said to have occurred at Broadhurst on 'Pensnet' [Chase] because of a careless miner with a candle. He quotes Dud Dudley as describing the layers of coal as: 'white coal' (so-called because of a white substance found in them which has been called arsenical); the 'shoulder coal'; the 'toe coal'; the 'foot coal'; the 'yard coal'; the 'slipper coal'; the 'sawyer coal'; the 'frisley coal', after which comes a layer of ironstone, and then further coal measures.

The location of Dudley's coal works at this time seems to have been chiefly at Knowle Hill in what we now know as Netherton but then considered part of Pensnett Chase, and in the two former parklands near Dudley Castle.[27] The most important was Knowle Hill, which could make almost £98 for the estate in a good month.[28] The Dudley rent rolls of 1701 show John Tandy as steward for Lord Dudley's land, including Himley Hall, Oliver Dixon his steward for the castle and its land, William Cardale seneschal for Rowley Regis, William Guest (also 'Geast') bailiff for the market tolls, and Oliver Dixon with Ferdinando Dudley in charge of the coal works at Knowle Hill.[29]

Dr Plot was also interested in the mining and processing of ironstone. He mentions a type of iron ore near Dudley which is very sulphurous and unfit to make into iron. Again he quotes Dud Dudley as describing this ore as 'red-share' on the ground, that it cracks in red heat. Just as there are names for the various types of coal, so 'redshare' seems to be an alternative name of one of the types he lists in order of their occurrence below the coal. First come the black, dun and white 'row grains', so-called from the earth in which they lie, then the rider stone, cloud stone, bottom stone and the 'Cannoc or Cannot Stone'. He contrasts these names with those used at Rushall and Walsall, where much the same configuration of the seams is implied but with variant names.

In his history section Plot repeats a suggestion of Camden's that Dudley Castle could have been founded in Anglo-Saxon times by a gentleman called Dudo.[30] No evidence has been found by archaeologists to support this, but it is a legend which has not faded. Describing the state of the castle in his time, Plot points out its high position: 'exposed to the ventilation of the Air … [its] magnificent ruins as well as habitable part (built on a lofty rock) notwithstanding the shrubs and trees all about it, are lifted so high above them all, as not only to afford a most wholsom air, but a delicat [sic] prospect over the County below it … notwithstanding its ruins remains the Seat of the right Honourable Lord Ward Baron of Birmingham, a person of most exemplary fidelity to his Prince, and a most noble encourager of this Work …'[31]

26 Dr Plot's illustration of Dudley Castle in the seventeenth century.

Where is the Vicar to Live?

During the last part of the seventeenth century the town was still trying to come to terms with the devastation caused by the siege of Dudley Castle in the 'late war'. St Edmund's had been the more important church, but still lay in a heap of rubble, from which parishioners were sometimes helping themselves to incorporate in their own new housing. As the churchwardens of the 1680s surveyed their heritage, they totalled up the church vessels: one pewter flagon, two silver cups, two pewter plates and no pails.[32] A new vicar, William Cleiveland (variously spelt), was inducted in 1684, and Jonathan Taylor and John Parkes could happily report that the church was in good repair and that inhabitants 'diligently frequent the church', a view which was surely unsustainable. The usual suspects, Thomas Osborne, John Higgins, John Bayliss and James Jucks, were still absenting themselves to attend a Catholic church, and it was only two years since, in 1682, 'Christian Lewis a stranger dissenter' was living in the town and teaching without a licence.

It may be that Taylor and Parkes had sought to present a positive initial view so that they could address with the diocese the issue of a new vicarage. William Cleiveland had nowhere to live. At the time, there were many pluralist vicars who would have no intention of living near their flocks, and the churchwardens obviously hoped to avoid this in Dudley. Despite the good state of the fabric of St Thomas', they reported that there was no vicarage since 'same was demolished by souldiers in the late Civil Warrs'.[33] It is not clear that the problem of the vicarage was solved, at any rate not for many years. William Cleiveland is recorded as living in various places, apparently not purpose built. The church continued to be repaired, however, and in 1699 the new churchwardens could report that 'our Books bells surplice and all ornaments to our church are in good repair'.[34]

Dudley Market and Trading

The market in the centre of the town, adjoining the new market hall, had struggled to compete with markets in other local towns. Now, in 1685, King Charles II granted the Lord of the Manor (Edward Ward) the right to hold two annual fairs, on 21 September and 27 April. By the early eighteenth century the additional date of 25 July was included. There was a further increase at an unknown later date. Accounts of the horse fairs are preserved and show people travelling from some distance to buy and sell horses in Dudley; however, much of the trade was with local people in such places as Halesowen, Handsworth and Oldbury.[35] It needs to be remembered how important horses were in those days as the only viable means of transport and for working in both farms and industry. These sales seem to have taken place in what is now Priory Street, and were clearly useful, though it is possible that little revenue passed to the borough from them.

The exercise of some trades was still jealously guarded. In 1683, a group of iron mongers, including Thomas Sergeant of Pilkington in Lancashire, reported that John Finch was carrying on the trade of 'iron monger' in his Dudley home and was buying and selling iron and nails.[36] He owed £500 to one of the petitioners, William Cardale. The chancery document lists Finch's holdings in Dudley, which included much property once belonging to Henry Finch, mainly in the area we now call Burnt Tree.

THE EARLY EIGHTEENTH CENTURY

During the reign of Queen Anne and the earlier part of George I's reign many developments took place which changed Dudley into the place we know today. Grand new houses were built in the centre of the town, industries to sustain them flourished, and a splendid modern church – St Edmund's – was designed and built.

The first detailed map of Dudley was produced, and when Robert Foley of Stourbridge died, leaving his Netherton Hall property to his son, North Foley, the latter married and a list of the Netherton properties was drawn up. Dudley residents were enrolled as manorial 'resiants' by the Lord of the Manor, and court rolls describe some of their doings. In the mid-century a disaster overtook the castle: fire raged, destroying much of the residential accommodation and invalidating the building for habitation. The earliest drawing of the old priory was made by visiting artists.

In 1701 there was a survey of all houses and residents in the town centre, not including the foreign and Dixon's Green.[1] This may be compared to a second list, printed by John Hemingway, and a 'bhurgers' list from 1703/4 described as being taken from court rolls. (A similar list from 1686 has mainly been destroyed.) By the side of the names are numbers, and it has been suggested that these were a primitive house numbering system for the main streets. This is possible, but these numbers are not used outside the survey, its later version or the derived burgage list of 1703/4, so that it does not seem that they were a way to identify houses *in situ*. Far the most populous street was High Street (also 'head street' and 'main street' at various times). There were 190 houses here, the whole road from the market to Queen's Cross being included. Forty houses were labelled 'burgages' in the 1701 version (perhaps forty-two, depending on whether adjacent houses were counted as one or more). Deeds constantly show burgages being sold, but there is evidence that the sale did not always imply physical properties: rights were being sold to individuals with the houses, but the land and house themselves appear not to have carried the title. (*see* Appendix)

Hampton Lane (Wolverhampton Street) contained seventy-one houses, of which three were regarded as burgages. Stony Lane (Stone Street) contained nine houses and one burgage.

Sheep Fair (Priory Street) included no burgages among its twenty-one houses; neither did New Street among its thirty-six. Next on the list was Back Lane, the name used at the time for the northern branch of High Street, above the market and east of the market hall. By this time the buildings in the centre of the market were called Middle Row (where today's market stalls are set up). We can identify one of the Back Lane houses as in Middle Row, and some others may have been, though many seem to have been on the north side, a continuation of High Street.[2] Soon this area would be called Queen Street, presumably in commemoration of Queen Anne (the first occurrence I can find of the name is in 1705). Four of these houses were burgages, including the first house, belonging to Richard Bolton of the Priory.

Back Lane is followed by Castle Street, part of the town where there is a great deal of evidence gathered from deeds. There were sixty houses in Castle Street, including Oliver Shaw's 'mault rooms', the house of Mr John Wowen, Robert Baylis' burgage, which became the site of Bayliss' charity school (all on the north side), and several houses belonging to John Payton. His 'dwelling-house' was on the corner of modern Fisher Street, later the site of Stanton's music shop. Also along the south side was the house which developed into the

28 Wolverhampton Street; an eighteenth-century creation.

Woolpack, then tenanted by William Bissell. Ten of these houses were burgages, possibly more if the survey's brackets are re-interpreted.

Hall Street had seventy-six houses, stretching as far as Waddams' Pool. Small-scale pictures of a slightly later date seem to suggest that most of these were Elizabethan-style timber-framed houses, but seemingly with brick casings. Seven were burgages. A final section of the survey lists houses in Vicarage Lane and Fishers Lane (Fisher Street). There was still no vicarage, and this road name refers to the old vicarage, which had stood on modern Birmingham Street, but was destroyed along with St Edmund's in the Civil War. Most of the houses here were tenancies of John Payton, whose Castle Street home backed onto them. At the east end were the Vicarage Croft and churchyard. It can be assumed that at this time some of the remains of old St Edmund's existed, but no illustration has come to light. There were no burgages here.

The Payton family were a considerable power in Dudley. They traced their descent from an early inhabitant of Rowley Regis, and included the Quaker John Payton, whose meeting house had been the subject of a churchwardens' presentment in 1679.

In 1703, the son of John Payton, also John, married Mary Fidoe of Wednesbury. A document endorsed 'our marriage certificate' was signed on 6 September by forty-seven people, who presumably attended the ceremony.[3]

They appear mainly to be Dudley residents, including the interestingly named Epaphra Bagnall and Cornelius Hawkes. Some cannot be identified, and presumably came from Wednesbury. John Payton gives his trade as a 'mercer' in the later marriage settlement, dated 3 April 1705, of his brother Henry who married Mary Stephens of Leominster. Henry was also a mercer.

Much property is listed in this settlement, giving us some idea of the closely interlocking buildings on the south of Castle Street. Henry Payton owns the cellar under the 'shop' occupied by his brother John, a malthouse adjoining the kitchen and the 'middle stable'. There was also a barn and a walled garden by a well. The Paytons kept pigs in their pigsty, and used the 'house of office' near the 'lower stable' as a toilet. Payton land stretched from Castle Street to the 'back lane', this time a name for what is called The Vicarage Lane in the 1701 survey. (The term 'back lane' is used in Dudley deeds to represent various unnamed streets). The same document contains an example of a common Dudley habit, to provide an alias for people with common names, in this case Thomas Henley 'alias horseshoes', the nickname doubtless indicating Henley's trade. The Paytons also owned land on the south side of this lane, part of which had the name Compton's Close. Some Payton land was situated on the road to Rowley on both sides of the road, described in a 1701 deed as 'the road from Dudley to Conney Hill'. Part of their land on Cawney Hill was called Amsley, a name which finally added a 'T' at the front and became Tansley.

We know a little more about Dudley residents in 1700-3 from the lists of confirmation candidates.[4] About thirty-six females were confirmed in June 1700, including 'Mrs Ann Corfield' and Elizabeth Cleveland, the vicar's daughter, who is put near the head of the list presumably on grounds of status. The list is unfortunately blotted and defective. About fifty males were confirmed, apparently including several adults: Mr John Wowen, who had been born in 1686, and Gilbert Shaw, born 1688. The vicar's son, William Cleveland, appears in this list. The fact that adults were among the confirmands suggests that the previous bishop had not been active.

Court Leet

The manor court was concerning itself with the inhabitants who broke manorial rules. Burgagers were fined 1d for breaking 'the assize of bread' and 2d for breaking 'the assize of ale'. Non-burgers were charged 2d for bread and

6*d* for ale. They continued to do so year after year, obviously considering that these fines were worth paying for the privilege of selling ale and bread which broke quality regulations.[5] The market evidently had fixed opening and closing times, and there was trouble with some stallholders who wished to start early. They were to be fined 6*s* 8*d* if stalls remained after eleven o'clock on a Saturday night. John Payton makes another appearance, with John Benson, John Henley and others, for not controlling their pigs ('swine'), which should have been yoked, ringed and tied up. New Street, Back Lane and Hall Street suffered from people making muck hillocks and dung hills on them, a habit which was forbidden. There was a problem with Nathellen Addoe's 'little house of office' and people were laying 'rubbidge' in the little lane leading from the Pinfold Gate to the Vicar's Gate (now King Street).

John Benson did not act to restrain his pigs. In 1702 the court threatened a 'peane' of 1*s* 6*d* to him and several others 'for Theayr Piggs going in Grestone [Greystone] field and for Damadg thear'.[6] There was a difficulty with people who would 'anoy' the market by tying their horses in or near the market or market place. In future they would be fined 10*s*. Efforts were made later that year to ensure that the market place was kept clean. Stallholders Banester, Pinly and Parkhouse must clean up the 'chanell by ye Towne hall' when they have removed their stalls on a market day. There are frequent references in these rolls to muck and dung being left in the streets. Further from the marketplace, the owners of hedges along the narrow lanes leading to it from Netherton and elsewhere were often told to 'plech' (pleach, 'lay') these field boundaries. Water supply on the ridge was a perpetual concern, with landholders trying to turn off water from its natural flow in the small brooks. An example in 1702 is that of widow Bate, who allows her tenants to turn water from 'the over church' (St Thomas') 'and through the vicarage gate which led to Church Field.'

Robert Foley of Stourbridge was the owner of Netherton Hall. When he died, a court called for the 'forrein' decided that his son North was the heir. When burgagers died it was customary to pay a 'black bill' to the lord, but this time the court were unable to be sure what was owing. Robert Foley did not hold a burgage, and though his hall could be described as a 'capital messuage', Netherton was not a manor. The court, meeting in October 1702, put off any decision until they had investigated further.

A major problem confronting the jurors of the foreign was the illegal enclosure of the commons. This was caused by squatters who had erected small cottages at the edge of the commons taking in small pieces of land adjacent to their dwellings. The process had been going on for many years and clearly could not be stopped. Though those who infringed manorial writ were 'amerced' (paid a fine), no real effort was undertaken to remove the enclosures, and in any case it would not have succeeded and was probably not economically desirable. In 1701, nine inhabitants took land at Cawney Hill: John Mallenn, John Diteridge, John and Edward Woodall, Thomas Danks, Edward Hanley, George Guest, and William and Edward Hubball. Their descendants stayed on Cawney Hill and can be found in the 1841 census. Far more inhabitants took land at Pensnett Chase, the large area stretching from the centre of modern Netherton to Mushroom Green, Darby End and Woodside. In 1701 there were twenty-six such infringements, and once again these cottagers tenaciously held onto their plots to the nineteenth century and beyond. A distinction is made between these cottagers and others who had taken 'plackes' (plecks) out of the common. They were given four months to take down their barriers.

On occasions the court summoned old inhabitants to testify about ancient rights of way or routes to or through the common fields. For example, in 1702 such an enquiry was held about ways to Newcombs Inage, in which Samuel Bowers (aged about 50), John Baleys (70) and John Holmer (80) were witnesses. Fights are occasionally mentioned in the court rolls, as when in 1703 Josiah Bach and Edward Attwood are fined for breaking Her Majesty's peace and 'Drawing Blood' each of the other.[7] More serious violence was dealt with at Worcester.

Another example of the issue concerning old ways into common fields was a matter for debate in 1705. This concerned a route from Dudley (near Castle Street) to Porter's Field. Samuel Robinson or Mason (70-plus) and William Southall (75) were called. Both had lived in Dudley all their lives. They gave evidence that there had always been two ways from the town to the field, one via lands of Lord Dudley currently held by widow Bond and also, more often, through a gate leading from Humphrey Bannister's house off Hall Street. These old men with their long memories were vital to the peace of the borough, their evidence always proving acceptable and decisive.

St Thomas' churchwardens were always aware of various kinds of defaulters. Church levies were an important issue for them, sometimes avoided by the better-off residents. In August 1703 they record default in this matter by widow Parkes of 'Withimore' Mill, Richard Parkes of The Lodge (Netherton) and William Prise of Pertrelane. It is interesting that all these are Netherton residents, who may have felt the parish church on the hill rather remote.

Possibly worse was the behaviour of Thomas Russen, who was presented for 'having a child by his late wife's daughter and living with her, it not being known wether they are married or not'. In the same memo John Jones, alias Green, was mentioned as having a 'bastard child'.

Queen Anne Mansions

Two splendid mansion houses built during the reign of Queen Anne still survive. Both were constructed by entrepreneurs of local families using bricks and incorporating plaques with the date and the initials of the owners. One was built by Hugh Dixon, who married Joyce Hodgetts in 1701 and had the house built shortly afterwards. This stands next to the art gallery, in what was then called Sheep Street, now Priory Street. It can be seen to its full effect from the square at the bottom of Stone Street. The other house was built by Joseph and Mary Finch, a short distance away in Wolverhampton Street. It dates from 1707. Mention must here be made of a third house in the area, just beyond The Innage, now unfortunately demolished. This was the property of Gilbert Gillians, drawn at least twice before its demise by Victorian artists. Made of stone, it pre-dated the Queen Anne houses just referred to, and had some medieval carving built into it, featuring a stone sculptured head. This

29 Cavendish House, Wolverhampton Street.

suggests that the stone had come originally from the priory, but possibly from
the ruinous St Edmund's Church. More
fine buildings were to join these in the
Wolverhampton Street area before the
eighteenth century was over.

This Hugh Dixon is almost certainly
not the same as the man from Netherton,
who gave land to the new Baptist chapel.
The Netherton resident is probably to be
identified with the Hugh Dixon who died
in 1721, 'far stricken in years', giving his
residence as Netherton 'in Dudley fforen'
and married to Elizabeth. He owned two
houses in Dudley High Street near to
St Thomas' Church. He was evidently a
nailer, since he left an anvil and bellows
and shop tools to his son Thomas. He
does leave 5s to a son, Hugh, a glassmaker,
who may be the once well-off builder of
the house in Sheep Lane.[8]

30 Mansion near St Edmund's.

Other People in Dudley and the Foreign

Wills give us occasional insight into the living standards of Dudley residents,
and at times supply information about new house building. When Christopher
Braznell died in 1705 he left his wife the 'three dwelling houses lately built at
Blows Green with gardens and a croft adjoining the said houses, in the holding of Nicholas Dayes, Ann Baker and Jonathan Lane, and myself, adjoining
lands of Mr Humphrey Colborne and Mr Leather of Birmingham, in possession of Thomas Hughes'.[9]

Catherine Bond, who died in 1709, was described as a 'barber chirurgeon'. It
is interesting to see a woman following this trade, probably taken on after the
death of her husband.[10] She left clothes and a cow to her dependants. Edward
Blunn, alias Wright, of Hall Street, left two old lame horses with their gear,
some hay and muck (a valuable commodity). To his granddaughter he willed

two yards of stuff, and to his own married daughter, Mary Dudley, a bed, some pewter and a brass kettle at Henry Williams' house if she paid 'the money that they lie in pawne for'. His son Edward would inherit an iron 'pott', old coffer, chaffe bed and some old clothes. The egregious John Payton was a witness to this will.[11] Many Dudley wills are similar, highlighting that the standard of living was not high in Queen Anne's day.

A little later, in 1722, Oliver Shaw Senior made his will, leaving to his son Samuel four good chairs, a little table, and a clock from his Hall House.[12] He also left to Samuel a silver tankard, three silver spoons, a box of linens and a quilt 'which my dear wife desired he should have'. Shaw gave £5 to the poor of Dudley, an amount which sounds little in the twenty-first century but was then quite a sum.

An estimate of population can be made from the manorial residents' list produced in 1726, which includes the foreign.[13] Not all streets are differentiated in this list, which appears to have been made for taxation purposes and used in the two following years for 'amercements', theoretically fines, which in practice amount to taxation. There are 347 dwellings identifiable in High Street, including Castle Street, Bannisters Lane and Porters Field (these may not all have

31 Finch House, Wolverhampton Street.

32 Finch House from the rear, showing eighteenth-century gables.

been separate houses, but may have included dwellings divided into two, as sometimes seems to be the case). Although sixty-five names are listed in Hall Street, this total includes some crossed through as though dead or removed. Twenty-two dwellings are in Queen Street, the northern, separated part of High Street/Market Place, including some which can be identified as in Middle Row. About seventy-eight houses are said to be in New Street, but this total includes some which can be shown to be in Stoney Lane and almost certainly modern Priory Street. In Hampton Lane there are seventy-four dwellings listed, including some away from the main street. The surviving Finch House is identifiable. This concludes the borough section, and gives a total of about 586 dwellings in the borough, though allowance must be made for some erasures and some unclear entries, but this total cannot be far wrong.

The foreign section of the list is undifferentiated, and cannot be checked against a list of taxes. Some residents can be located from other documents. The list covers Springs Mire, Woodside, Netherton Hall, other parts of Netherton, Bumble Hole, Baptist End, Dixon's Green and Cawney Hill, but none of these place names is used. About 312 residences are on this part of the list, though it is hard to be totally accurate since the document has some missing pieces. Adding the borough and the foreign together we get a total of 898: the total may actually be as much as 900 or as little as about 895.

Dudley Schools

In 1714 it was recorded that a new schoolhouse had been erected, which was later to be called Dudley Grammar School.[14] An inventory of school property was taken, showing that the school itself was on the corner of what is now King Street and High Street, with a croft at the rear fronting King Street. The school owned a stable situated between Castle Street and St Edmund's churchyard (there was still no church on the site of the ruin). Also in Castle Street were two houses on the north side, next to a house belonging to Robert Bayliss. Further west along High Street were three small houses and gardens, and there were four houses on the west side of Stoney Lane. There was further property in Stoney Lane, including a timber yard adjoining The Horsepool in possession of Samuel Clement. Near to Queen's Cross were some more small tenements fronting the Stourbridge road. The school owned several plots in Hall Street, on the north side of the road. In Church Field there were a number of small pieces

33 Tansley Hill, now a suburban road but once the Portway to Birmingham.

making about 3 acres altogether. The inventory concludes with a mention of another small plot near St Edmund's and another half acre near St Thomas'.

A new school was founded early in the century, which would eventually become the Bluecoat School. Its foundation may have been as early as 1705 or 1706, but documentary details become available in the will of Samuel Taylor, dated 1733.[15] He owned a considerable amount of land in Tansley Hill and near Dixon's Green, as well as in small parcels elsewhere in the open fields and near the town. He says that 'there are 50 poore Boyes called the Charity School Boyes yearly taught and Instructed [...] to read write and cast account in a house rented of Mr Joshua Finch by one William Geast a Schoole Master there ...' He leaves a group of fields to the trusteeship of Edward Lord Dudley, North Foley, the Revd Thomas Olliver (vicar of Dudley), Richard Bradley, Ironmonger, Oliver Dixon Gent, John Cardale, Apothecary, Daniel Shaw, Mercer, John Hodgetts junior, Yeoman, Daniel Payton 'of the Towne of Dudley Yeoman', James Hincks of Sedgley Gent, John Parks of The Holt in Halesowen, Edward Paston of The Hawn and William Freeth of Oldbury to buy a house 'fit for a School House and a School Master'. William Geast's name appears in the 1726 suit roll near the beginning (near Queens Cross) but it is not possible to pin down exactly where this house was. The house purchased by the trustees was in the lane which later became Stafford Street.

Not long after this, a further charity school was founded by Samuel Bayliss, occupying land between the north-east of Castle Street and Pease Lane (Tower Street), where the forerunner of the existing Baylies' School building was located.[16]

North Foley Marries into the Holtes

The Holte (occasionally Holt) family were one of the major gentry families in the area. They owned Aston Hall, now within the Birmingham boundary, about 10 miles from Netherton. In early 1719 it was announced that North Foley, whose strange name recalled that his grandfather was Lord North, was to marry Anne Holte, eldest daughter of Charles Holte. He had been baptised at Oldswinford in 1677 and trained in law at the Middle Temple. Correspondence from his mother at Worcester includes chatty letters about the seeds of kidney beans which she will send him along with cabbage, cucumbers and lettuce.[17] She also tells her son about clothing she is buying, showing that she followed fashion and relied on her own mother to engage women to do alterations. A marriage settlement between North and Anne Holte was drawn up, with the agreement of the heir to Aston, Clobury Holte, and John, who was at Christ Church College in Oxford. North lived in a house in Stourbridge; his messuage in the High Street there is mentioned in the settlement, as are some fields in the same town. There was some property in other parts of Worcestershire, including neighbouring Oldbury. [18]

In this document we get a rare inventory of Netherton Hall estate. The house itself had outhouses and other buildings, gardens, orchards, a foldyard and of course many fields surrounding it. There were also a number of farms and other houses: a dwelling house tenanted by Thomas Pargiter, a farm and houses tenanted by William Pitt and another farm tenanted by Edward Pitt; there were three more houses and land held by Edward Shirt, William Griffin and Daniel Littley. On the side of the hill, now bordered by Buffery Road, were more lands in the holding of Henry and John Payton. This area was and is called Sledmere.

Near Blowers Green were Flax Leasow, Watery Leasow and Fitch Leasow, names all describing the terrain. Further down Peartree Lane were the divided Ox Leasows, not to be confused with Ox (or York's) park on the other side of what is now Cinderbank. The name of the Ox Leasows recalls the original inhabitants of these fields, from a time when oxen did all the heavy work on

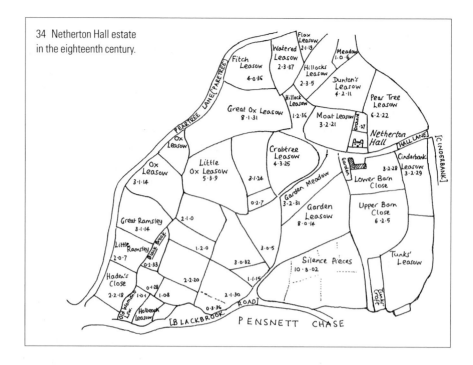

34 Netherton Hall estate in the eighteenth century.

Flax Leasow 2-1-13
Watered Leasow 2-3-37
Meadow 1-0-6
Fitch Leasow 4-0-36
Hillocks Leasow 2-3-5
Dunton's Leasow 4-2-11
Pear Tree Leasow 6-2-22
Hillock Leasow 1-2-36
Great Ox Leasow 8-1-31
Moat Leasow 3-2-21
Netherton Hall
[PEARTREE LANE/ PEARTREE]
[HALL LANE]
[CINDERBANK]
Ox Leasow
Crabtree Leasow 4-3-25
Garden
Cinderbank
Cinderbank Leasow 3-2-28
Leasow 3-1-29
Lower Barn Close
Ox Leasow 3-1-14
Little Ox Leasow 5-3-9
3-1-24
Garden Meadow
Upper Barn Close 6-2-5
2-1-0
0-2-7
3-2-31
Garden Leasow 8-0-14
Great Ramsley 3-1-14
Little Ramsley 2-0-7
0-2-33
1-2-0
3-0-5
Silence Pieces 10-3-02
Tunks' Leasow
Haden's Close
2-2-20
3-0-32
1-1-15
Old Meadow Low 2-2-18
1-0-1
1-08
2-1-30
0-3-36
[ROAD]
Holbeach Leasow
[BLACKBROOK]
PENSNETT CHASE

the Netherton Hall estate. Crabtree Leasow tells us about the trees in a close near the hall, as does Peartree Leasow near the main road. Opposite the hall is Moat Leasow, recording a landmark which was probably lost by this time.[19]

Cottagers on the Dudley Estate

In 1720 an energetic steward for Lord Dudley determined to take in hand the rents paid by cottagers on the directly administered sections of the estate.[20] Most of these seem to be on what had once been the lord's waste, and some of the inhabitants can be identified as those mentioned in the court rolls for encroaching on the commons. Twenty-three cottages were on a small area of land at Cawney Hill, in the dip on the western side near modern St John's Street and East Street. Seven of these have illegally enclosed land by 1710, and there is no record of this land ever having been released. Among the twenty-three cottages were five tenanted by members of the Woodall family and four families named Danks. There were two Henley families and two Hanley families: it is anyone's guess whether they originated in Hanley near Stoke or Henley near Stratford, but these names were probably two variants of the same.

A number of cottages had been built near Woodside (part of Pensnett Chase) by the side of the road leading from Holly Hall. At Mushroom Bank were members of the Troman and Nicklin families, but many of the locations of these small cottages cannot be known for certain. Cottagers generally left no wills which might tell what items they had to pass down to the next generation. However, there is evidence that they could transfer the cottages themselves to a near relative. When John Price died his widow kept on the cottage and John Haden's cottage passes to his son, also John, at his death. These cottages continued to be owned and rented out by the Dudley lords until they were mainly sold off in the nineteenth century.

St Edmund's Rebuilt

The growth of the town in the early eighteenth century turned some minds to the question of the lack of church accommodation, especially since the ruins of St Edmund's at the foot of the castle was still derelict and its stone a quarry for those wanting to repair their houses. In 1724, Richard and George Bradley were the prime movers in its rebuilding. The new church resembles St Thomas' in Stourbridge, built two years later by the stone carver

35 St Edmund's Church from the south-east.

Thomas White of Worcester. It seems possible that White also designed and built St Edmund's, though there is no proof and very little is known about the event. An alternative architect might be William Smith of Warwick, since Baroque detail in St Edmund's is similar to detail in Smith's church at Whitchurch, Shropshire.[21] There are vaults below the church, one belonging to the Wooley family which was also used by members of the Hancox family.[22]

A certain degree of mystery surrounds the large house adjacent to the church on Castle Hill, which seems to date from this time and was surely intended for a vicarage. No document yet discovered refers to it as such, but its imposing design suggests that it was intended to provide a house for a clergyman here. However, there continued to be one vicar in Dudley, attached first and foremost to St Thomas'.

Dudley's First Large-Scale Map

Parts of a plan of Dudley, showing fields, land ownership and some houses, are preserved at the Dudley Archives. Though now partially faded, the plan is well drawn and is evidently based on some detailed surveying, since acreages of the various fields are given. There seems to have been little interest in the buildings and the town centre is omitted, so unfortunately no record of houses in the town appear. There are about thirty small drawings of houses in the rural parts of Dudley, but in other places where it is known there were houses, it has been left blank. The plan has been attributed to Harry Court, the Stourbridge surveyor, who was appointed as surveyor of the Stourbridge to Bromsgrove turnpike road in 1762 and surveyed the whole of Stourbridge, including Lye, in 1782. The Dudley plan under consideration formed the basis of another in the 1780s, and has possibly been confused with it. Various attempts have been made to date this plan, without success.[23]

Many of the fields surveyed carry the names of owners or occupiers and from these we can deduce an approximate date of the plan. Gilbert Haughton, or Horton, recorded as proprietor of a field on the north-east side of modern Tower Street, died before 1726, as did Richard Parkes, shown on the map as proprietor of land near Netherton. Richard Parkes is cited as owner of land in the will of Jonathan Taylor, dated 1720. The current plan was therefore made between 1720 and 1726. Hugh Dixon of Hampton Street also died before 1726, leaving his property to his widow.

The remaining parts of the plan do not include the centre or south of Netherton, though they do show Netherton Hall. The Withymoor area, which trailed down in a long extension at the side of Pensnett Chase, is missing. It seems that the surveyor originally intended to show the houses from the front, and a certain amount can still be deduced about the appearance of some of them. At the top of what is now Buffery Road, two taller houses are shown with a shorter one between, but in the orchard opposite, on the north-west side, there is only one building which appears on the plan. Netherton Hall barn, south of the hall street, is

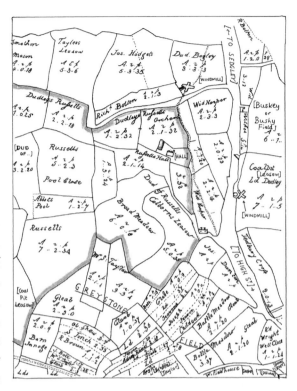

36 Plan of Russell's Hall estate at the end of the seventeenth century.

shown in plan only, though a rudimentary drawing of the hall, with its round doorway, is shown opposite the barn. An apparent barn is shown at the far north of the parish, near the site of the present Black Country Museum, with a high entrance and a clearly marked window. Many other thumbnail sketches show schematic windows as a row of dots. In some cases there are two rows, in others only one; this may mean that the latter are one-storey houses, but there can be no certainty. Despite these problems, it is useful to have some indication of the siting of some Dudley houses at this time.

Many interesting facts about Dudley in the early 1720s come to light from this plan. For example, at Holly Hall, running across land which was part of the section of Lord Dudley's estate owned by the Russell's Hall branch, was a way (not a road) marked 'way from ye Cole pits'. Paretree Lane was a fluid name, at this time attached to the route from the bottom of Woodside to Blowers Green. The Finch house and others fronting Hampton Street are shown as blanks, and there is no delineation of the market area.

Glassmaking in the Eighteenth Century

Hugh Dixon, whose house still stands in Priory Street, was the first known glassmaker in Dudley. Despite his fine house, he became bankrupt in 1713, and his wife became head of the household in 1726.[24] In another house nearby lived Edward Dixon, his youngest son, who had evidently salvaged something from the bankruptcy, and is listed as a glassmaker in the 1726 residents' list. Precisely when the glassworks was established near Priory Street is not known, but it continued there for many years. Glass manufacture had expanded to Dudley from Oldwinford/Stourbridge, where it had been established for over 100 years. It appears that the Dixons, who had other works elsewhere in the Midlands run by other members of the family, moved the manufacture into Dudley, perhaps to keep it closely under surveillance from their ancestral home at Dixon's Green.[25]

37 Hugh Dixon's house, The Horsepool (Priory Street).

Turnpike Roads

The early eighteenth century was a time when road transport became a crucial issue. Coal was no longer consumed locally, and the glass and nails which Dudley produced required routes out of the parish in better condition than the old unpaved Portways, of which the Stourbridge and Birmingham routes were examples. Rising entrepreneurs combined to put pressure on Parliament to create toll roads with guaranteed minimum standards of repair, no longer carried out by the parish but by new turnpike trusts. They were paid for by tolls collected in toll houses along the route. A route through Dudley town centre was turnpiked early; this was a main road from Wolverhampton to Birmingham via Sedgley. Other early examples in Dudley included the route to Halesowen and Bromsgrove and that to Kingswinford (both

ANNO DUODECIMO

GEORGII III. REGIS.

An Act for enlarging the Terms and Powers of Two Acts, made in the Thirteenth Year of the Reign of King *George* the First and the Twenty-first Year of the Reign of King *George* the Second, for repairing the several Roads leading from *Birmingham*, through the Town of *Wednesbury*, to a Place called *High Bullen*, and to *Great Bridge*, and from thence to the End of *Gibbet Lane* next adjoining to the Township of *Bilson*, and from *Great Bridge*, through *Dudley*, to *King Swinford*, and to the further End of *Brittel Lane*, in the Counties of *Warwick*, *Stafford*, and *Worcester*.

WHEREAS by an Act made in the Thirteenth Year of the Reign of King *George* the First, intituled *An Act for repairing the several Roads leading from* Birmingham, *through the Town of* Wednesbury, *to a Place called* High Bullen, *and to* Great Bridge, *and from thence to the End of* Gibbet Lane *next adjoining to the Township of* Bilson, *and from* Great Bridge, *through* Dudley, *to* King Swinford, *and to the further End of* Brittel Lane, *in the Counties of* Warwick, Stafford, *and* Worcester, several Tolls and Duties were granted and made payable, and divers Powers given for repairing the said Roads and for putting the said Act in execution; which said Act was to have Continuance for and during
A 2   the

38 Turnpike Act: first page of the Act for repairing turnpikes.

1726–7), and the route to Lye and Pedmore (1727). The Dudley to Brettell Lane turnpike was initiated in the same year.[26] Worcester remained an important destination for Dudley men; this was reached by following the Bromsgrove route through Halesowen and Romsley. The several recognised routes to Birmingham caused some confusion in defining in deeds the position of properties, which are said to adjoin the road to Birmingham, without specifying which route. The high road via Cawney Hill was still important, but roads via Oldbury and West Bromwich were being improved. A later turnpike trust linked Dudley with Rowley, via Oakham: the present road south of Warren's Hall was a nineteenth-century development.

Meanwhile, the old market roads were still heavily used by pedestrians and packhorses. Court rolls continually urged landowners and tenants to scour ditches and trim hedges along these routes. In 1711, Cornelius Abiss is commanded to 'mend' the road leading from 'Walkey well' (Oakeywell) to 'Black acker', and at the same meeting Mr Samuel Baylis is told to remove the old tree lying in the road near Springs Mire.[27] A little earlier, John Hunt had been ordered to remove 'carrion' from Fishers Lane. In 1703 the roadway between

Over Swines Croft and 'Caulfs Craft' needed repair. This formed part of the Market Road from Netherton, which cut off the steep hill near Queens Cross. However, these roads would not be recognisable as roads in modern times; they were muddy tracks, their potholes filled in haphazardly with grit and small stones.

Advice for a Dudley MP[28]

At the Parliamentary election in 1742 Edmund Pytts was elected as MP for Worcestershire, and travelled to Dudley on 21 October to thank the freeholders for electing him. He was met 'about a mile from the town' by a large crowd of freeholders, who escorted him to the Town Hall and entertained him, giving him their thanks for his previous 'constant attendance in Parliament'.

However, their lavish entertainment and thanks had a purpose. They were there to express very forcefully their views on how the country should be run. A report in the *Worcester Journal* for November 1742 records the speech to which Mr Pytts listened as follows:

> Never was more need of standing up in defence of our country than now; for the filling up the House of Commons with placemen and pensioners (like the locusts of Egypt) if not timely prevented, must soon devour every thing in the land we may presume to say that standing armies and heavy taxes in time of peace for several years together, the repeal of the Triennial Act, the many breaches and violations made in another important act, with an infinite number of penal and excise law must inevitably bring on the destruction of all our liberties and constitution; and therefore beg you will please to concur with all such measures that may be taken to redress these abuses, and to bring us once more to our old and excellent constitution. And for that purpose we recommend you to vote for a strict inquiry into former mismanagements, in order to bring those to justice who besides other black enormities, have pillaged and plundered the nation, and then employed our own money against ourselves to corrupt and influence elections, and then to chuse such members as would most readily betray their country and its trade and liberties ...

Mr Pytts thanked the freeholders and 'assured them he would give constant attention in Parliament and faithfully observe their instruction in opposing corruption in whatever shape, and without any private view of enriching himself or family, in promoting the true and real interest of the country'.

At the time, just over 200 Dudley freeholders are listed, most of whom would presumably make time to listen to Mr Pytts and give him the benefit of their instruction. The speech, strongly criticising 'excise laws' and financial mismanagement, emphasises the Dudley interest in trade. Many of the freeholders are recognisable as Dudley inhabitants, though freeholders did not have to live in the parish: the list includes Richard Bolton of Rowley, John Dyke of Bromsgrove, Gilbert Shaw of Birmingham and John Bond of All Saints', Worcester.

Most of the Dudley residents give no hint of their address, though there is mention of William Pearkes (Parkes) of Netherton.

Events at the Castle

By this time, the Dudley lords, the Wards, were living mostly at Himley Hall. The castle itself was apparently occupied by stewards such as Mr Tandy, who was told by the court to put a hedge round an open pit in the Farthings in 1705, but died later the same year. He was followed by John Tandy, who may have been his son and who owned or rented land near modern Trindle Road. Offshoots of the baronial family owned Russell's Hall and a house near Woodside, where there lived Ferdinando Dudley, who claimed a debt from Richard Jones in the Court Baron of 1709. He is located in a house at Woodside in the residents' list of 1726.

About 1700 a two-storey building was erected near the gatehouse and is generally called the stable block. It has been suggested that this was the first building in an attempt to rebuild and make habitable a considerable section of the old castle.[29] The intention was never fully carried out. It is possible that the castle was left with only an occasional visit from a steward, since it has been alleged that the cellars and dungeons were occupied around 1750 by coiners making counterfeit money.[30] At any rate, in July 1750 a fire broke out, for which coiners were blamed, and raged for three days through the castle. It is also alleged that no one dared to help put out the fire because it was supposed that a store of gunpowder was kept there. Red-hot lead ran down from the roof and soon the whole hill was aflame. This spectacle proved to be a memorable if disastrous end to St James' fair day in Dudley town.

six

THE LATER EIGHTEENTH CENTURY

By 1760 there had been very significant rebuilding of Dudley's half-timbered Elizabethan buildings. The market area now contained mainly three-storeyed houses, not always occupied by their owners but rented out to traders, and in some cases divided into two or more dwellings. A contemporary view of the centre of the town shows some properties with gable ends facing the street, perhaps refacings of timber-framed houses, and some with parapets. A few earlier buildings still remained.[1] The Town Hall was a prominent feature, with its large working clock on the tower and its arches on the ground floor, leading to a covered area which could be used to store goods in bad weather. Many houses had shop fronts by this time, still using small panes of glass, but with overall dimensions suitable for exhibiting clothes or household goods.

Houses in Middle Row were not as tall as those on Queen Street and High Street, and there is evidence of earlier buildings surviving. There were also two-storey buildings in Castle Street. High Street, also called the Turnpike Road, was 15ft across, and there were channels through the market place to drain off water and probably many other things, including offal, blood and decayed vegetable matter. Chief among the property holders mentioned are James Shaw and Mr Nightingale. The corner of the Long Entry, still in existence today, can just be seen in this picture opposite.

A little later than the view of the market just mentioned, a view of Dudley from the east was painted, showing the castle on its commanding hill and the road into the town from Dixon's Green to Hall Street.[2] This gives us an idea of the houses on the north-east side of Hall Street, showing them as small cottage-style buildings, with dormer windows and gable ends. Hall Street was not as prestigious as the market area.

Nearer the forefront of the picture is a mansion which appears to have three storeys and an attic. It is plastered, perhaps over bricks, and has an eighteenth-century pediment over the front door. This may be Dixon's Green House, with its estate including tall trees behind it, and a wall skirting the road in the direction of Waddams' Pool. Just possibly it could be Hill House, though there seems to be no map evidence that the house existed at this time. The viewpoint appears to be from a spur of Cawney Hill.

39 Market Place in 1760.

Some twenty years later there was to be another view from a similar viewpoint, but on that occasion from a lower level. This view, said to be from Easey Hill, shows the Hall Street glass cone in operation. The name Easey Hill does not occur in any other context, and it may be that Cawney Hill is meant. Towards the town end of Hall Street some three-storey houses are shown, the top storeys being lit by attic windows. This view also shows gable-ended houses surrounding St Edmund's Church. Part of Hill House is shown in this picture, with a female figure walking across the lawn to a gate into Dixon's Green Road. The house has three storeys and is certainly of eighteenth-century construction.

One family that continued to exercise influence in the town during the second part of the eighteenth century was the Paytons. In 1751 a plan was made of property belonging to Henry Payton on Cawney Hill, and another of his land in Porter's Field.[3] The Cawney Hill plan shows a mansion and gardens, none of which appeared on the so-called Court plan earlier in the century, detailed previously. Because of the absence of many buildings on that plan, it is impossible to tell whether the Cawney Hill house or its attendant buildings, probably cottages, had been built since then. There is unfortunately no explanation of the various shapes on the plan. Adjacent to the main house are four fields, totalling just over 9 acres.

Payton's land in Porter's Field is more easily located. It lay next to Birmingham Road, the lane which has had many different names over the years and is currently represented by part of Birmingham Street and part of the bus station. This property consisted of just under 2 acres, with land belonging to Mr Bodily (Baddeley) and land of Lord Dudley making up the rest of this portion.

An insight into the administration of manor land is given by a cottage rental of 1768.[4] Details of rents to be paid are given, with some information about what happens if the rent is not paid. William Haden paid 10s for a cottage, the late Jane Scott's, but 'unless he repairs the buildings he is to be turned out'. Of William Stinson it is noted that 'he has a pleck – never paid […] he to be turned out'. The pleck was to be let to Samuel Foley. Benjamin Timmins' cottage was 'very badly out of repair. If John Taylor repairs it, he to have it.' Of widow Homer, 'By my Lord's orders the widow is to pay 20s a year from Lady Day 1768, the arrears to be forgiven.' Arrears were also forgiven for Joseph Cartwright. At the end of the rental are some accounts which show how the steward himself charged. He notes a charge of 1s 4d for the survey of the manor, and 1s in Dudley town. He paid William Bunch £1 4s 7d for sawing timber to repair Richard Moore's house at Netherton, and among other items for the repair of the same house, £3 14s 9d for mason work and just over £3 2s to Peter Homer for bricks and tiles, with the carriage.

A Printed Directory

The first printed directory of Dudley inhabitants was published by Sketchley in 1770. It contained ninety-seven names, along with their trades and in most cases the name of the road where they lived. Selection for inclusion in the list seems somewhat haphazard; only two inns of the many are recorded: The Swan on the south-east side of what became Union Street and the Old Bush on the opposite side. Adam Read Shaw, surgeon, is given as Adam Readshaw and there is a vague entry for 'Hinton's, Nailors' in Bannister Lane.

Glassmakers feature as 'Geast, Hawkes and Seager, High Street' and 'Jonathan Green, Dixon's Green'. There are several threadmen, including Richard Crane and Thomas Willington of The Horsepool. Joseph Wainwright, who was to become a force in town politics, was another surgeon, and there were two attorneys in Thomas Seager and James Shaw. There is no mention of clergy or school teachers, though there is plenty of evidence elsewhere to supplement this omission.

Last Days of the Manor Courts

Manor and borough courts continued during the 1770s, but their supremacy was entering its last years. The court was now meeting at The Swan, the public house on the corner of Union Street owned by Mrs Sarah Aston. Clearly the upper room in the Town Hall had ceased to be large enough to contain the members of the courts, who perhaps cheered their deliberations with a drink. The market was still a main concern of the borough courts. For example, the court of 19 October 1778 made the following points:[5]

   (i) Hucksters were not to buy butter or cheese on market day before one o'clock

  (ii) The bailiff was to test the weights and weigh the butter every three months; if an alleged pound of butter did not weigh the full 16oz, it was to be given to the poor

 (iii) Butchers must not buy meat until it had been put up for sale in the market, or sell it the same day

 (iv) No one must buy 'dead victuals' to sell

  (v) No one must slaughter beasts in the main street

 (vi) No one must fire any barrels or casks in the main street

 (vii) No one must leave their 'blocks' out after 6 p.m. except on Saturday, and then only until 10 p.m.

The court fined Joseph Tompson 3s 4d for putting up a stall on the footway.

Four other provisions were made by the borough court that day, but it is clear that the conduct of the market was their chief interest.

The manor jury still dealt with the foreign and had rather different concerns. Apart from fining people who should have attended but did not, their orders all had to do with keeping roads open. These roads, even the major ones, seem to be in poor condition, apt to be blocked or narrowed by the activities of frontagers. They were increasingly important because of the growing coal and mineral traffic. Even the surveyors of the highways could not always be relied on to keep on top of the problems: 'the bridge under the causeway at Scots Green' needed repair. Prudence Caddick, a member of an influential Dudley family living near Shavers End, was constantly being encouraged to amend the road through her property, the Little Meadow, which led to Parkes' Hall in Sedgley. John Robinson of Holly Hall was called upon to mend the road near his house, and John Southall must remove or repair his 'necessary house' (privy) which was fouling a minor lane near Mr Fieldhouse's property at Caddick's End. In the following year the surveyors of the highways were told to mend a bridge which led over a ditch from Yoakes Park to Blows Green, and even Lord Dudley must attend to the road to Burnt Tree.

In 1779 the surveyors of the highways were told to repair the 'lane called Finche's Lane and the lane called Little Lene leading from Sinderbank to Baptist End'. Footbridges were always causing trouble, presumably because they were made of wood, led over small ditches and rotted way with time. Samuel Fullwood was fined for a nuisance at Queens Cross by laying timber in the main road, and placing wagons, carts 'and other things' there. In the town, Selmon Wilkes caused people to trip up by leaving a hole leading to his cellar open in the footpath. In 1786, Stephen Fisher of Blowers Green opened a drain in Dudley High Street and left it open, while there was much difficulty over dung hills left by the sides of houses as a resource which would later be spread on the fields.

After 1791, when the town commissioners began their work, the borough court effectively lapsed, though the manor still dealt with the recovery of small debts. To the very end the borough court was trying to pursue those who committed various nuisances such as cattle collecting near the pathways and inhibiting passage, or the eternal problem of dung being left near houses.

Enclosure of Pensnett Chase and Dudley Wood

By an Act of Parliament, Pensnett Chase was enclosed in 1784. The territory affected in Dudley parish was mainly in Woodside, Netherton and Dudley Wood. Maps were prepared before and after the enclosure, and a detailed schedule ('the award') is to be found in Dudley Archives.[6] Under such acts, large landowners were allotted tracts of the former commons, the lord of the manor generally being the chief beneficiary, but others, including charities, also benefited. The map drawn up before the enclosure process was based firmly on the Court map already mentioned, using the names of landowners who had been alive at that time, and omitting most buildings, even those which had appeared on the earlier plan.[7] It gives field names, but is little help in pinning down land ownership. A major error is committed in describing much of Netherton as in Rowley Regis parish, an attribution which would have alarmed the vestry at Rowley Church. The enclosure map produced after the allotment was more accurate. The allotment process was completed by the end of 1786.

Before this enclosure, Netherton village had ended at the site of the present marketplace, opposite the present Netherton Arts Centre. Almost everything beyond this was common. A thin tract of land in individual ownership ran down the boundary brook to Withymoor, but almost everything south of Northfield Road was common. The cottages listed in 1720 were mostly at Newtown, Mushroom Green, Saltwells, Woodside and, in a different direction, Cawney Hill. Cawney Hill was never part of Pensnett Chase. On the chase were the coal mines at Knowle Hill, and more recently at the far end of Peartree Lane. Islands in the chase were Saltwells Wood, Lodge Farm and a small area at Yew Tree Hill.

Another duty of the enclosure commissioners was to specify the roads and lanes across the newly enclosed area. They began by listing turnpikes: Brettell Lane Turnpike from Holly Hall; Kingswinford Turnpike also to Holly Hall; Pedmore Turnpike from Holly Hall to the bridge over the Dudley Canal 'near the Level Colliery' and then to Tipsyford Bridge. These turnpikes were 60ft wide, as were the Northfield Turnpike (Northfield Road) and the Halesowen Turnpike. Peartree Lane had existed for many years, but was now to be connected southwards and westwards with new roads, or roads developed from small tracks. A canal bridge had been put over it, and this was used to lead a road from near the Level to the centre of Netherton where it joined the Halesowen Road. Two or three other roads were linked to this.

On the Windmill End side, 40ft roads led from Northfield Road to Windmill End itself, and a road was built from Bumble Hole across Northfield Road to Darby Hand and thence to Halesowen Road. This is one of the earliest occurrences of the name Darby Hand, which appears to be a corruption of Darby End. Near to Cradley Heath and Old Hill, three roads led across the new fields to Reddall Hill Road, Whitings Holloway and Mushroom Green. In the same area was Lodge Farm Road, connecting Halesowen Road to Cradley New Pool. All these new roads were to be 40ft in width. A series of what were described as 'private carriage and drift roads' was also planned, each 20ft in width. These were all for the benefit of the Dudley-Ward family. Firm designations were also given to eight public footways which may well have existed before as unofficial routes across the chase.

Land was awarded to the vicar as 'glebe', church property which could be farmed for the benefit of the church or the incumbent. Some of this was near

St Thomas' Church and some on the newly enclosed moorland which had been part of Pensnett Chase. The opportunity was also taken by the commissioners to rationalise some small areas of land in and around the town centre. This was sometimes effected by exchanges of land, and sometimes by the addition to the freeholdings of small strips which had been lining tracks or roadways. Thus for instance the grammar school gained 0-2-37 acres and the 'gown charity' 0-2-4 acres: tiny patches adjacent to their existing properties. Some landholders quickly took the opportunity to sell their newly acquired allotments.

Canals[8]

The first canal to be built in the Black Country, the line from Birmingham to Wolverhampton, did not pass through Dudley, and indeed the hilly terrain of the parish was to make canal transport difficult. There was, however, urgent need for bulk transport of coal, iron, and finished wares to markets within and outside the kingdom.

In 1775, Lord Dudley initiated a private canal cut from his limestone works at Castle Hill to join the Birmingham route. In 1776 an act was passed to allow building of a canal from Dudley (with a similar act for Stourbridge) to take produce and raw materials to the Severn. It would terminate at Ox Leasow on the Netherton Hall estate. These canals do not feature on the pre-enclosure map, but they surely must have been built before it was produced.

40 Netherton Hall estate: 'Silence' pieces with distant view of Dudley town.

Left 41 Canal basin near the entrance to Dudley tunnel.

Below 42 The high bridge over the canal at Netherton.

In 1784 it was decided to join the Dudley canals to the Birmingham canal by means of a long tunnel, and surveying took place. This tunnel was to connect the previous canal at Peartree Lane via the limestone mines under Castle Hill with the Great Pool at Castle Mill and so to the Birmingham canal. Surveying was done by John Snape and a plan was drawn up.[9] The plan shows the tunnel, which still exists, passing under the turnpike east of Scots Green, under the Wolverhampton Road near Caddick's End and so to Castle Hill via the former priory lands. There was a branch to the Wren's Nest, with a stair-case entrance completed in 1840. Altogether, the Dudley tunnel is 5,208yds in length.[10] The tunnel was (and is) narrow and had to bear too much traffic, especially as through boats were hampered by the limestone boats using the Tipton end of the tunnel. The tunnel mouth can still be seen at the edge of the Black Country Museum, and trips are mounted into the limestone caverns.

Canal transport was soon perceived to be easier and more efficient than the old method of moving large quantities of minerals by packhorse. In 1792 it was deemed desirable to find a way to connect Netherton with Birmingham by canal, so that Netherton coal could be carried directly there. It was decided that the canal would go from Netherton via Halesowen and Weoley Castle to join the Worcester canal at Selly Oak. The proposal was opposed by the Birmingham Canal Company, which had spent money on the previous Dudley connection from Castle Mill. Nevertheless, an Act of Parliament dated 1793 secured the proposed pathway through Halesowen, with two short branches in

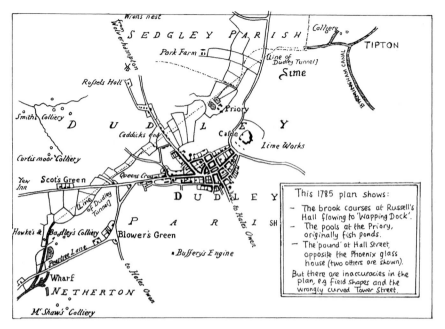

Within the map:

SEDGLEY P/A R I S H

Wren's nest

Wolverhampton Road

Park Farm

[Line of Dudley Tunnel]

Colliery

TIPTON

Lime

BIRMINGHAM CANAL

Russels Hall

Smith's Colliery

D   U   D   L   E   Y

Caddicks end

Priory

Castle

Lime Works

Curtis moor Colliery

Yew Inn   Scot's Green

Queens Cross

Line of Dudley Tunnel

D   U   D   L   E   Y

to Hales Owen

Hawkes & Badleys Colliery

Blower's Green

P   A   R   I   SH

Peartree Lane

to Hales Owen

Bufferys Engine

Wharf

NETHERTON

to Hales Owen

Mc Shaw's Colliery

This 1785 plan shows:
- The brook courses at Russell's Hall flowing to 'Wapping Dock'.
- The pools at the Priory, originally fish ponds.
- The 'pound' at Hall Street, opposite the Phoenix glass house (two others are shown).
But there are inaccuracies in the plan, e.g. field shapes and the wrongly curved Tower Street.

43 Part of Dudley in 1785, developed from Snape's canal plan.

Dudley parish, from Windmill End to Baptist End and from Cabbage Hall to the previous branch. Considerable problems were encountered in making the canal, especially in the Lappal Tunnel, which was the fourth longest in England, at 3,795yds. However, the canal was opened as far as Halesowen by 1797 and all the way to Selly Oak by 1798.

The Dudley Arms

Until the mid-eighteenth century the Town Hall had sufficed for meetings in Dudley, and The Swan had provided for any traveller who wished to stay in the town. These were both old buildings, without modern facilities. There were a number of other public houses in the marketplace, but none suitable for expansion. In keeping with Dudley's enhanced position as a new centre for manufacturing and mineral exploitation, it was felt that there should be more prestigious accommodation for visiting businessmen and others, and this could only be a new building. The process was begun at a meeting of principal inhabitants in 1786.[11]

Old houses between the Bull's Head, owned by the grammar school, and the Rose and Crown, bordering the Long Entry, were demolished and a completely new hotel built on the site, the width of two houses that had originated as burgages in medieval days. The hotel was run as a company, with shares being issued by public notice. For a while no name seems to have been allocated to it, but it eventually became the Dudley Arms, as such lasting until the 1960s, when Marks & Spencer wanted to extend their shop.

Lord Dudley's Estates and Others

Under the Enclosure Act, large tracts of land had been allocated to the Dudley estate by the commissioners. These, mostly in Netherton, were soon divided into viable fields and farmed. Meanwhile, a revised rental was produced, providing a further insight into premises belonging directly to Lord Dudley in the town centre and elsewhere.[12] Seventeen houses are listed in town, together with a dye house at 'the Nether Trindle' and a skin house belonging to Thomas Hawkes. The Hen and Chickens public house at the corner of Castle Street and New Street was also part of the estate. There were still farmed fields near the town centre, especially along the Birmingham turnpike, and sheep walks existed on Castle Hill. The Dudleys did not own the windmill at the back of High Street near the modern Stepping Stone Street, but several houses are

44 Late eighteenth-century houses, with Earl Dudley's statue.

noted on Windmill Hill and in Field Lane (Stafford Street). Gads Lane contained six dwelling houses occupied by Edward Jukes, Joseph Field, James Hadley, Thomas Wakelam, John Parkes and Thomas Mumford.

Out of the town centre, the survey noted David Bagley's tenancy of Lodge Farm 'and three cottages at the Rookery'. At the other extreme of the manor, Henry Hurst farmed 13 acres at Short's Mill (on the site of the present Black Country Museum), and there were four houses attached. (Short is probably the original spelling, though 'Shirt' is more common.) John Keeling's executors still had a lease of the priory. The areas where long-term cottages survived and increased in number – Cawney Hill, Mushroom Green, Newtown, Holly Hall and Dudley Wood – had their land augmented by new allotments under the Enclosure Act. Thomas Cowper is mentioned as renting four closes called Clewes Lane at Cawney Hill and there were older houses at Newtown and

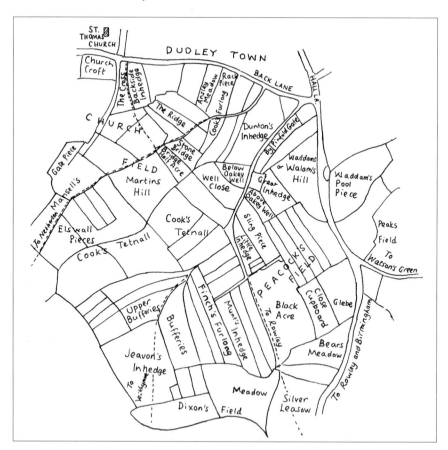

45 Parts of Church Field and Peacocks Field in the 1780s, based on the pre-enclosure plan.

Dudley Wood. Edward Robinson possessed a new enclosure there and Peter Pitt lands by Woodside. The farm of Joseph Dudley at Peartree Lane included a barn, stable and nine closes as well as his house. Thomas and Benjamin Gibbons, ironmasters, rented more than 77 acres to the west of Holly Hall.

There were other landholders in Dudley and Netherton, though of course nominally under the manorial lordship of the Earls of Dudley. Oldswinford Hospital owned a large tract of land to the west of Peartree Lane, which had originally been part of the Netherton Hall estate. Six fields were let to Hawkes and Badley for their coal and iron company. The firm rented farmland which had once been Leather's Farm, contiguous to the previous land and close to Blowers Green. They also owned land in their own right stretching from the hospital land to Scots Green, and a little area in which there was a quarry near Russell's Hall. George Jones, the builder, owned houses in and around Field Lane. The widow Foley still farmed land in Netherton, both on the east and west sides of Buffery Road and Swan Street. The Shaw family let land adjacent to this to Joseph Granger, and Gilbert Read Shaw had land in Church Field. Part of the Russell's Hall estate was leased to Daniel Nicklin, who apparently lived in the hall in the 1780s. Two areas of land belonged to Sidney Sussex College in Cambridge: the northern end of Sledmere (fields then called Slademoor) and a tract of land on the other side of the turnpike from Scot's Green, called Ashen Coppice.

Town Commissioners

With the vast industrial and commercial expansion of the West Midlands it was becoming clear everywhere that old institutions could no longer cope. The old manor courts had little power to enforce their will, and were flouted by such determined individuals as Prudence Caddick, who neglected to abide by the court ruling and simply ignored it. A more representative body was needed, and it was hoped that this could be remedied by the formation of a group in 1791, the Dudley Town Commissioners. They met on 5 July and appointed clerks, Thomas Burne of Himley and James Bourne of Dudley, and a surveyor, James Kennedy. James Bourne would also be the treasurer, and Joseph Bourne the scavenger. Their first aim was to remedy a number of nuisances which had been festering, beginning with a house in Hall Street which had become 'old and decayed' and had to be purchased for the improvement of the town.[13]

But what was meant by 'the town'? Dudley parish included the original street that had formed the borough all those years ago in medieval times, and its offshoots including Hall Street, the area round Fisher Street and Porter's Field, which had now been mainly built over, New Street leading to the Horse Fair, Stoney Lane (Stone Street) and Wolverhampton Street. Where were the limits to be drawn, when the High Street continued to Queen's Cross and Wolverhampton Street almost to Russell's Hall? Could the settlement at Dixon's Green be included as part of the town? Rules were to be made about premises in the town, involving such matters as street lighting and water supply: there must be some coherent definition. The borough limits had been fairly well understood, as courts dealing with the foreign were separate from it.

Town limits were eventually agreed as follows: from the Horse Block adjoining the Dog House at Queen's Cross Hill along the land belonging to the Free School (Saffron Close) to the house at the top of Windmill Street (leading off modern Stafford Street), across the Innage down Gad's Lane to the Plough and Harrow in Wolverhampton Street and across the fields on the priory estate (Stockwell Field) to the castle wall at the end of Pease Lane (Tower Street). Then along the wall to the Birmingham turnpike and up a footway through Porter's Field to Waddams' Pool, including 'the uppermost Club House' (club houses were on the north side of Hall Street), along Dunton's Field to the end of a malthouse belonging to Richard Southall and then back across the fields to the Horse Block, excluding the Free School House and buildings in possession of W. Jackson.[14] This definition seems very similar to the previous extent of the borough, and leaves out most of the newer developments. However, within a few months the commissioners found the limits needed to be altered to include buildings on Back Lane (King Street) and behind Stafford Street.

Water Supply

A very serious problem now had to be faced. Situated on the ridge between the castle and the steep hill leading to Netherton or Holly Hall, the location of Dudley was a splendid place for defence in the Middle Ages, when the population was small and there was no concentrated industry. Water was supplied from wells, marked up to the nineteenth century by the names of small fields such as Well Close. The population had now grown enormously, with many small traders using water to produce ale and many larger firms dying, tanning, cooling metal products and other processes, not to mention the catering trade and the needs of private houses. Dudley's water supply, largely provided from small brooks, could not cope with this demand. Manufacturers pressed the commissioners to remedy the situation. The whole matter of water supply became an issue that Dudley had to solve, which would need cooperation from landowners and manufacturers, as well as taxes which were hard to collect.

It was easy enough for the commissioners to see a solution: a reservoir must be made at a high point on one of the hills near the town, and the obvious choice was Cawney Hill. As early as July 1791 a Mr Hateley was required to draw up a plan of a proposed watercourse from Cawney Hill to Waddams' Pool. It does not seem to have been practical to use Waddams' Pool as a reservoir: plans show that it was a very small pool, in a hollow alongside the road to Dixon's Green. The main water pound would be at a section of Cawney Hill called in the minutes 'Rounds Hill'. In March 1792 it was agreed that Mr Hateley would estimate the cost of water pipes.

The commissioners, meeting at the Dudley Arms, found that it was none too easy to get a quorum to attend their meetings. Between 1791 and 1800 many meetings had to be adjourned, the worst year being 1793, when six meetings running had to be cancelled between January and June. It may be inferred that though the residents and businessmen wanted action on the prevailing issues, including the water problem, they shrank from personal sacrifices which would be necessary to achieve their ends. Voluntary work would be necessary; there were no rich donors to help in setting up the reservoir and conduit, and it seems likely that the commission members all had their own affairs to attend to at a time when the French War was damaging trade.

Negotiations were nevertheless entered upon with Thomas Shaw Hellier to allow the water to be brought through his property behind the White House, his residence in Hall Street. The discussion turned on how far the conduit could be culverted and how far it should be left open. A sub-committee was set up, consisting of two clergymen, Mr Cartwright and Mr Perry, with the influential Joseph Wainwright, the entrepreneur Mr Dixon, the banker Mr Amphlett and others to work out the positions for the proposed reservoirs and to estimate the cost involved. It is not clear how far the reverend gentlemen's theological skills qualified them to decide on the locations for reservoirs. We can, however, see that the power of the Church was still important at this stage.

Early in 1792 Mr Hateley reported that the watercourse was ready for reservoirs to be made.[15] The minutes do not necessarily imply that the watercourse was excavated, but perhaps means only that the course was settled and negotiations complete. Two months later agreement was made with James Winnington to build the reservoir and 'basons', and in the summer Abraham Lees was appointed to survey a dam at Freebody's, with the clergyman Mr Perry and others to supervise. The report does not seem to have been encouraging, as the following year a Mr Kerby was to put the dam in order and estimate the cost and damage to the watercourse. A little while previously, in June 1793, Isaac Badger and Thomas Homer were deputed to make bricks for the culvert from Waddams' Pool to the 'bason'. In 1795, Edward Jessop was appointed to work out suitable compensation for those affected by the building of the watercourse. It is not clear what happened next, but in 1800 the minutes note that a surveyor, Charles Roberts, had surveyed the proposed watercourse and declared the scheme to be ineffectual. Mr Hateley's confident assertion of 1792 seems to have been premature. Instead of the water supply, it was now suggested that pumps be installed in the town centre.

Much of the commissioners' work replaced that formerly carried out by the courts. There were constant disagreements with property holders who had built small extensions to their shops, projecting onto the footpaths of the already narrow streets.

Fourteen orders were served in March 1792 upon such persistent offenders as Prudence Caddick.[16] Stoney Lane was to be widened, and this affected grammar school property; John Martin refused to take down 'bulk windows' from the front of his shop, and the commission decided to do so by force. An interesting and important decision was to provide a route from King Street (by this time so-called) to the High Street between The Old Bush and The Swan. This became Union Street. The owner of The Swan, Mr Nicklin, agreed to take down his parlour window before 29 December 1792 and replace it as desired by the commission.

Other towns in the West Midlands were acquiring street lighting, and the amount of traffic moving by night made this necessary for Dudley. It was agreed that a number of streets would have 'lamps with lamp irons … erected at the corner of streets'. Mr Sheldon made and exhibited a specimen lamp in October 1792, and soon afterwards made and began to erect fifty lamps round the town. The widening of Stoney Lane proceeded and it was renamed Stone Street. Mr Sheldon made seventy more lamps, and a committee was set up to decide which houses they should be placed on. These events took place at the end of 1792, and there followed a period when no meetings occurred.

Every effort was made to tidy up the centre part of the town, dealing with inappropriate extensions which had been allowed to proliferate over the years. A notice to remove these 'nuisances' was issued in October 1793 to eleven householders: Edward Parkes, John Hartill, Joseph Moss, Benjamin Jackson, Eleanor Gorton and John Abbis were to remove penthouses, and in three cases windows, from their houses in High Street; Joseph Bourne had to remove a bulk window, James Raybould likewise, while James Laker had also to remove some projecting steps. These orders are not repeated, and it seems that they were obeyed.

The problem of Middle Row began to be addressed. The large number of houses which had accumulated there had constricted the market, which needed to grow. In June 1796, a Mr Edward Hancox was asked to sell three houses near the Town Hall so that they could be demolished to widen the street. There were problems collecting the rate for the town, which had been assessed by Edward Jessop in 1792. By 1797 there was a sum of £221 still outstanding from the years 1792–25.[17]

Industrial Development

During the latter decades of the eighteenth century a number of furnaces were erected in Dudley. As an example, we can take that of Messrs Gibbons, situated on the borders of Dudley and Kingswinford parishes, partly on land newly enclosed. The transfer of this land began with a lease by Viscount Dudley in 1784.[18] By this document, land was leased to William and Richard Croft, ironmasters, to build a furnace and other necessary buildings for processing ironstone. The end product would be cast iron. The document describes the property as: 'All that piece or parcel of land or woody ground as the same was marked and staked out', containing 2 acres more or less on the east side of the Dudley canal 'adjoining to the towing path of the said canal at or near a place called the Level Colliery, being parcel of a certain wood called Arch-hill als Hartsell Coppice.' The land appears to be just inside the Kingswinford boundary.

In such leases care was taken to ensure access for 'horses, cattle, wains, carts, waggons, etc.' from the site of the mine or furnace to the main roads, in this case the 'public way' from the Level Colliery to Pensnett Chase. As in this case, minerals (coal and iron) under the ground were usually exempted from the lease. Here, timber and fish in the canal were also exempted. Messrs Gibbons intended to erect another furnace, and to this end land described as 'at The Level' measuring slightly over 18 acres was leased to the firm. In describing the boundaries mention is made of 'the Level wood', showing that at this time there was little conflict between industry and country features. By 1801 Gibbons' firm was completing the furnaces and paying not less than £1,500 on them, processing ironstone they had mined in their own fields from land in Dudley and Kingswinford. The recovery of heathen coal under the ironstone was subsequently allowed in separate leases from Lord Dudley. The Gibbons brothers were able to exploit a large area here, stretching from Holly Hall to Saltwells and beyond the boundary under land in Kingswinford (Brierley Hill).

Dudley Trades in the Last Quarter of the Eighteenth Century

Eleven years after Sketchley published the first Dudley directory, a rather more comprehensive one was printed by Pearson and Rollason of Birmingham in 1781. This showed an increase in the numbers of 'ironmongers', whose industry was not confined to small iron objects, but could include the sale and even manufacture of machinery and equipment made of metal. Some metal objects were more specifically mentioned: John Chambers and Dixon & Son made

47 A view of Dudley from Easey Hill, 1775.

patten rings, John Packwood hinges, Edward Wilkinson was a locksmith and members of the Woolley family made special locks for horses. Lewis Blews made padlocks. Among those catering for food were Joseph Bourne, prominent on the town commissioners, who lists himself as a grocer and chandler, Stephen Brinton a butcher, and William Hughes a baker in Queen Street. Clothes could be bought from James Sansom of Hall Street, haberdasher, while George Dunton and James Moore provided shoes in their trade as cordwainers. There were also whitesmiths, maltsters and a sailcloth maker. The glass industry was represented in the directory by Abraham Hawkes of High Street, Jonathan Green of Dixon's Green and William Penn of Hall Street. The last mentioned owned the glass cone occurring in the 1775 picture from Easey Hill.

Uses of the Priory

The priory ruins had been despoiled in the centuries after its dissolution, but the wholesale thieving of the stone abated during the eighteenth century.[19] Though Richard Bolton tenanted the property during the early part of the century, there is little known about his possible use of the buildings. A drawing of the 1730s by Samuel and Nathaniel Buck shows the chapel standing up to half its height, and some of the cloister still above ground. The Buck drawing shows

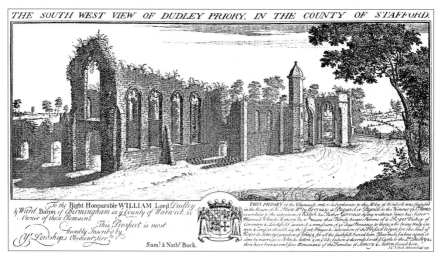

48, 49 & 50 Buck's view of the priory in 1731 (*above*); the priory in the late eighteenth century (*right*); and at the end of the eighteenth century (*below*).

no ancillary buildings, such as a lean-to residence, which may have been built there; his view may have been selective. The cloister stone was later plundered and little remains in the Molineux picture of around 1764.[20] By this time there were certainly living quarters attached to the old chapel structure, apparently more than one and perhaps some kind of manufactory.

A stone cottage was built on the site of the twelfth-century south apse. The roof was high pitched and the upper floor had dormer windows. This extension seems to have been added at some time to a previous pitched roof building occupying most of the south transept.[21] Grose (1775) claims that the cottage addition was erected about four years previously, but he may have been referring to the dwelling, not an apparent barn. The probability that this was a barn is strengthened by the fact that a haystack appears in front of it in the illustration published by Grose. At this point, and into the nineteenth century, the priory pool reached almost up to the buildings. The dam for this pool remained in existence until it was demolished when Priory House was built.

At least four dwellings are rated in the 1787 poor relief survey as belonging to Lord Dudley and located at the priory, but this survey does not clearly distinguish between houses and workplaces.[22] By the beginning of the nineteenth century a steam mill in the priory ruins was used for polishing glass, and perhaps for other uses in finishing metal products. There was little interest in the history of the priory except from non-local antiquarians, and – a notable exception – the local writer John Payton. Meanwhile, the former priory estate, consisting of fields running from Wolverhampton Street to the castle grounds, was being successfully farmed.

Methodists and Baptists

John Wesley had visited Dudley on many occasions. His visit in 1749 was the first, during which he preached in the marketplace. He was mobbed, as often happened when Wesley preached:

> At one [o'clock] I went to the market place and proclaimed the name of the Lord to a huge, unwieldy, noisy multitude, the greater part of whom seemed in no wise to know wherefore they were come together. I continued speaking about half an hour, and many grew serious and attentive, till some of Satan's servants pressed in, raging and blaspheming, and throwing whatever came to hand. I then retired to the house from which I came. The multitude poured after and covered over with dirt many that were with me, but I had only a few specks. [23]

An interesting light on the state of the market place, which despite the efforts of the borough court, still contained sufficient dirt to cover 'many'. Wesley returned in 1751, to be welcomed by a 'dismal screaming': 'I began preaching in a yard not far from the main street. Some at first seemed inclined to interrupt, but when they had heard a little they grew more attentive, and stayed very quietly to the end, though it rained a great part of the time.' Few details of the earliest Methodist church remain; it was clearly too small to hold a growing congregation, but in 1761 Wesley uses the word 'congregation' of the crowd who met him, and on 23 March 1764 he says that the Dudley people, 'formerly a den of lions', were now as quiet as Bristol. He was able to make a final visit in 1790, to a meeting house newly built (in 1788) in King Street. He describes the building as 'one of the neatest in England', and adds that his visit proved 'a profitable season'. The Methodists were to become influential in the town as a force for rationality and education.

It is not certain whether the Baptists at Cinderbank were originally classifiable as 'Particular', i.e. Calvinist, but it is known that a Baptist group was formed in Dudley proper in 1772.[24] The Midland Association of Baptists held a meeting in 1775 with delegates from the New Street Baptist meeting present. Church members may have met in little more than a room. The Midland Association issued a doctrinal statement which included the belief in 'eternal and personal election'.

In 1780, the church called its first minister, Abraham Greenwood, coming to Dudley from Rochdale where he had been working for five years. He is recorded in the 1781 residents' list in a house just below modern Tower Street as 'Rev. Mr Greenwood', with Richard Harper, a whitesmith, as his next-door neighbour. He departed in 1786 for a church in Rutland, leaving behind him the reputation of having been energetic and enterprising, founding a daughter church in Coseley in 1783, though this separation was not without disagreement. The Coseley residents considered the distance to be travelled was too great, but they left New Street with debts incurred in the building of the chapel. Mr Thomas Barber is recorded as Baptist minister on the 1787 Land Tax, but by 1788 Thomas Williams had become the minister for two years until he moved to Eastcombe in 1800.[25]

Quakers

Dudley Quakers had long occupied land between Back Lane (King Street) and High Street, parallel to what became Union Street. This was purchased from Robert Nayle in 1674 for £10, leaving a space for a footway from Back Lane to High Street.[26]

The group bought a house on High Street for £85 and a cottage at the end of the garden. These premises became the Quaker Meeting. For many years the Payton family were pillars of the church, which drew its membership from a wide area, including Rowley Regis, Hagley, Tipton, Nethertown [sic] and even such places as Bromsgrove. It is recorded that in the seventeenth century complex statements were required from the participants in a marriage, such as that given in 1693 by Sarah Payton when she married John Clarke of Tarporley in Cheshire: 'Friends and all people in the fear of God, and in the presence of the Assembly, which I take to be my witnesses, I, Sarah Payton, do take this my esteemed friend John Clarke to be my husband, Promising to be unto him, through God's assistents [sic], a faithful, loving and obediend [sic] wife until death.'[27] A similar declaration was made by John Clarke.

The hegemony of the Paytons had waned by the last part of the eighteenth century, but the Quaker Meeting continued, owning three houses in the same location by the time of the 1781 survey, which were tenanted by John Johnson, John Pinnock and Joseph Shore. Twenty-five Quakers died between 1762 and 1796 and were buried in the burial ground adjacent. Among them were 'Caleb Baker, who had forfeited his membership in the society' but was nevertheless allowed to be buried in the graveyard in 1783, and in 1796 a small daughter of Edward and Phebe Bridgwater, aged 3 years, 11 months and 19 days, was buried on 23 August. By this time, the Quakers seem to have reluctantly agreed to name the months, which had previously merely been numbered, though this time the register cautiously calls this '8th month called August'.

Among distinguished members of the congregation was Catherine Phillips, who published, in 1797, memoirs of her life.

Independents and Unitarians

An Independent chapel had existed in the centre of Dudley since the beginning of the century.[28] It occupied a position in the prestigious area of Wolverhampton Street, next to Horseley House, a splendid Georgian mansion. James Hancox was the minister during the mid-century; his sermon welcoming back the prince after the victory at Dettingen, 'The Safety of a good Prince, the Joy of a grateful People', was published in 1744. According to the evidence of the 1763 residents' list Mr Hancox apparently lived in Horseley House, with distinguished neighbours in Mr Charles Dixon, Mr John and Mr William Finch of the

Finch House, and Mr Samuel Caddick.[29] By 1781, and probably well before this, the fine house was the property of the Meeting trustees, occupied by the Revd William Wood. Mr Wood was paying 12s land tax on the house in 1787.

The following year a doctrinal disagreement arose between members of the Wolverhampton Street Church, relating to the same issue as vexed the Baptists, the question of 'election' for certain humans as compared to Wesley's (now Methodist) view of potential salvation for all. As a consequence the dissenting members formed a new church based on the previous Countess of Huntingdon's congregation in King Street. Many respectable inhabitants of the town were involved in the purchase of the King Street building from the Huntingdon sect: Edward Davies, ironmonger; Joseph Johnson, baker; William Penn, glassmaker; Thomas Hateley, gentleman; George Jones, builder; William Hartell, cordwainer; Benjamin Vanes, ironmonger; John Underhill the elder, hingemaker; Henry Blews, gentleman; Samuel Hammond of Birmingham, gentleman; William Whiley, gentleman; George Macmillan, buttonmaker; Thomas Sidaway, ironmonger; Joseph Edwards, carpenter; Samuel Loynes, bucklemaker; John Cardale, gentleman; John Skidmore, mercer; Joseph Linney, mercer, and Samuel Edge, potter. The list shows how influential Independent churchmen would be in the next years as Dudley grew: a number of them served on the town commission. The new meeting house was built on land in King Street on the opposite side of the road not far from the newly cut Union Street. It was some years before the Revd James Dawson was inaugurated as minister.[30]

Among other householders in Hampton Street (the name was not always lengthened to Wolverhampton Street) in the mid- to late eighteenth century was Samuel Cardale, who lived next to the site on which the Crown Hotel was later built. In 1755 he sold 'all that messuage in Hampton Lane heretofore in the possession of John Fauckes, now Edward Price and Thomas Thornton, with shops, barn, garden and small close belonging, called Moat Close'. Cardale was also the owner of a small close on the northern side of Sheep Lane (Priory Street), on which many years afterwards the post office was built. This close, called Sheep Close, also became the location of the county court in the nineteenth century.[31] The field name suggests that sheep were herded there before being sold to butchers on market days.

seven

BEFORE VICTORIA

During the first part of the nineteenth century Dudley was to grow until its population reached 18,211 in 1831. By this time industry had overtaken the commerce of the market place in importance, and large numbers of additional houses had been built, changing the nature of the eighteenth-century town beyond recognition. Dudley had spread to the south, down the slope towards Netherton, and to the north along the line of Wolverhampton Street. Netherton itself had burgeoned, becoming almost a town in its own right, covering fields which had been enclosed from Pensnett Chase only thirty years ago. Yet public services such as the water supply struggled to keep up with the expansion.

Increasing population meant increasing numbers of graves required, and several attempts were made to find more room for burials. The first was an exchange of land between Lord Dudley and St Thomas' Church, in which Lord Dudley gave land near the church 'adjoining the Back Street ... near the vicarage' on the opposite side of what became King Street, measuring just less than half an acre. St Thomas' gave Lord Dudley some land in Rowley Regis.[1]

St Thomas' vestry minute book is still concerned with parochial administration, such as the production of gowns for the 'gown charity'. Mrs Woolley is paid 12s in 1804 for making these clothes and Lucy Whitehouse 15s in 1812. The Revd Joseph Cartwright was the vicar in the early years of the century. St Thomas' is still thought of as 'the old church' and St Edmund's 'the new church', but both are under the control of the vestry meeting at St Thomas'. For fifteen and a half days' work at 'The New Church Yard' Richard Wilkes was paid over £2 in 1805. At Christmas, St Thomas' was 'dressed' by Edward Edwards, who also supplied coal. New rope for the church clock occurs as an item of expenditure in 1808, but the church also looked after the public clocks in the town at a cost in 1809 of 3 guineas. Church bells are mentioned, though it is not clear how many were installed. A subscription list was opened in 1811 for a new chandelier, to which James Bourne paid £5 and Miss Bennitt of New Street 3 guineas. Mrs Dixon at Horzely (Horseley) House paid 2 guineas. There is little hint in the vestry book that the physical state of the old church is deteriorating, but very great changes were about to take place.

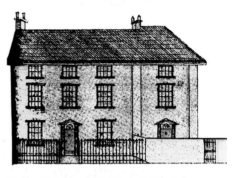

51 The grammar school at Queen's Cross, 1794–1826.

In 1812, the Revd Luke Booker was appointed to the parish, though he had been master at the grammar school and is recorded as having rented land at 'Cooks Tetnal' in 1801.[3] An autocrat with literary leanings, he was not perhaps well suited to Dudley, but was a man of enormous energy who was determined to make his mark. Already he had written poetry and prose, and during his life married no less than four times, his wives dying at comparatively young ages. In 1785 he had published *Poems on Subjects Moral and Entertaining, Volume I*, and within ten years had added *The Highlanders* and *Miscellaneous Poems*, following these with *Malvern: a descriptive and historical poem*. There were more poems and sermons to be published in the following years. It appears that on his arrival he took one look at the 'historic' St Thomas' and disliked what he saw. As a result, almost all trace of the old building would be erased. As a temporary measure repairs were carried out in 1813 and iron railings erected later that year.

Dr Luke Booker (trained as a lawyer) was determined to enhance the impact of the Church of England in Dudley. Before tackling the major development of St Thomas', he was concerned to remedy some difficulties at St Edmund's. In 1815 he sanctioned a free gallery at the 'new' church at a cost of £50. Up to that time, St Edmund's had four bells, but a fifth was added in 1817. Meanwhile, the old St Thomas' Church was completely demolished, leaving only the crypt, one memorial and a minimum of gravestones in the churchyard, all of which related to people who could claim kinship with those buried in them. Many of these memorials were later removed to the new Dudley cemetery: among dedications were the names of Elizabeth Morris (often spelt 'Maurice') the bookseller's wife who died on 2 August 1809, and members of the Shore family who died in 1803.

The foundation stone of a new church was laid in October 1816 by workmen belonging to Mr Evans, whose pay for the day amounted to £5.[4] A pageant

52 A view across the
fields to Netherton Church.

was arranged, with a band (paid £3 5s) and a feast at the end of the day. Luke
Booker is described as dressed in black, with a long-tailed coat, silken hose,
silver buckles and a broad-brimmed hat. A special guard was mounted, and a
brass plate incorporated in the foundation stone. Some of the cost of the new
church was supplied by revenue from church lands, such as the sale of coal
mines at Queen's Cross.

The new St Thomas' Church was an interesting building designed by William
Brooks, who had also designed the London Institution (now demolished). The
church was made of Bath stone and cost £24,000.[5] The outside walls form an
octagon, but not a symmetrical one, and instead of a chancel there is an organ
space; the archaeological detail is described by one commentator as 'uncon-
vincing', but the high spire dominates and can be seen from a considerable
distance.[6] The Gothic elements are mainly based on fifteenth-century appearance, as was frequently the case with Gothic-style churches at the time.

The Town Commissioners Continue to Struggle

Early in 1800 it was decided to abandon all hope of a communal water supply
in the town. This decision seems to have dispirited the commissioners, who
failed to meet for months. The meetings were by now taking place in 'the public
office', the Dudley Arms having been deserted. It is not clear what building is
meant by 'the public office', perhaps the Town Hall, but in 1803 the commissioners returned to the Dudley Arms. Considerable problems were found in
collecting the town rate and when the collectors discovered this they generally

resigned. The total collapse of the plans for a water supply presented great difficulties, and pumps were authorised for individual streets, such as that proposed for Priory Street in 1806, to be sunk near the garden ground of J. Keeling's executors. New buildings were rising every day, and there was discussion of new boundaries to include these. On the south side Mamble Square was designated, and near it additional buildings for William Penn the glassmaker at Oakey Well Lane. On the north, more buildings were being erected at Shaver's End and Caddick's End. The Inhedge was being built up, with new houses at Field Lane (also called Mill Street after the windmill, now Stafford Street). Owners of the new buildings did not always want their property included in the town boundaries, since this would put them within the jurisdiction of the commissioners, and they feared that rates would be raised accordingly.

Land tax itself was feared. In 1807, £20,619 was raised by this tax, though many inhabitants were exempted.[7] Lord Dudley still owned the greatest amount of land, including Stockwell Fields near the Priory, land by the road to Burnt Tree, land at Parkhead Colliery and in Dudley Wood, with some new allotments. The estate had been revalued in 1801.[8] Eleven tenants held the revalued land and buildings, and the detail in the account shows that the Dudley estate aimed to be fair to old tenants as well as obtaining a reasonable return on the land. Joseph Spurdle rented 24 acres near Queen's Cross. This was land which had been in the Pitt family, with old Daniel Pitt paying £48. The barn and stable were 'in a bad state of repair' and the court had recommended the rent be raised to £51, but Lord Dudley settled on £50.

At the new evaluation, Charles Norton paid rent for 9 acres 'below Castle Hill' and James Gibbons land at Burnt Tree. Joseph Clarke had land near the Trindle, and Joseph Moss land at Cawney Hill. William Penn rented 2 acres of land and Abiather Hawkes 9 acres at the Priory. Lodge Farm and a farm in Peartree Lane were two larger areas, Lodge Farm being almost 90 acres at a rent of £81 and Peartree Lane 40 acres at a rent of £37. The description of Lodge Farm mentions a farmhouse, barn, stable, wainhouse and two tenements and 'shops' (workshops) in an 'indifferent state of repair'. Ann Dudley was a widow whose son now helped her on the farm, also bringing coal from Parkhead. Ann's husband had died very recently and she was in arrears with the rent, but her son, described as 'industrious' though in 'indifferent' circumstances had promised to pay about half a year's rent in 'about a fortnight and one year at Lady day'. Apart from these tenants, Benjamin Silvers at Dudley Wood rented no buildings but 12 acres of land, and Edward Robinson at Holly

Hall about 30 acres including an old house and shop in a bad state of repair. Most of these properties appear in the 1807 land tax.

The land tax assessment gives an idea of some of the kinds of property to be found in Dudley at the time. There are many malthouses, some claypits as well as dyehouses, nail warehouses and the remaining farms. The names of tenants are given, but there are many subtenants whose names are omitted, such as the ten whose houses adjoin a stable at Dudley Wood in the holding of John Whitehouse and the eleven subtenants of Daniel Parsons in Wolverhampton Street.[9] Many of these houses would be very small, speculative buildings. William Penn's glasshouse is mentioned, with two tenants in Hall Street. He has a void house and land at 'Balper' glasshouse and there are eleven other tenants. Penn, whose residence is given as Birmingham, also owned land at Blackacre and 'Oaky' Well, with his small allotment under the Enclosure Act at 'Waddam's Hill'.

Edwin Blocksidge, the Dudley printer, included a map in his printed work on the castle and town. It has evidently been derived from a manuscript plan, for which Blocksidge gives no date. However, it shows the newly erected Bluecoat School premises in Fisher Street, and so must be from about the 1820s. It seems likely that it is based on the parish survey which had been made by order of the parish given on 15 July 1824.[10] The east end only is shown, with the newly cut Birmingham Road running by St Edmund's churchyard. Lettering on the street names is clearly by Blocksidge, but the outline of buildings is likely to have been traced from the original.[11] Tower Street and Upper Tower Street are included, and the name Queen Street is applied only to the northern branch of High Street, running behind the marketplace. In this plan, the Town Hall has a small passage behind it, separating it from the other buildings in Middle Row. New Street is very narrow. Birmingham Street has many courts leading off it, their plots leading to Porter's Field.

Castle Street, so named, has its new hotel, The Castle, featured, supplanting a row of small houses. Public buildings seem to have been coloured in a darker colour, so that the workhouse, fourth building from the west end of Tower Street, and Baylies' School are picked out, as is St Edmund's. Baylies' School was rebuilt in 1824 and the plan appears to show this building. The narrow plots originating in the medieval burgages are clearly to be seen; some of these still exist in this plan, presenting thin frontages to High Street but occupying lengthy areas behind the frontages. These are particularly noticeable behind Queen Street, their plots stretching in a number of cases back to Tower Street.

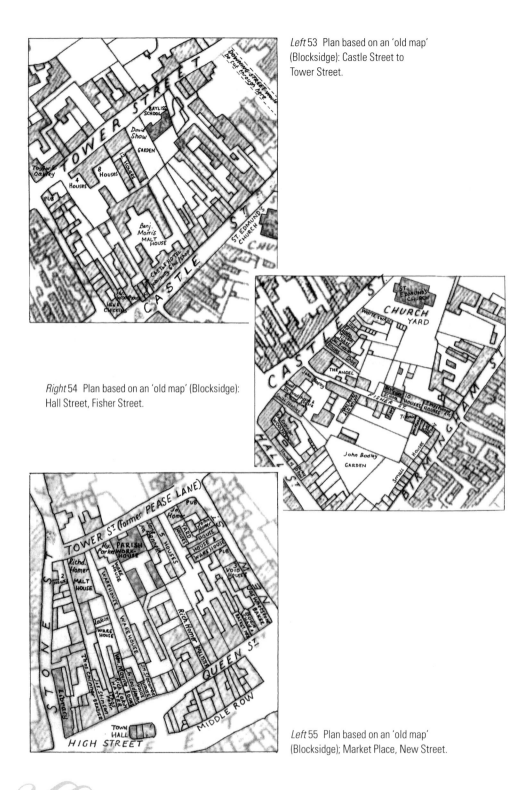

Left 53 Plan based on an 'old map' (Blocksidge): Castle Street to Tower Street.

Right 54 Plan based on an 'old map' (Blocksidge): Hall Street, Fisher Street.

Left 55 Plan based on an 'old map' (Blocksidge); Market Place, New Street.

A good deal is known about the history of the Fisher Street site of the old Bluecoat School, now part of Dudley bus station. In the early eighteenth century it had been part of the large estate of the Shaw family. The plots at the north end of Fisher Street were already owned in part by Stephen Fisher, when he bought further land on the east side of the lane from the Shaws in 1764. The close on which the school was eventually built seems to have had only a stable on it in the mid-eighteenth century, but on the death of Stephen Fisher in 1814 the land was obtained by the charity that ran the Bluecoat School. (It should be noted that Fisher Street, or Fisher's Lane, carried the family name many years before this, and Stephen Fisher was merely returning to a road where his ancestors had probably lived.)

Here it might be appropriate to discuss the hotel called the Woolpack, fronting Castle Street on the south side. This rather fine building appears from illustrations to have dated in its most recent form from the eighteenth century. It was notable for its archway, leading to a yard for horses and coaches to remain while their owners were in the hotel. Further down the yard was a row of houses, the yard and houses sometimes occurring on plans and surveys as 'Dunton's Yard'. Like the other houses on the south-east side of Castle Street, the hotel was owned by the Paytons and passed to the Baddeley, or Badly, family (also sometimes written 'Bodily'). In 1739 the premises were described as a 'dwelling house' or tenement with 'gatehouse' as well

Above 56 Statue of an orphan at Baylies' School.

Left 57 Inscription on Baylies' School.

as gardens and other appurtenances.[12] In 1759 the tenant was Hurst Dixon, the previous tenant being given as Thomas Baker, known to be a trader and publican. It seems likely that the dwelling house of 1739 was already a hotel, though this is difficult to prove conclusively.

In the 1790s the four houses in the yard were occupied by Samuel Burton, James Bowater, Isaac Wharton and Benjamin Dudley, and the occupier of the Woolpack, William Rolinson, described himself as a butcher. This does not preclude him from being an innkeeper as well. Rolinson was succeeded in 1810 by Edward Grainger, while a few years later, in 1815, the yard is called Dunton's Entry and the position is described as 'near the Horse Fair', which had been transferred there from the area round what is now the art gallery. In 1824 one of the buildings in the yard is a slaughterhouse. By 1835 the hotel was kept by Thomas Allendale, though the property remained in the Grainger family.

The parish survey of 1824, made to enable a poor rate to be levied, is enormously detailed, giving owners and occupiers of all premises with a degree of precision which had not been attempted before.[13] Eighteenth-century maps had omitted most buildings, so that the 1787 survey mentions houses and manufactories which cannot be identified. The 1824 survey, however, identifies most houses, though it does at times give in and list the occupiers with the term 'and others'. For example, in Upper High Street (not so-called; the denomination of streets is very vague) Samuel Jones owns what became No. 78, with Samuel Cook and others occupying the fourteen houses in this block. Lower down the street, J. Pensotti (who can be identified from the 1820 directory as an umbrella maker) is listed with five other tenants, names not mentioned. The Dudley Arms Hotel, the most prestigious hotel in town, is owned by 'the Dudley Arms committee', while The Bush is owned and tenanted by James Cartwright.

The market place naturally provides considerable interest, though it is a little difficult to match the premises shown on the map with what existed before the 1960s redevelopment. On the east corner of New Street, Elizabeth Bennett tenanted the Hen and Chickens, owned by Sir Horace St Paul, who had inherited some property from Lord Dudley. William Maurice, bookseller, was the owner and occupier of what became No. 225, while No. 235, later the Miner's Arms, was owned by Barnet Hinton and tenanted by Joseph Harper. The other tenants on the north-west side were two basket makers, a baker, a hatter, a maltster, a clothier and a draper.[14] Queen Street (Middle Row) had not yet been demolished, and included sixteen properties with various tradesmen occupying them. The owner of the Town Hall is given as the Earl of Dudley.

58 Upper High Street, showing early nineteenth-century houses, once prestigious.

On the corner of Stone Street, the library was apparently combined with an engine house, and was owned by the Dudley Arms company. Between Stone Street and Wolverhampton Street an auctioneer, a brazier and a seedsman were among tenants, and at the house which became No. 211 was the Salutation Inn. By this time there were a number of fine houses in the upper part of High Street, including that of Abiather Hawkes called The Mansion, at what became shops Nos 203 and 204, a wide house with a large garden owned and occupied by John Robinson, attorney (later No. 194) and Cornelius Cartwright's house which later became No. 188.

Directly opposite St Thomas' Church was the Blue Bell, which had been a burgage as early as 1703, and almost certainly before. A row of houses at High Side features on the map. The 1824 survey does not mention a new venture on the priory grounds, the building of a fine new house called Priory Hall. By 1826 it was complete and was occupied by Francis Downing, the Earl of Dudley's steward. Unfortunately the access road cut through the priory ruins, demolishing some medieval work and complicating discovery by later archaeologists.

Development of Netherton

Identifying properties in Netherton from the many deeds surviving is hazard-ous. A survey taken in 1701 for the quarter sessions would have helped, but has disappeared.[15] It mentioned the old Baptist chapel at Cinderbank, which can be located on a field called Austin Barbers (variously spelt). With very few Netherton buildings shown on either the Court Map or the 1780s updated plan based on it, the 1824 map we have been studying is the earliest except for the enclosure map itself, which was made before the major developments took place in Netherton.

Prior to this, clusters of dwellings were situated at Mushroom Green, Withymoor, near the present Netherton market place, at Baptist End and fur-ther afield at Woodside. Lodge Farm and Saltwells were prominent outposts. A good deal of fresh information can therefore be gained from this survey of 1824. However, the survey is vague in its naming of streets even in Dudley town, and becomes worse in Netherton.

Baptist End Chapel occupied land to the east of the junction with Swan Street, with five houses adjoining. Beyond this there were no further houses until High Street was reached. The British Iron Company was established by this time in Northfield Road, owning nine houses lining the road. Most devel-opment here was on the south side of the road, with eight houses facing the nine belonging to the British Iron Company.

East of the canal in Windmill End, Lord Dudley still owned some land, though the trustees of Windmill End chapel owned the land on which their meeting house stood.

Nearer Northfield Road was Withymoor Brick Works with its kiln, ware-house and rough land. On Northfield Road lived members of the Darby clan. It is difficult not to link the name Darby End with the numbers of this family living here: Sophia, Joseph, William and Daniel each had a house between the two turnpike roads.

New houses had been built at the crossroads where Halesowen Road meets what is now Saltwells Road, on land owned by William Hodgetts. Further south, in Newtown, the settlement was dominated by the Truman family with houses clustered along Mousesweet brook (sometimes called Newtown brook at this point). On the north side of the lane, John, Mark, Thomas and 'Captain' Truman each had houses, while Elijah Truman had a workshop and garden opposite. Amos and Richard Truman had a house and garden at the end of the lane, and Anna also had a garden just below these. Two members of the Sidaway family also lived in Newtown. The clannishness and self-sufficiency of the inhabitants of this hamlet can be imagined.

The western part of Netherton, stretching to Woodside, is listed in 1824 under the name of Yew Tree, using the ancient name of the Yew Tree Hill through which an old lane roughly on the path of present-day Marriott Street wound its way. The land enclosed from Pensnett Chase had been divided up into fields by this time, with names such as Beauty Bank, Little Coppice Piece and Nursery Piece. In the centre of Netherton the British Iron Company owned land at Sweet Turf, but on the western side of the old village Lord Dudley's cottagers included Benjamin, Thomas and Ann Round, Sarah and Edward Lavender, Sarah Shakespeare and Samuel Rushton: all names present in Netherton for many years.

St Andrew's Church

As early as 1825 concerns were being expressed about the lack of Church of England facilities in the growing town of Netherton. The Parish Order Book records on 8 January of that year a proposal that drawings should be prepared for a new church. The site, given by Lord Dudley, was described as a desolate spot, from which the coal had been removed from its surface, being far removed from the population at this time.[16] It is certainly true that in 1825 there was no sign of houses between the church and Netherton village centre. Objections were made to any new building by the redoubtable draper Samuel Cook, but his fears that ratepayers would be called upon to pay for the new building were groundless. The church authorities were able to apply for a grant from the Ecclesiastical Commissioners, a body set up following the Napoleonic Wars to build churches in developing areas. The church was built of brick faced with Gornal stone, the foundation stone being laid by Dr Luke Booker on 30 November 1827 (St Andrew's day). Just as when St Thomas' was rebuilt, there was a band and a procession, with the now merely ceremonial members of the court leet and local inhabitants lining up.[17]

St Andrew's was completed in 1830 and consecrated on 16 July by the Bishop of Worcester. Luke Booker was still in charge, as this was only a chapel of ease, not yet a parish. His new chapel was of Early English appearance, 98ft by 54ft, with galleries supported by iron pillars. The organ was installed in 1835.

59 St Andrew's Church, Netherton.

Details of the wall round the churchyard were agreed at a parish meeting on 8 January 1830: it was to be 9ft, made of brick with supporting pillars. It was agreed later in the year that a beadle must be employed, and his salary was fixed.[18] St Andrew's stands at a height of 650ft above sea level and can be seen from many miles around. The location is so natural that it is surprising that no church was built there previously; in this context one has to remember that this was formerly part of Pensnett Chase, and though coal had been dug on Knowle Hill for centuries, there were no habitations nearby.

Samuel Cook, who had been a principal opponent of the new church at Netherton, continued his campaign against the domination of the Church of England, Dr Luke Booker, and church rates. He began by issuing two posters and in the following year on 8 December 1824, he issued a new poster called 'The Duties of Parish Officers'.[19] Church rates were an issue up and down the country at this time, with the increasing influence of Nonconformist churches in new industrial towns, whose members resented paying rates to the church when they classified themselves as 'chapel'. To this was added a controversy over the emancipation of Catholics, which in Dudley caused a petition to be raised. There had been, and still was, a Catholic presence in Dudley and district, exemplified by a small number of Italians who had settled in the town.

Gas Lighting

The lamp brackets which had been attached to street corners using oil as a fuel soon became obsolete, and the town commissioners sought ways to illuminate Dudley streets more effectively. In 1818 a meeting took place in the Town Hall determined to press ahead with new lighting plans by establishing a new gas company.[20]

60 Turnpike gate ticket.

James Bourne, the long-serving clerk to the commissioners, became the new company's secretary and the invitable committee was formed. In contrast to the situation over the water supply, the supply of gas was very actively developed. Cook's Tetnall, which had recently been turned down as a new site for the town workhouse, was chosen as the right place for a gasworks and an Act of Parliament was promoted to incorporate the Town of Dudley Gas Light Co. Its success had been anticipated by the commissioners, who had already authorised the laying of gas pipes throughout the borough section of the parish. Samuel Clegg, who had experience of gas lighting in a number of other towns, was chosen as the gas engineer. He had already written several books on the subject, as well as, surprisingly, some Old Testament studies. The new company allowed lighting to be extended to Stone Street, Queen Street and along the west end of High Street. The lights were fixed on tall poles so that light could travel some distance, but they were still few and far between. In other respects the town commissioners were less successful, having great difficulty in keeping the streets clean. In 1824 it was decided that this task should be performed by the Turnpike Commissioners. As in the late eighteenth century, one major problem was that of dung, resulting from the increasing horse traffic. The Turnpike Commissioners were to be allowed to take the manure for their own use, presumably for sale to neighbouring farmers.

Political Reform

The years leading up to 1832 saw agitation throughout England for reform of the political system, which left large towns and cities without any kind of representation in Parliament except as part of county constituencies. In Dudley, this movement was bitterly opposed by the richer inhabitants. As early as 1819 a meeting was called by the Mayor, Francis Downing (Lord Dudley's steward), to pass a resolution against any such change.[21] The vast majority of Dudley inhabitants had no voice whatever, even in choosing the mayor, who was an official chosen by the old court leet. One of the organs through which the anti-radicals exerted influence was the Dudley Pitt Club, supported by Dr Luke Booker and other church members, and often opposed by the Nonconformists. A small local paper called *The Patriot* publicised the radical cause, but a copy of this was ceremonially burnt on the Market Cross. It was in the same year that Samuel Cook opened his drapery at Gibraltar House in Upper High Street, a business which provided him with the resources to fight for 'liberty' (for such was was the continual cry).

Cook was in the habit of displaying political posters in his shop window. In 1827 he was committed for trial at Worcester on a charge of publishing 'a certain scandalous libel' on government ministers which might incite the populace to insurrection. One of his many objections to government policy was that they spent 'a million and a half' on new churches, and that the 'tax producers' were starving, while the tax eaters were living in abundance. Cook claimed that the poster which he had exhibited had been stolen from his front window, and in any case it was not written by him. He was bound over to keep the peace. However, he did not retire from the political field and became one of the founders of the Dudley Political Union as part of a network of unions in the West Midlands and beyond, working towards a reform of the Parliamentary system. Dr Luke Booker continued to oppose any reform, commenting on a rick-burning that a rick burner 'commits an injury which is justly punishable by death'. The Earl of Dudley was also opposed to the Reform Bill, but Cook continued to issue and display posters in favour of radical change. The first attempt at reform failed, but this made the Unions more determined than ever to gain representation for the people.

The Reform Bill was finally passed in 1832 and Dudley was granted an MP for the first time since the Middle Ages. Sir John Campbell was the reform candidate, and was opposed by the veteran ironmaster Sir Horace St Paul, who still owned much property in Dudley and Netherton. Horace St Paul had origins near Coventry and married Anna Maria Ward, an illegitimate daughter of the second Viscount Dudley. Through her he inherited a small portion of the Dudley estates.However, he seems to have lived far away in Northumberland, or during the season in London.When Sir John Campbell was nominated as the reform candidate, Samuel Cook lobbied him in support of further reform measures: would he give the vote to working men? The replies were not promising. There was no question of a secret ballot and the electorate voting was not much more than 500. There was a considerable difference in the vote between Dudley and Netherton, the latter being much more favourable to Horace St Paul than Dudley itself. In two days of voting, carried out in public near the market place, there was a majority of sixty-five for Sir John Campbell, who thus became Dudley's first modern MP. It seems that many of the population were not impressed, since they still had not obtained any voting rights.[22] Nevertheless, a procession escorted Campbell into the town, with a live cock in front, garlanded with blue ribbons (Campbell's colour) and a dead cock on a withered branch representing Sir Horace St Paul. However, two years later Campbell was made attorney general, and Thomas Hawkes, from a well-known local family, stood for the Tories and was elected. The Political Union had won its case, but not to the satisfaction of the bulk of Dudley inhabitants, who soon demanded again the voice in Parliament that they had hoped and worked for.

Dudley Appears in the Topographical Dictionary

One of the first comprehensive national surveys to be published was produced in 1831 by Samuel Lewis, and entitled *A Topographical Dictionary of England*. One and a half pages were given to Dudley, reciting details (sometimes conjectured) of its history and describing its current state. Its account was perhaps a little optimistic:

> The town is pleasantly situated in a tract of country, the surface of which is finely varied, though in several places disfigured by mining operations, which are extensively prosecuted in the vicinity; the principal street is spacious, and the whole town is well paved, and lighted with gas; the houses are in general neat and well built, and many of them are large and elegant; the inhabitants are supplied with water from wells of considerable depth; and the environs beside the castle hill, which is a favourite place of resort, abound with pleasant walks and rides.[23]

Information for the article was clearly supplied by one of the wealthier inhabitants, but we do not need to doubt the point about well-built houses in central Dudley, since many of them survived to be photographed. It is also interesting to note that Castle Hill was regarded already as a place for leisure.

After describing the subscription library opening in 1805 and the Dudley Arms (not by name), the article continues to discuss mining and iron production, mentioning the production of agricultural equipment and nail making. Limestone, we are told, is used in iron production, but also burnt for agricultural use and made into chimney pieces; there is reference to the canal tunnel, its length given as a mile and three quarters. The dictionary gives details of the two town churches and St Andrew's ('recently erected') and Nonconformist chapels. Turning to education, the article deals with the grammar school, the Baylis (so spelt) foundation, ascribed to 1732, and the 'Blue-coat school … founded in 1708, in which there are now about two hundred and thirty boys'. An infant school and a 'school of industry' for 220 girls also existed.

Cholera and its Aftermath

The cholera morbus, a water-borne disease, first devastated Asia and Europe in 1829–30, and arrived in England at Sunderland in 1831. Soon it had arrived in the Black Country, where water supplies had not kept pace with the increase in population. Efforts to supply Dudley with a sustainable water system had stalled many times, and there was still great reliance on pumps in the main streets, as well as in Netherton.

Not suprisingly the disease spread alarmingly, and no one knew why. The general feeling was that the disease was airborne. By mid-1832 there were so many deaths that the graveyards in Dudley could not cope, and on 1 September the Board of Health directed that people dying from cholera must be buried in the new churchyard at Netherton.[24] An unnamed local source reported:

> During the Asiatic Plague, 1831-2 … the bodies of the victims were collected and buried in the north-east side of Netherton Churchyard. So dreadful was its effect that it was found necessary to bury them in large common graves deeply dug. The bodies were collected at night in carts, the wheels of which were muffled, having had straw tied to their wheels. The drivers of the carts on their rounds, raised the fearful cry: 'Bring out your dead.' The bodies were buried uncoffined and unnamed.[25]

Churches and chapels were appalled by the spread of the disease and communal prayers were held. A poster from 22 September 1832 ordered that 26 September, a Wednesday, was to be kept as a 'day of humiliation'. This was

signed by the churchwardens, John Williams and Joseph Bennitt. During the previous week the Committee for the Relief of the Poor issued an appeal, with the preamble acknowledging the depression of the iron trade and the families of workers having been 'brought to a state of extreme destitution'. Of individuals, Francis Downing gave £10, Cornelius Cartwright and Mr (John) Badley each the same.

An alternative explanation for the spread of cholera was poor food, and a subscription was set up to provide 'the poor of this parish with wholesome food and other comforts they may require'. By a coincidence it was only a year since attempts had been made to develop Saltwells as a health spa, depending on the special qualities of its mineral waters. A London chemist was employed to analyse the water and pronounce it 'one of the best Mineral Waters in the Kingdom, for almost every disease incident to the human body'.[26] With cholera raging in the parish, this claim looked dubious. Even the alleged miraculous cure of Mr Oxford of Brettle Lane could not encourage large numbers to partake of the waters. The name given to the spa, Ladywood, did not indicate a medieval provenance and had nothing to do with the Virgin Mary, but derived from the previous interest of a Lady Dudley.

The Dudley Waterworks Company, which had been inaugurated in 1810, had proved incapable of organising a water supply, and the year before the cholera outbreak the town commissioners had decided to make a cistern under St Thomas' Church to 'afford the inhabitants of this Town a supply of soft water' by collecting the rain water 'from the roof of St Thomas' Church'.[27] It was not likely that this supply could answer the needs of the whole town. A Parliamentary bill was promoted in 1834 to provide a new reservoir, which was subsequently built at Shaver's End, but even this made little difference to the major water-supply problem which was to haunt Dudley for many years to come.

Dudley in 1835

The state of Dudley in 1835 can easily be assessed from Treasure's map and Pigot's Commercial Directory.[28] Pigot is able to elaborate on the information given by Lewis four years previously. He adds flint glass to the account of manufactures, and supplements a point made by Lewis about the amazing sight of fields on fire, which Lewis calls Fiery Holes, at Queen's Cross, where Pigot says smoke and gas may be seen issuing from the interstices of the rock: 'These subterranean fires generally continue until the fuel which supplies them is nearly exhausted.' The whole area, however, is lit at night by flame:

> A stranger who approaches the town of Dudley in the evening will be much surprised at the innumerable lights, seen in every direction, issuing from furnaces, forges, collieries, imparting not only to the face of the earth, but also to that of the firmament, an appearance of one universal illumination.

Pigot naturally describes the castle and its history, 'now become a charming place of resort for inhabitants and visiters [sic]'. He mentions the priory and the newly built Priory House, 'a handsome building'. Ladywood Spa is described as 'valuable', and is alleged to possess similar waters to Cheltenham and Leamington. However, it demands 'much better accommodations than are at present afforded'. A note of warning is sounded: 'The only want hitherto experienced by the town has been that of water, which is being remedied by an affluent company' piping water from Sedgley. The new reservoir at Shaver's End is doubtless in mind, but this provided water for a small area only, and it was many years before the problem was remedied.

A much larger list of schools is provided. Baylies' Charity, Tower Street; Blue Coat, Fisher Street; a Catholic subscription school; the grammar school, now

62 Priory House, New Street.

in Wolverhampton Street with Proctor Robinson in charge; an infants' school
in Stafford Street; the Girls' School of Industry in Fisher Street; and a further
School of Industry in Wolverhampton Street are the public institutions, but
there are also about twenty private schools, including a ladies' boarding school
at Netherton. The directory lists many named public houses and even more
beer retailers. Among long-term survivors are the Blue Bell, The Swan and the
Hen and Chickens in Castle Street, the Miners' Arms and The Lion in Queen
Street. Thomas Allendale now kept the Woolpack.

By this time most of the Dudley open fields had been enclosed, sold off and
united with other small patches of open land. Farming had retreated to Cawney
Hill, Netherton and the area round the priory. Many farmers seem to have concentrated on fattening cattle and sheep for butchers, and this is the trade label
under which they are found in the directory. A number of members of the Cole
family had small farms at Netherton: Benjamin at Bumble Hole, and John and
Thomas at Darby End. Peter Pitt continued to run cattle at Woodside and John
Price was a butcher at Freebody's.

Agricultural land was spoilt by coal extraction, not only above ground but by
subsidence, causing water to accumulate and stagnate. Seventeen coal masters
are listed in the directory, among them Sir Horace St Paul at Windmill End,
working through his agent Richard Bradley, with Withymoor Colliery close by.
The British Iron Company owned Netherton Colliery, and Joseph Haden
Dixon's Green. Perhaps the largest share in the coal business was the Earl of
Dudley, with his agent Francis Downing. Though chain making was mainly

63 The cattle bridge over the canal near Netherton.

centred in the next parish at Cradley Heath, fourteen chain makers are listed in Dudley, including Benjamin Hancox at 'Mursham' (Mushroom) Green. A copy of the enclosure map shows that his family owned fields there in 1819.[29]

The Progress of Nonconformity

Dudley Baptist Church continued to expand.[30] There were forty-six members in 1817; the number increased to 175 in 1833. Important work took place in the Sunday school, which had 227 children by 1833. This work should not be dismissed as affecting only the children's religious progress: through these Sunday schools children learned to read and thus became literate members of society. There were, of course, differences of opinion on doctrine and other matters. An assistant to the minister, Mr Passmore, was allegedly in dispute with him and was finally expelled. The meeting house was enlarged in 1828, and during this period the Baptists were able to use the Unitarian schoolroom in Tower Street in the morning and the Wesleyan chapel in the afternoon, while two new side galleries were built. A degree of ecumenism clearly existed between different nonconformist groups in Dudley, though it is doubtful whether this extended to the Church of England during the incumbency of Dr Booker.

In 1829 the Baptist minister, Mr John Hutchings, became unwell, and as the church members wanted to increase the size of the chapel by adding the space occupied by the manse, they offered to pay Hutchings a salary if he would resign his office. Mr William Rogers, his assistant, was described as 'designing' in these negotiations, and John Hutchings did not resign. He died in office in 1829, but his wife refused to leave the house. Nevertheless, William Rogers succeeded to the ministry.

During these years, Baptist members were encouraged to assist in services, particularly in preaching, a vital part of nonconformist worship. In March 1814 William Bridge was invited to 'exercise his talents for the ministry' every evening, and in 1829 Edward Moss Milton was approved as a preacher; he was recommended to 'go to proclaim the glad tidings of salvation' wherever a door might be opened to him. In 1831, Mr Pickering was 'considered as possessing talents for the ministry' after preaching his probationary sermon before the church. The church was governed by a system of deacons, chosen at a meeting where important decisions were made.

Methodists

The Wesleyan chapel in Wolverhampton Street was for many years a landmark in Dudley. Its first stone was laid on 10 June 1828. It was an impressive stone-faced building with a portico supported by Ionic columns, approached through the graveyard, latterly lined with trees. There was a large gallery, lit by both round-headed and square windows. Building took just over a year, and the church opened on Sunday, 16 August 1829.[31] The inaugural preacher was the nationally famous Jabez Bunting, and the celebrations continued with more services on Tuesday. From the first there was an organ, supplemented by a cello. The first burial in the graveyard – that of a 9-year-old boy – took place while the church was still being built. It was decided at a meeting in the same year to call the building Wesley Chapel.

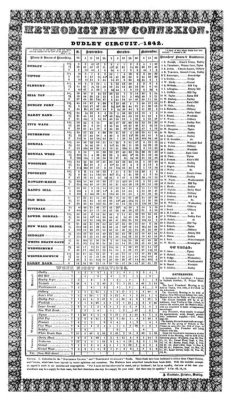

64 Methodist New Connexion Circuit plan, 1842.

65 The Methodist Church, Wolverhampton Street, after rebuilding.

The make-up of the congregation of Wesley was socially mixed, with Stephen Dunn, fender maker, Richard Attwell, bricklayer, James Kent, miner and William Dunn, cordwainer, among trustees.

A Methodist 'new connexion' church was founded on land at Caddick's End, next to Badgers' Nail Warehouse, in 1820. The street in which the chapel was erected became known as Chapel Street. As a result of disagreements between the Wesleyans of Dudley and the Wesleyan Connexion Conference, it was proposed that the Wesley church in Wolverhampton Street should join the New Connexion group. The grounds of the dispute are not clear, but the proposition succeeded, and in 1836, in a 'numerous meeting', Wesley members agreed to join the New Connexion, with the chapel joining a New Connexion circuit.[32] Wesley Chapel being the more prestigious building, it naturally became the focus. The disagreements with the larger Wesleyan Conference were gradually solved.

A glance at the register of Wesley Chapel shows that in 1831 eight children were baptised (following fourteen in 1830). Eli, son of Daniel and Elizabeth Willett, nailer, of Darby Hand; John William Paskill, son of William and Eliza, tailor; Eliza, daughter of George and Ellen Preece, carpenter; Hannah, daughter of John and Elizabeth Parsons, engineer of Netherton; Hannah, daughter of Benjamin and Hannah Careless of Netherton, engineer; Joseph Edward, son of Joseph and Mary Ann Histon, nail factor; Daniel, son of Herbert and Sarah Hancox of Musham Green, frame maker; and Ellen, daughter of James and

Prudence Weaver of Dudley Wood, miner. Trades are also represented, with a boatman's child being baptised in 1833 and many miners or colliers' children also mentioned in the same period. From 1834 more children born in the town centre are featured, and Church Street, Minories, Flood Street, Stafford Street and Oakywell Street all make an appearance.

The Badgers and Phoenix Glassworks

Phoenix Glassworks in Hall Street was originally the empire of William Penn, who owned much of the land around it and features in all the land tax documents. By 1820 it had passed to the ownership of Isaac and Thomas Badger.[33] The first of the family to move from Oldswinford was Isaac Badger senior, who died on 16 December 1808 and was buried in a vault in St Edmund's Church. His nail warehouse was in Eve Hill, recorded in the 1807 land tax as near to school land there. His wife, Sarah, followed him in 1820. Two of their sons were Isaac junior and Thomas, the latter of whom occupied The Hill, the old mansion near Dixon's Green. When he died in 1856 it was recorded that during his long connection with the trading and mining operations of the town he had been an upright magistrate, discharging the duties of that office 'with zeal and integrity'.[34] His memorial tablet claimed that he had been a liberal benefactor to the poor. This was not quite the experience of the radical Samuel Cook, who frequently clashed with the Badgers. Even the masters had their sorrows, however; Thomas and Mary Badger lost their fourth son, Edward, at the age of 18: 'a source of heart rending affliction' to them.[35]

Progress at the Grammar School

Thanks to Dr Trevor Raybould, we now have a very detailed picture of the running of the grammar school in the early nineteenth century.[36] Over the years the administration of the school had been haphazard, but the early nineteenth century was a time when rules were tightened. The very generous founding gifts of land had not been carefully preserved, though Dudley was not a special case: administration was lax in other places, such as in the case of the Free School (later King Edward's) in Birmingham. As in that case, headmasters were often pluralist, and in the early nineteenth century this was so with the Revd Proctor Robinson being both headmaster of Dudley school and vicar of St Edmund's. 'This being a commercial place', Robinson introduced a whole series of modern subjects to the curriculum, though it is not clear how they were all taught.[37] Neither Proctor Robinson nor the vicar preceding Dr Booker, Joseph Cartwright, could keep track of what was occurring with the rents supposed to be paid by the tenants of school lands, and indeed some were being sold off.[38]

A list of trustees from 1815 reads like a roll call of the influential members of the town commissioners, the church attenders at St Thomas' and St Edmund's, and the social clubs of the town which met at the Dudley Arms. John Badley, or Baddeley, we have already met as a contributor to the fund for poor relief in the cholera epidemic. He owned property in Castle Street and Blowers Green. Thomas Wainwright was among the list of mayors (who were not elected by the people), James Bourne of the town commissioners, Cornelius Cartwright, who had inherited the property of the earlier vicar, and of course Dr Luke Booker, who had previously been master of the school. The truth is that there was only a small clique of men with sufficient education and time to serve on any such group, and they were in constant demand for various official purposes in the town. Naturally, these men wielded great power.

School premises were never quite adequate at this period, and they suffered at times from the prevalence of mining, which was becoming a hazard in many parts of the parish. During the tenure of Thomas Jackson, in 1787, the school is recorded as being on the north-west corner of Stone Street, and it remained there during Dr Booker's headship in 1797. Its location is harder to identify a decade later, when it is simply described as High Street, but it seems likely to have been in the same place. Though the school trustees owned land at Queen's Cross and a building was almost certainly there in earlier times, it is not clear exactly what this building was; Luke Booker had a house on the

66 The grammar school, south side of High Street, 1840–99.

site, but mining operations made it unsafe. The school moved to property in Wolverhampton Street between 1827 and 1832.

In 1834 the trustees purchased a house in Upper High Street with a garden, and a considerable history. This can be identified with the later No. 60 High Street.[39] In 1744 it had belonged to Thomas Hawkes, the deed recording that it had previously belonged to Thomas Finch. Hawkes became bankrupt in 1749 and the land was vested in the Revd Joseph Dixon.[40] By 1804 it was transferred from Edward Hancox to Benjamin Parker of Oldbury. An old drawing shows that the house and adjacent schoolroom were of stone and the garden stretched to King Street. There was also a front garden, the house standing back from the general building line in Upper High Street and constituting one of the larger mansion houses which had been built along this turnpike road before the Georgian expansion of the town.

Netherton St Andrew's School

The year before Queen Victoria entered her reign, the state of education in Netherton came to the attention of John Badley and his family, whom were among the more liberal of the Dudley bourgeoisie. Working through the charity that had administered the Bluecoat School, they gave land to build a new school in the centre of Netherton to serve the growing need there. The land was described as:

> 1985 square yards ... adjoining the Turnpike Road leading from Dudley to Halesowen, bounded by the said Turnpike Road, by a newly made road thrown and dedicated to the Public as a common highway leading thereout to or towards Netherton Church [...] to use and apply and appropriate the same as and for Schools for the education of poor boys and girls resident in the neighbourhood according to the principles and doctrine of the Church of England.[41]

The Bluecoat trustees took out a mortgage to pay for the building of the school, which was single storey and in the rural school tradition, with drip-moulds over the windows and the master's house adjoining. He had a garden in front of the house and there was a bell tower on one of the school roofs, important in those days to call children to school, before the local inhabitants had watches or clocks.

eight

DUDLEY IN A SEA OF MUD

Within the next few years, Dudley and Netherton were to be engulfed in a tide of rubbish, mud and sewage, which encouraged some of the worst health in the country. The totally ineffective measures adopted to secure a plentiful water supply were one of the chief reasons for this. Civil unrest added to the problems of a town which had become a large industrial centre but still operated to some degree with the institutions of a village.

Samuel Cook was still a leader of the radicals. He and his fellow leaders organised a meeting in 1838 under the new banner of Chartism, to be addressed by London Chartist, Henry Vincent.[1] Cook followed up Vincent's speech with a call to reform the Dudley Political Union; one aim of the Chartists was universal male suffrage, so that working men could at least influence town and national policy. Riots broke out in Birmingham in 1839, and the mood was quickly reflected in Dudley. At a further meeting, Samuel Cook was arrested and a trial took place at Worcester. It was clear that he had advocated the abolition of the monarchy and the House of Lords and he was sent to prison for six months. Meanwhile, Dudley magistrates, led by Thomas Badger and W.H. Cartwright, wrote to the home secretary asking for arms to be sent to the town to supplement the work of the four permanent constables. The national government was sceptical, and though they sent cutlasses and pistols, they were reluctant to employ muskets. As for the trial and imprisonment of Samuel Cook, the home secretary wrote that he himself would not have pursued the matter. Attitudes began to change, and an enhanced police force was formed in the town, increasing the number of constables, who used a cell in the workhouse as a prison.[2]

Census of the Town Centre

The 1841 census was the first to give names of all inhabitants, though it still did not record details of their place of birth, and ages of the over-15s were rounded down to the nearest five. Nevertheless, the account of Dudley provides a window into the state of the town, though unfortunately only the main streets can be featured here.[3] Names of public houses are not generally given, but it is possible to find out their licensees from contemporary directories. For example, in Stone Street William Humphries kept The Griffin; Mary Adams was the tenant at the Bull's Head; the Saracen's Head was kept by John Mantle, who gave his occupation as a maltster, and the nearby Holly Bush, formerly The Roebuck, was in the hands of William Brown. Two other public houses were to be found in the street, kept by Charles Caswell and Benjamin Whitehouse.

Castle Street is full of interest, being one of the shorter streets in which changes of ownership of property can be traced. Despite this, when numbers were introduced, the numbering of Castle Street, Market Place, and Upper and Lower High Street were all run together, with the north side of Castle Street, starting at the Hen and Chickens at No. 244 and ending in the 270s. These numbers are not given in the census. There were eight houses before the Castle Inn, which was clearly functioning as a hotel to judge by the numbers of different names recorded there. A little lower down lived two generations of William Fellows, both attorneys, and behind the main street was Bloomer's Yard, an enclave named after its former owner, Caleb Bloomer.

On the south side of Castle Street the numbering began at Hall Street and went backwards to the corner of Birmingham Road. Thus the Woolpack became No. 15, with the houses in Dunton's Yard (not so-called in the census) unnumbered. John Badley, the well-known surgeon, lived in the house on the corner of Fisher Street which many years later became Stanton's music shop. He gave his age as 57, unusually not rounded down. On the opposite corner was The Angel, and

67 The old market hall.

68 View from the castle in the nineteenth century.

at No. 7 Samuel Packwood, a provision dealer. Number 3 was another public house, The Swan, or White Swan, to distinguish it from the old public house in the market place.

By this time the demolition of Middle Row was proceeding, though not complete. It is not possible to identify houses in this row which still occupied some space in the middle of the road where stalls have later been erected. Beginning at the junction with the recently opened Union Street, Joseph Cartwright kept the Old Bush and five more houses before the Dudley Arms. These were all occupied by shopkeepers, as were almost all the houses in the market place. Next door to the hotel, Charles Hancox was a wine merchant, one of several in this area. There were three drapers' shops, an ironmonger and a silversmith, before the wooden-framed Seven Stars. On the corner of Hall Street were a haberdasher and a grocer. These were premium commercial locations.

There were many public houses on the north side of Upper High Street (not so-called in the census).We note The Bell, or Blue Bell, opposite St Thomas' Church, now kept by Aaron Hughes, with the sexton, Edward Woodhall, living next door. Two major gentry houses were No. 188, where Henry Antrobus Cartwright lived, and the house called Beaconsfield House (later No. 194) and lived in at this time by William Robinson, attorney. Beyond Stafford Street were the Three Crowns, The Peacock, the Black Horse and the Plume of Feathers. At High Side Thomas Hodnett ran a small school and beyond, described as at Queen's Cross, lived the carpenter and cabinet maker Joseph Baker.

The south-east side of High Street began west of King Street, and housed employed workmen. Houses on the High Street east of King Street, some of which still survive at the time of writing, included Ann Fletcher's small school, a brewer, a tailor, a locksmith, a plasterer, a currier, a beerseller and a confectioner. Below Vicar Street at No. 74, William Ford kept The George, and Elizabeth Gray, widow of Sheldon Gray kept The Barrel. Proctor Robinson gave his age as 60 and his occupation as 'clerk' (clergyman). He lived in the school house with a garden in front of it. As Union Street was neared, the traders became more prestigious: a druggist at No. 55, then a jeweller and Zacharaiah Bloxcidge, corn dealer, then a woollen draper, hairdresser and grocer.

Nail Makers on Strike

Many, perhaps most, cottagers in Dudley existed on the proceeds of the nail trade. This was carried on not in large factories but in the small outhouse generally called in deeds 'the shop'. Here the whole family took turns at producing nails, made from nail rod which had been collected from the nailmaster's warehouse and would be returned to the same master at the end of the week in the form of nails, of various types according to the area where they were made. Isaac Badger of Eve Hill owned one such warehouse. Payment was niggardly: one example quoted suggests that a man needed to work from 4 a.m. to 9 p.m. to earn 1s 6d.[4] By 1838 nail masters were trying to force down wages even further, and this finally caused the nailers to strike throughout the Dudley area, within and beyond the limits of the town itself.

Matters reached boiling point in 1842 when large numbers of nailers marched to the main warehouses and took some of the masters prisoner, forcing them into the market place and keeping them there to be joined by more of their profession. They were released by a contingent of militia. In the following month of May the home secretary sent a London police officer to Dudley to try to induce 'well disposed' nailers to go back to work. A major influence was that of the Chartists, by now well organised. National government was reluctant to become too closely embroiled in the situation, and dragoons who had been sent to keep order were withdrawn in 1842.[5] Samuel Cook remained an active Chartist, though his attention soon turned to colliers and their problems. The hand-made nail trade declined as machinery developed and nails came to be made in factories in Birmingham.

Church Rates and New Churches

Before and since the nailers' strike, Samuel Cook had been conducting a long campaign against church rates, which had to be paid by all, whether Church of England, nonconformist or Catholic. These contributions to the upkeep of St Thomas' and St Edmund's seemed grossly unfair when so many Dudley inhabitants' belonged to other denominations. Cook described this process as 'Church Rate Oppression'; rate collectors found it hard to collect the money and had resorted to distraining goods instead of money. Joseph Pitchfork was the inhabitant concerned, and issued a handbill to explain the injustice of his case. Many other posters and handbills testify to the conflict.[6]

A major item of expenditure for the Church of England was the founding of two new churches, St James' at Eve Hill and St John's at what was then called Freebodies, but is now known as Kate's Hill. The building of these two very similar churches was inaugurated in October 1838. St James' was begun on 22 October 1838 and consecrated on 21 July 1840. At first it was a chapel of ease, but gained its own parish in 1844. St John's was two days older, its foundation stone having been laid on 20 October. Like St James', the church cost £3,000 and was built of Gornal stone to local design. Unlike St James', however, the church had sandstone pillars.[7] The attractive lych-gate was added much later, in 1920.

69 & 70 St John's Church: the lych-gate (*above*) and the tower (*right*).

A New Chapel at Darby End

The Methodists in Netherton built a church at Cole Street in 1821, with Sunday school accommodation and a house adjoining. But Netherton's growth was rapid, and the Darby family of Darby End were determined to build their own chapel on land at Northfield Road. The work began in 1828, but the church was not ready for use until 1837.[8] It was opened on 21 January of that year as Providence Church, affiliated to the New Connexion. As the chief social institution in Darby End (often called 'Darby Hand' in documents and on notices), the chapel did great work in raising the aspirations and self-confidence of very ordinary people in that area. William Thompson was probably typical when he was asked to be a Sunday school teacher: 'From the very first day I undertook this work I resolved to become a good man. This I felt was essential if I was to become a fit person in the Sunday school.'[9]

Short Lives in Netherton

Statistics on life expectancy can be gained from a study of St Andrew's registers.[10] Records in a typical year (1843) show that 105 people were buried that year. Of these, forty-nine were adults of 18 or over. Their ages were as follows: 18–27, fourteen people; 28–37, eleven; 38–47, six; 48–57, three; 58–67, seven; 68–77, four; 78 and above, four – the oldest claimed to be 96. As may be expected, autumn and winter months were more dangerous than the summer: seventeen people died in October, ten in November, while only six died in May. However, the distinction was not clear cut, as ten people died in April. Children buried were often extremely young: Mary Chambers was only 3 days old, while a considerable number of children numbered their lives in weeks. Some survived until 11 or 12, by which time they had probably been worn out by disease and hard work in the nail shop.

Most of those buried at St Andrew's this year were recorded as simply from Netherton, but there were some more particular addresses. Ellen Walker, 2 years and 6 months, was from Primrose Hill, and four others were recorded from there. 'Mushroom' was the address of two children, and Benjamin Hancox, early the following year, came from Mushroom Green. Darby End provided a number of burials: the name is sometimes Darby Hand and sometimes Derby Hand as well as the standard Darby End. Elizabeth Parker, aged

70, was from Baptist End, and George Henry Bennett, 7 weeks, was from Bumble Hole. Woodside and 'Cinder Banks' are names also found in the register, while 18-year-old Mary Woodward was from Blackbrook.

Hardly any burials at this period were from outside the parish, though John Worrall, 57, was buried from Cradley Heath in February. A few more burials during these years were from Cradley Heath and Old Hill, suggesting that links between Netherton and the parts of Cradley Heath just across the Mousesweet brook were strong. Christian names recorded do not include many from an Old Testament background, showing that such names, regarded as common in Dudley, were mainly adopted by Nonconformist families.

71 St Andrew's Church, Netherton: the tower.

The Railway Comes to Dudley

The Oxford, Worcester and Wolverhampton Railway Company began its operations in the Dudley area in 1845.[11] By the next year work had begun on digging out the tunnel between what is now the Station Hotel and Blowers Green. There was also some activity to the north of this, on the stretch of line leading from Dudley to Tipton. Work was very slow and took place during a time when railway companies were in sharp competition with each other. Negotiations and alliances were made between directors, and Parliament's attempts to control the process did not always succeed. By 1849 the cuttings and embankments were finished, but there was still no track. The viaduct at Stourbridge had still not been completed. There was also delay in building the line from Dudley through Tipton to Priestfield and so to Wolverhampton. As a result the South Staffordshire Railway arrived in the town centre first, reaching the station in May 1850.[12]

The final opening of the Dudley to Stourbridge section took place in December 1853, with another station in Dudley parish called Netherton but actually near Blowers Green. During the next decade a railway was added connecting Dudley with Halesowen via Windmill End and Old Hill. This left the Stourbridge line at Blowers Green and had halts at Baptist End and Darby End as well as Windmill End. Much of the traffic was industrial, and a branch to Withymoor was later constructed. In the 1860 directory Isaac Osborne is the station master at Tipton Road (Dudley station) and Thomas Hibbert the goods manager. Pickford's are listed as general railway agents with links throughout the United Kingdom.

Dudley's Appalling Squalor

In the mid-nineteenth century there seem to have been two Dudleys. There was the Dudley of the elite houses, such as Hill House, Priory Hall and some mansions in Upper High Street and Wolverhampton Street, but there was also the dark and squalid Dudley of the courts and alleys, even in some of the better streets, where lack of drainage and water supply meant a continual fight against disease and poverty. In a devastating report of 1852, William Lees itemised street by street and building by building the dreadful state of affairs he had discovered into which Dudley had descended under the aegis of the town commissioners.[13]

In Upper High Street Samuel Cook's premises had no sewer leading out to King Street. His refuse was put in buckets, then taken out through the kitchen. Dr Brown, the vicar since 1845, said that there was no drain in the vicarage; there was an open cesspool between the yard and the garden. Mr Harrison stated that the privies in his house were emptied during the night though the living rooms. Richard Bowen kept the Three Swans; next door was a butcher whose drainage went into Bowen's public house, carrying pigs' offal and blood. His water supply was a well in the cellar, into which a small stream fed. At The Hope tavern there was a cesspool and a pump. The refuse was pumped away once a week, but then it ran along the surface to Stafford Street on the corner of High Street, causing an offensive smell.

Visiting the Queen's Cross area, the report noted that Mrs Mary Westwood's yard was saturated with drainage from the stables, and that 'all behind the property in Queen's Cross Hill are the most abominable privies and refuse passing under buildings', while on the hill the buildings were undermined and the coal underneath was on fire. Local inhabitants had no water at all except what they could steal. Brandy Row, near King Street, had a yard in which lived 'twenty bad girls'. Their language was disgusting as were the privies, and there was no water. On the other side of High Street, Gad's Lane was the worst in the town for cholera. There was no water supply and the privies were filthy. In this area were many Irish immigrants, but anyone wanting water was charged 3d per week from the Castle Inn. Near Eve Hill was Badger Square, where there were twenty-five houses with shocking privies. There was a draw-well in the yard, but there were bodies of dogs and cats in the water.

Nearer the old castle at the east end of the town was the Green Man Yard. It was described as a long place, like a lane, perhaps 100yds long. 'All the filth comes down on both sides in channels to Tower Street, and then does not get away well; it is complained of by the occupants of the houses in front of Tower-street as a nuisance.'

Some attempts to remedy the terrible sanitation had been tried. In Vanes' Yard, Birmingham Street, there was a 'beastly privy' for seven houses. The owner of some premises below this had been told to build a privy for houses that had none, but 'the tenants pulled it down, because they said they should have all the people in the district coming to it if they did not'. The owner built three more, and had locks put on; these were still standing. These conditions existed not only in the town but in the foreign. The inspector said of Cawney Hill, where

72 Cawney Bank Lodge, part of nineteenth-century suburban Dudley.

very old cottages had stood for centuries, that most of the inhabitants were very poor. They had depended on Watson's well for a supply of water, but it had now dried up because of alterations made by Lord Dudley. Money would be needed if a new well was to be sunk on Cawney Hill; this would be possible but costly.

As a result of the report, a Board of Health was inaugurated in 1853, with fifteen members elected by local ratepayers.

Dudley Poor Law Union

Dudley Poor Law Union was formed in 1836.[14] Dudley workhouse in Tower Street was becoming much too small for the large number of poverty stricken people in the town, which had been the case nationwide. Unions were formed by law, Dudley taking in Rowley Regis, Sedgley and Tipton as well as Dudley parish. Nevertheless, little was done as the usual hierarchy took control, among them Isaac Badger, chairman of the Board of Guardians. Such people thought that poverty was the fault of the poor themselves, and were determined that they should have no comfort in the workhouse. Fear would keep them out. Old workhouses were not amalgamated, with Tipton, for example, continuing to cater for its own poor. In nearby Kingswinford Mr Foley refused the poor any beer, allegedly pulling the plugs out of the barrels and letting the beer go to waste.[15] Local crops ailed in 1845, causing near starvation.

The 1852 health report had been scathing about the state of the workhouse. William Lee had found that there were seventy-two inhabitants in the Tower Street building. Little or no alteration had taken place under the aegis of the Board of Guardians; the accommodation seems to have been just as it was in the eighteenth century. One room had been used for the gaol and was now a mortuary. Rooms were all small, and there was little separation between the sexes or ages.

In 1853 a further report recorded the dreadful state of the workhouse in a twenty-two-page letter to Isaac Badger, written by the Poor Law inspector, Andrew Doyle.[16] He had visited the workhouse and saw old and young, men, women and children crowded in the small yard, across which drying washing was hung on lines, and a large heap of dirty clothes lay in the corner of the yard. A small room with an old sloping roof was the bedroom for thirty women. Doyle went on to describe the state of provision for the sick. In the two men's wards he saw a man called Perry, violently insane and strapped to his bed. This room was only a passageway to another room where there were three sick men, one of them dying, with his friends surrounding his bed. They could hardly be heard because of the shouts of Mr Perry in the corridor.

Irish Immigration

Early immigration from Ireland was doubtless a factor in the foundation of St Joseph's Church. After occupying various small buildings, the town's Catholics were able to take possession of a fine new church built in 1842, the church of Our Lady and St Thomas of Canterbury (continuing the tradition of the Anglican St Thomas'). This was consecrated by Cardinal Wiseman and soon had a school added, St Joseph's School.[17] Gad's Lane was not the only location favoured by Irish immigrants. In Wolverhampton Street lived Richard Griffiths from Ellesmere in Shropshire, who had married his wife, Mary, from Ireland; their daughter Cathline had been born four years earlier when they lived in Birmingham. Bridget Doyle was a lodging-house keeper in the same street, whose lodgers included two Irishmen, a Scot and George Cooper from Hinckley. These men were bricklayers. A little further along the street lived Michael Concarnen with his wife Cathline, a rag and bone gatherer, and Edward Nolan, a rope maker. A large group of Irish people lived very near, all bricklayers; next door were John McNaughton, shoemaker, and Lucy

73 Church of Our Lady and St Thomas of Canterbury.

his wife, with an Irish blacksmith and his wife as lodgers. Members of the Hart, Cahalan, Egan, Carty, Quinn, Hardiman, Cody, Holmes and Goodwin families, all from Ireland, also lived in this part of Wolverhampton Street. There were many bricklayers, but others were labourers, tinmen, shoemakers, carpet weavers, glaziers and bone gatherers. These details from the 1851 census show that however insanitary Dudley was, it was better than trying to live in Ireland. Children of these workers are often described as 'scholars'; in the Hardiman family, Isaac was an apprentice at aged 12, Martin was a scholar at 10, and Rose was stated as merely at 'home' at age 6.

Dudley in 1860

The population of the town had been 37,954 in 1851, and by 1856 it had risen to about 40,000. The growth was to continue for many years. Kelly's Directory of 1860 provides an account of Dudley and its facilities at this time. It reviews the churches and chapels: Unitarians in Wolverhampton Street, Baptists in New Street, Wesleyans in King Street and elsewhere, New Connexion Methodists in Wolverhampton Street; Primitive Methodists had a chapel in George Street and several other chapels are mentioned.

Schools are thought important enough to describe. The grammar school was by this time in King Street, with the Revd Robert Harper as the headmaster. The Bluecoat School remained in Fisher Street, with an infants' department in Stafford Street. Jesson's School in Salop Street is mentioned, and the Catholic Free School (St Joseph's) is described as in Porter's Field, with its head Mr Joseph Thompson. Baylies' School remained in Tower Street. Each church, St Edmund's, St James' and St John's, had a school attached, and there was one at St Thomas' simply described as 'The National School'. Unitarians and Wesleyans each ran their own school, and there was a British School in Stafford Street, while girls were catered for at Cartwright's Charity School.

The Local Board of Health was by this time well established, with its offices in Wolverhampton Street. At the Saracen's Head was the local Inland Revenue office, while the new police station had been opened in Priory Street. It was in this year that the Earl of Dudley laid the foundation stone for what was to have been an 'asylum' for the blind and maimed workers from the limestone quarries. This consisted of a row of cottages on Tipton Road, but its usefulness was compromised by the fact that the blind worker could not take the rest of his

74 The White Lion, Baptist End.

75 The Bull's Head, Netherton.

family with him.[18] However, a general hospital was much needed, and when Joseph Guest died in 1867 he left £20,000 for the foundation of such a hospital. It was decided to use the redundant blind persons' cottages as a base for the hospital, and by 1871 this had been accomplished. The Guest Hospital, named after its chief benefactor, was opened by the Countess of Dudley on 25 October.

Netherton warranted a separate entry in the 1860 directory. The book accepted the spelling Darbyhand (all one word) for that area, listing thirty or more traders, including Benjamin Bissell, cooper, Benjamin Bourne, shopkeeper, James Hill, blacksmith, two members of the Taylor family, nailmakers, and Levi Willetts, shoemaker.

76 The Dudley fountain.

Only eleven private residents are featured in Netherton, of whom Mrs Fletcher lived at Netherton Hill, Mr Joseph Griffiths at Mushroom Green, Mr Henry Parkes Skidmore at Netherton Hill House and Mr Joseph Griffin Walker at Primrose Hill House. There were many taverns and public houses by this time, including the Rose and Crown at Darbyhand, The Crown at Cinderbank, the Bull's Head at St John's Street, The Swan at Baptist End, the Golden Cross at Dudley Wood, The Loyal Washington on Halesowen Road, The Dog and Partridge at Bumble Hole, and The Cottage Spring in High Street. Barnsley's Jews' harp manufactory and Thomas Coley's chain and trace works, both at Dudley Wood, the Fisher Brothers, traders in grease, oil and gunpowder at Blackbrook, and James Trowman, chainmaker at Newtown, show how industrialised Netherton had become. Withymoor was particularly industrial, with the canal at hand for transport: here were located William Henry Dawes' furnaces, Swindell and Co., manufacturers of scythes, shovels and other agricultural equipment, with Samuel Lewis' chain cables at Withymoor works; not far away was the Windmill End works of Samuel Woodall, iron boat builders. However, another member of the Woodall family was a music teacher at Sweet Turf. Thus

77 Dudley Mechanics' Institute, Wolverhampton Street.

culture struggled to live side by side with industry. So also did a few farmers, such as Benjamin Whitehouse at The Buffery.

Middle Row had by this time been completely demolished, but the Town Hall still stood. Its condition had deteriorated and it too was demolished. In its place the Dudley Fountain was erected, made of Portland stone at a cost of £3,000 in 1867. It was opened by the Countess of Dudley. This was not merely a decorative work, but symbolic of the townspeople's dependence on water and the need to continue improving the supply. A new Town Hall was built in 1858 by Lord Ward, but sold to the town rather than given. A further development was the opening of the Mechanics' Institute. This was built in Wolverhampton Street in 1860 on the site of a stone house that had once belonged to Gilbert Gellians. (Drawings of this old house seem to show that it was built from fragments of the priory. What became of these fragments is unknown, but they included sculpture as well as dressed stone.)

nine

THE LATER NINETEENTH CENTURY

I t wasn't until 1864 that the Board of Health constituted the main governing institution of the town, but in that year Dudley was incorporated as a borough, thus renewing a status which had not been evident since the Middle Ages. Precisely how it had been lost is not clear, and we have seen that the court still preserved the name of borough throughout all the years that this was not a politically apt description. Dudley had become an enfranchised borough after the 1832 Reform Act allowing one member of Parliament. In 1864 it became an Incorporated Borough, leading to much securer administration and a wider distribution of influence. The town commissioners had failed in their task because they were the better-off property owners, who had a strong interest in keeping down the rates. Authority was divided between the churches, the commissioners and the old court leet, and little public progress was made.[1]

Dudley in the Late 1860s[2]

The 1869 directory updated previous descriptions of the town, its landmarks and inhabitants. It was able to note a new workhouse, on Burton Road, with frequent guardians' meetings to avoid the dreadful state of the previous Tower Street premises. There were now 757 paupers in the new building, drawn from the various local parishes forming the Union. Mr and Mrs Stillard were the master and matron.

The directory was, as usual, most interested in churches. St Thomas' had been restored in 1862 and the vicar was the the Revd James Caulfield Browne, whose superior residence is also mentioned. St James', Eve Hill, and St John's, Kate's Hill, are mentioned as fine buildings, each with its own vicarage. The Catholic church in Porter's Field is described as 'handsome'. There were the following

78 Former St John's School, Kate's Hill.

79 Victorian houses in Fir Street, Kate's Hill.

nonconformist groups: Presbyterians, Wolverhampton Street; Unitarians, tracing their ancestry back to 1701; Wesleyans, King Street, Salop Street and Woodside; Congregationalists, Abberley Street and Woodside; Independents, Salop Street and Woodside; New Connexion Methodists, Wolverhampton Street, Kate's Hill, Woodside and Hartshill; Primitive Methodists, George Street, Kate's Hill, Hartshill, Woodside and New Dock; Baptists in New Street and the Friends' Meeting House in High Street. One year before the passing of Forster's Education Act in 1870 there were many small schools linked to the various chapels. In King Street was the School of Art, forerunner of the terracotta building which still stands opposite the library. There is also mention of the

80 The Crown Inn, corner of Wolverhampton Street and Priory Street.

Dispensary, which had recently been erected in Priory Road. The resident surgeon at this time was George Clement Searle. Like the Guest Hospital, the Dispensary was founded through the philanthropy of Joseph Guest, originally a nail master but later a proprietor of Castle Foot glassworks with other members of his family. He had been born in 1793, and died in 1867 at his home in New Street.[3]

A large number of industries and trades are recorded at this time. John Barnsley's Jews' harp works flourished at Cradley Road, Netherton. Not far away at Mushroom Green were Coley and Hancox, chain, cable and anchor makers; Jesse Hancox was one of the proprietors. D. & S. Davies made furniture in King Street. John Finch was an ironfounder, specialising in fenders and trading in Priory Street. The Gas Light Company had its headquarters in Spring Gardens at No. 13 Fountain Street. Samuel Holbrook made account books and was a bookbinder in Old Mill Street, while Ebenezer Hutchings sold books and stationery as well as pianos. Samuel and William Lewis advertised their horse nail, chain and cable made at No. 12 Northfield Road, Withymoor. William Henry Meese was a blacksmith and sheet-iron worker, also making rifle tubes at Queen's Cross. At No. 77 Wellington Road, a recently developed

81 A chainmaking forge, from a postcard.

link between Queen's Cross and Stafford Street, William Nelson was a brick-layer, stonemason and timber merchant. Some doors away at No. 57, Joseph Robinson made sacks and bags. Netherton Furnaces were run by James and George Onions at Northfield Road, Withymoor. It is worth noting James Rutland's shop at No. 63 High Street, since Rutland Passage was named after this enterprise. Rutland was a wine and spirit merchant, and sold 'Dublin stout' as well as beer from Burton.

Moses Spittle manufactured chains, nails, cables and horseshoes, and was also a contractor for railway carriages, with works in Hall Street. Electro-plating also took place in Hall Street at the works of Suter & Co. The Thompson brothers were maltsters and hop merchants in Oakey Well Street, while another Thompson was the agent for the Great Western Railway, with his office in High Street. Vices, hammers and anvils were made by Joshua Wilkinson in Churchfield Street. He lived in Wellington Road, one of the Dudley manufac-turers who had not fled the town for greener pastures; indeed, this fashionable street housed a number of such fairly well-off residents. However, many of the old elite had gone to places such as Kingswinford (Cordy Manby, iron mer-chant), Edgbaston (Henry Stringer, iron merchant), and Smethwick (Charles

Kettley, local manager for Pickford's). Within the parish Dixon's Green and Tansley Hill were favoured retreats.

A surprising number of private schools had been opened in Dudley by 1869, including four boarding schools. Miss Caroline Carter had a school at No. 267 Castle Street, Mrs Eliza Harper at Oak Villa, No. 62 Dixon's Green, Mrs Loxton's school was in King Street, while it is not surprising to find Wellington Road the site of another boarding school, Miss M.S. Robinson at No. 57. However, the same address was used by her relative, the maker of sacks and bags, Joseph. The grammar school also took boarders at this time, giving its address as No. 60 High Street and the head as the Revd Robert Harper, surely a relative of the proprietor of the school in Dixon's Green.

82 Advertisement for Rutland wines in 1890 (next-door shop to modern Rutland Passage).

There were ten other private schools in the borough, including one at Hartshill. The nationally run school at Woodside was called Cochrane's School.

More Trouble with Sanitation

The shocking report of 1852 led to activity designed to cure the santiation problems in Dudley. In 1853 the new Board of Health appointed the surgeon John Houghton as its first medical officer.[4] He proved much too enthusiastic and the old guard got rid of him three years later as a 'useless and unnecessary officer'. This action did not make the sanitary problems go away.

Meanwhile, water supply in the town had been provided since 1853 by the South Staffordshire Waterworks Company, but they were unable to provide the quantity really needed if the existing water problems were to be remedied. In 1862, water arrived fom Lichfield, being stored at the early Shaver's End reservoir. There were many problems with the supply, with much of the water being stolen from the genuine outlets. Men who had a plumbing background were employed as turncocks, with headquarters in Tower Street. As well as the Shaver's End site, there was still a reservoir at Cawney Hill.[5] Sewage disposal remained a major difficulty, and various attempts were made to find solutions.

They all foundered on lack of investment, and if implemented would have fouled Cradley Pool disastrously. Many of the town's rich citizens still wished to avoid any responsibility for sewage disposal. Two reports were authorised, the first by Dr Thorne Thorne in 1871 and the second by Dr Edward Ballard in 1874. These were nationally commissioned reports, to the newly established Local Government Board, which had written many times to Dudley Town Council, but the council still delayed any action.[6]

Dr Thorne had noted the high death rate from infectious diseases and from diarrhoea, the bad condition of parts of the town which had not been paved and had no gutters, and worst of all the fact that there was no sewage provision at all in some parts of the town, and that what had been done in this respect was poorly executed and inefficient.

Privies were still too rare and there was a 'great neglect of excrement removal'. Some houses were using wells which were polluted, and the South Staffs Waterworks Company sometimes provided poor quality water. Some areas were overcrowded, with too many cottages, themselves also overcrowded, huddled together on small plots. Pigs were kept all over the town in an 'unwholesome' manner. The same conditions applied also to Kate's Hill and Netherton.

By 1872 the national Local Government Board was reasonably satisfied on some of the points raised by Dr Thorne, but there were still issues outstanding, the chief of which was the matter of sewage and water supply (street cleaning had improved).

The borough council stalled. It raised a series of objections which could have been anticipated: mining operations had destroyed the contours of the land (and indeed subsidence continued to do so); there were canals intersecting the parish which would hinder disposal; no suitable place for outfall could be discovered – it all added up to extreme cost. So far as water supply was concerned, the council passed the buck, alleging the poor service of the South Staffs Company. The Local Government Board pointed sharply to powers for compulsory purchase which had existed since 1848.

Dr Ballard gave a description of the political division of the town into seven wards, of which four covered the town itself and three the surrounding villages. St John's contained Kate's Hill, while Netherton included many small hamlets: Netherton, Windmill End, Darby End, Primrose Hill, New Town, Mushroom Green and Dudley Wood. Woodside covered Woodside and Hart's Hill. Ballard made use of statistical tables to assert that 'the labouring class of the population' greatly preponderates in Dudley. Woodside, St James', Netherton and

83 A view from Kate's Hill across Trindle Road.

St John's were the most heavily populated by the labouring class. Many women were employed in weaving nail bags in workshops where 'an irritating dust' was prevalent. This industry was mainly confined to Castle and St Thomas' wards.

Dr Ballard made a careful study of the works being undertaken by the council. Work was proceeding in Wellington Road, which was a road mainly inhabited by the better off. Some work was also being done in Netherton, to divert sewage from a point near Cresswell's Iron Works, which at present was running into a local pool created by mining. Here the sewage was supposed to dry off spontaneously. No plan of existing sewers existed, but there were also open sewers in various places, including Birmingham Road and Farthings Lane. Particular problems were associated with Greystone Passage, where a deep natural channel was full of sewage emanating from several houses. Dudley council had promised to deal with some of these nuisances, and with the problem of surface water after rain, which spread the nuisance from sewage.

In the early 1870s there was no efficient system of 'scavenging' (cleaning the roads), despite the employment of forty men partly in mending roads and partly in scavenging. Night-soil men were supposed to remove the waste from privies, but they were not always able to do so because of lack of time, and privies could become so stopped-up as to become unusable. Night soil was removed to 'depots', one of which was near Russell's Hall Colliery weighing machine, where it constituted a 'most intolerable nuisance'.

Much of Dudley town still had to be supplied by water from wells which had once been perfectly satisfactory but by now were much polluted. Inhabitants told the surveyors that they could use these for cleaning yards, etc., but not for drinking. A particular example was Court One on Newhall Street, where there were seven houses all belonging to one gentleman 'who is Alderman of the Borough, a Justice of the Peace, and the Chairman of the Public Works Committee, and who ought therefore, to have set a better example'. The single well here had sewage from neighbouring houses brought to the base of its pump, so that the water in the well was tainted with sewage and unfit to drink. Despite this, the alderman in question refused to have South Staffs water brought to the houses. The houses themselves were very dirty. With such men controlling the council, there was little hope for the residents.

Typical Dudley Houses in the 1870s

Ballard's report gave evidence of the type and condition of many ordinary houses in Dudley at the time. Many were back-to-backs, with pervasive damp. Others were 'exceedingly dirty' with yards unpaved, undrained and overlaid with slops. Filth was everywhere, pigs roamed around, and there was stored pig-swill smelling by the side of the house. No one cleaned the courts, and at The Mamble there was no drainage, and the single privy was choked with filth. Scarlet fever had recently been reported there. In Bond Street was a lodging house with a cellar in occupation, while in an outhouse there were people living in a room over a large and 'stinking' privy. The building had been reported to the council as unfit for human habitation, but was still lived in.

Turning its attention to Netherton, the report noted a sewage swamp which flowed out into Hill Street from King Street. Four of the houses were especially dirty and neglected, and one was inhabited by a labourer with thirteen children, four of whom had recently had measles. Some cottages in Halesowen Road had been the site of a typhus outbreak, though water had now been supplied. One bedroom was occupied by six people at night: a grandmother and her grand-daughter aged 17, with a boy aged 5; a girl aged 7 with her brothers, aged 8 and 12, in another bed. The other bedroom was occupied by two boys and a small girl. The council had taken no action after the typhus. Not much better were conditions in Baptist End, Bumble Hole or Windmill End. One well sufficed here for many people.

This enormously depressing account of Dudley requires some explanation. Landlords and councillors knew much of what was happening, but did little. There seem to have been two main causes. One was the enormity of the problem, caused ultimately by the location of Dudley on a ridge with totally inadequate natural water supply. This had been exacerbated by the excavation of minerals haphazardly without adequate plans being drawn up, so that sewage pipes and water supply would have to be carried through uncharted territory, some of which was still sinking year by year. It was beyond the powers of engineers to find ways to lay pipes which would cure the problem, and any such action would have been enormously expensive. The other problem was the concentration of power in the hands of too few people, who were councillors, mine or factory proprietors, and justices. Some of them lived outside Dudley. They hardly saw the ordinary people as of their own race, and in diaries or accounts of their lives they hardly mention them, themselves living distinct existences, even sometimes promoting cultural and artistic causes but ignoring their fellow townspeople.[7]

Crime could be a problem in this period. In 1879 there was a sensation at Woodside, where Alfred Meredith was shot in Pit Lane (Cochrane Road).

84 The Glede Oven, engraved by Chattock.

The publican at the British Lion had heard the shot and was called to be a witness at the trial. The murder was the result of a robbery that had gone wrong, causing Meredith's death during the theft of £200. Alfred Meredith had been a clerk at Hill and Smith's Hart's Hill works, entrusted with the firm's money, a situation which was often the case in those days. Such employees had little protection.[8]

Transport in the Late Nineteenth Century[9]

It was during the late 1870s and early 1880s that the foundations of public transport in the Dudley area were laid down. An important decision was the predominant gauge of the tramways – 3ft 6in in contrast to the standard gauge of most parts of the British Isles. The result of this decision was that tramways in the Black Country became unviable before they did in such places as Sheffield and Leeds, so that buses became the preferred mode in the West Midlands. These were more flexible and provided good competition with the railways, so that the rail system was less developed. But all these matters were far in the future.

An early route was that from Dudley to Sedgley and Wolverhampton, beginning at Parson's Street and following the old turnpike road, and it was to be a standard gauge tramway. This predecessor of the 558 bus was at first horse-drawn, forty-seven horses being eventually available. However, the steep hills on the route made working very difficult and it was not long before steam trams were substituted. Steam trams began working on the route in 1883.

A little after the Wolverhampton route was opened, the Dudley, Stourbridge and Kingswinford Tramway Company Ltd secured permission to open a line from Dudley market to Stourbridge via Queen's Cross and Springs Mire. A link was soon made with the end of Tipton Road near Dudley station, and the tram depot was located here. By this time Birmingham Road had been included in a route from Burnt Tree; these routes were available from 1884. In the mid-1880s there was a half hour service on the Stourbridge route. The speed of these trams was very slow: 4mph was the limit at one time. The passenger cars had seating on top (outside). The destination, Dudley-Brierley Hill and Stourbridge, was exhibited above the saloon windows; there was no other route on which these trams could run so the destination could be fixed.[10]

By 1898, Dudley council was concerned about the poor quality of the tracks used by steam trams throughout Dudley. On the Dudley to Hartshill route,

Queen's Cross Hill was a particular worry. 'The turn-outs are ... useless and the joints between them and the rails are at present made up of short lengths which are not properly secured.' As for the track up Castle Hill, the rails on the southern track protruded above the stone setts and were very badly worn at the joints.[11] The report on the tram situation was presented on 3 Feburary 1898 and recommended a change from steam to electric traction, with a change to a universal 4ft 8in gauge. It suggested a survey of the road from Queen's Cross through Netherton to Bishton's Bridge, a distance of 2½ miles, and estimated the amount of electricity which would be used.

Most of the track would be single, but nevertheless a 7½ minute service would be possible between Castle Hill and Queen's Cross, with trams then diverging towards Hart's Hill and Netherton. Consideration was given to beginning a municipal tram department, as was happening at Wolverhampton, Walsall, West Bromwich and Birmingham. When this suggestion was turned down, a crucial decision was made, leaving Dudley as the only main authority in the Black Country without its own municipal transport, and leading eventually to the local dominance of the Midland Red bus company.

Little change occurred in the railway system round Dudley after the construction of the line from Blowers Green to Halesowen. Though Dudley station was now connected to the town by tram, it was inconveniently situated because of the hill, a disincentive to foot passengers. By the end of the century there were extensive sidings on a branch at Withymoor. There were also sidings and a goods shed at Blowers Green (Netherton Junction).

Almost the final development on the canal system had been carried out in 1855 when the Netherton tunnel had been initiated. It was much more modern in design than previous tunnels, having towpaths on each side, and being lit by gas, later replaced by electricity. It was wider than other tunnels in the rest of the country.[12] Meanwhile minor improvements to the Dudley Canal took place at Park Head, the lock system being simplified, and further modifications were carried out here in 1893–94. Canals were still viable, especially in this area where both road and rail transport failed to cover all the needs. Bulk transport of coal was a main preoccupation of the canals. A typical invoice from 1890 records 4,025 tons of coal transported by the Birmingham Canal Company from Saltwells Colliery and Warren's Hall (just in Rowley Regis) to Birmingham via the Netherton tunnel at the cost of £58 13s 11d.[13] At this time most of the hauling was done by horses, though there are instances of men also drawing canal boats.

85 One of Lord Dudley's coal mines.

86 Saltwells Coppice, from an old postcard.

The Progress of Churches

The vast increase in the population necessitated more church building both by the Church of England and the nonconformities. Two new parishes were formed, St Luke's in 1876 and St Augustine's, Holly Hall, in 1884. Many new houses were built at Kate's Hill, turning the old Freebodies area into a closely packed suburb, for which St John's was responsible. At St Thomas' Church there were two long incumbencies, William Reyner Cousins, who was vicar from 1870 to 1892, and Adam Gray Maitland, who became vicar in 1892 and remained until 1918.

St Edmund's remained the less important church in Dudley town, but it had now been administering its own parish once again since 1844. Among the more philanthropic and respected people buried there was John Badley, whose marble memorial bears witness to his outstanding qualities. He had been born in 1783 and been a surgeon in Dudley for sixty-five years. His memorial talks of his 'unvarying honourable conduct', and for once this tribute seems to be true. An outstanding doctor, he was also interested in many fields of knowledge, being praised in the memorial for his love of literature in all its branches. He died in 1870 at the age of nearly 87.

An important descendant of the Amphlett family, bankers, was also buried in St Edmund's. Edward Amphlett was the son of Joseph Amphlett of Horseley House in Tipton. He had lived at Broome in Worcestershire, but then retired to Cheltenham, where he died in 1867. Edwin Poole, a churchwarden and secretary of the Guest Hospital, is commemorated by a plaque recording his death in 1894. Members of the Bourne family were buried in the churchyard, among them William Bourne, his wife and daughter.

At Netherton, St Andrew's took some time to be accepted, but this was finally achieved after the appointment of the Revd S.J. Marriott in 1874.[14] Until his incumbency, Netherton had really been the preserve of the Nonconformists, but Marriott earned general respect. He ran many activities, such as garden parties and tennis tournaments, as well as overseeing many additions to the church, such as the new altar installed in 1887, a chancel screen in 1892 and a new lectern in 1897.

The Methodist New Connexion Church in Wolverhampton Street had grown too small for the congregation, and it was decided to enlarge it at a meeting held in 1861.[15] Money was quickly subscribed, including £330 at a 'Tea Meeting' in 1863 and more than £750 at a bazaar held at the Mechanics' Institute in the

87 The Guest Hospital, Tipton Road.

same year. By 1865 there was enough money to put the work in hand. The most important operation was taking down the rear wall and rebuilding it far enough beyond its earlier limit to provide room for the organ, choir seats and pulpit to be included in the new section. This was a period when many people felt moved to join churches and chapels, and took the new life they were entering seriously. (It is said that a mission in 1885 became the talk of Dudley.) Church Union was beginning to be an issue, and in 1889 a committee was set up to try to agree union with the United Methodist Free Church. Ministers in those days walked considerable distances to preach. One gentleman, the Revd T.T. Rushworth, describes in a letter how he walked from Oldbury to Cradley Heath one Sunday morning, then to Knowle on the side of the Rowley Hills and in the early evening to Wolverhampton Street, Dudley, finishing with a walk back to Oldbury, as he put it 'prepared and ready to welcome the blessing of the night's repose'.[16]

Cooperation between Nonconformist groups in Dudley was good during the mid- and later nineteenth century, and when the Revd David Evans had arrived at Dudley Baptist Church from Newtown in Montgomery, his inaugural service was led by the Revd D.K. Shoebotham of King Street Independent Church. Evans was a prominent figure in local life, urging factory workers to 'improve their intellect and invest their money wisely'.[17] He shared a platform with Joseph Chamberlain in Birmingham and was active in Liberal politics. The Dudley chapel cooperated with other Baptist churches in the Midlands Baptist Association, and in 1879 joined in united evangelical services in the Birmingham area, a procedure followed again in 1886. The New Street Chapel was becoming elderly and suggestions were made that it should be replaced. Instead, it was decided to alter the existing building at a cost of £600. Further joint action with other free churches took place in 1896, when the Baptists joined in a visitation scheme with the Free Church Council. Meanwhile, the Sunday school had grown to 172 scholars in the afternoon, a library was run, and there was a flourishing Band of Hope.

At Netherton, Providence Chapel at Darby End continued to flourish in the Cradley Heath circuit.[18] A succession of excellent ministers spent time talking to miners in the local pits, encouraging them to come to the church. Once there, they would find lively services, with excellent music led by a very competent choir. The organ was replaced twice, first with a second-hand organ, but later with a new one on the occasion of a total refit of the church and its furniture. Many other local chapels boasted excellent choirs and enthusiastic singing. A Sunday school Union existed in Netherton, its specially composed hymn being recorded for us by M.H.W. Fletcher. It recorded the nine Sunday schools assembled in Netherton market place in the following lines:

88 Wesleyan leaders in the 1920s, in front of the chapel.

89 Wesley Church Trustees

90 Rose Hill Sunday school.

91 A mysterious scene in Netherton churchyard, with late nineteenth-century monuments.

May Sweet Turf join with Cinder Bank, and Ebenezer swell the rank; and may St John's and Primrose Hill, with Noah's Ark their stations fill and may Church Road, and Darby Hand, all join in one harmonious band; to spread the triumph of our King, who did for all salvation bring. [19]

The hymn is ascribed to 'J. T. of Darby Hand'.

Municipal Progress

A landmark was reached when in 1865 Dudley once again became a borough, receiving its charter on 3 April of that year. A new constitution replaced the old confusion of duties, and seven 'wards' were designated. However, this dispensation was not destined to last, as large towns everywhere began to outweigh their surrounding counties, and it became obvious that they needed greater powers to administer their areas successfully. Accordingly, in 1888, Dudley was given county borough status, which enabled it to run many services previously in county control. This followed a confirmation of Parliamentary borough status in 1885, though Dudley still merited only one seat in the House of Commons.

Even before this there had been a great change in the attitude of Dudley's principal inhabitants to public services in the town. As long ago as 1853 there had been the beginnings of a School of Art, fostered by the Revd Dr James Browne and by 1860 provided with dedicated premises. A fee was charged, however, and this had the effect of putting off artisans who could not afford the outlay. Coupled with the need for design, education was the matter of public reading facilities. For a while the growth in literacy had been satisfied, so far as Dudley was concerned, by the collections at chapels and at the Mechanics' Institute. By 1878 these provisions were proving inadequate, and Dudley adopted the Public Libraries Act. A site was found at the junction of Priory Street and the new St James' Road for both library and the new School of Art.[20]

A grand procession was organised to open the new building on 29 July 1884, led by a band and including council committee members, magistrates, clergy and members of the Board of Guardians. Both institutions flourished. The library was allotted the proceeds of a penny rate. It was run on the then current system of choice from a list, the books being requested and librarians fetching them for issue. Newspapers were also supplied. In the following year, branch libraries were opened in Woodside and Netherton. At first premises for these two were rented, but permanent buildings were erected in 1893–94. Netherton also included a public hall. The library ser-vice became very popular, with 50,000 books being issued in 1889.

Meanwhile, the School of Art was going from strength to strength. It had been recognised nationally that drawing skill was essential in the newly mechanised manufacturing economy, and drawing was introduced as a subject in schools. Teachers flocked to the School of Art to gain quali-fications to enable them to teach art and technical drawing. Outside Birmingham there was little availability in the West Midlands to study original works of art, and it was a natural extension of the functions of the school that an art gallery should be established. A joint committee of the Public Libraries and School of Art representatives

92 Ebenezer Baptist Church, Netherton.

93 St John's Road, Kate's Hill: a mixture of housing styles.

94 Dudley Art Gallery.

95 The Earl of Dudley's statue and castle gates in the nineteenth century.

96 Church Road, Netherton.

agreed policy for the gallery, and it was opened in 1888. A technical school was set up during the 1890s and later moved to Stafford Street.

The changed attitude to public works had begun to be evident for fifteen years or more, and can in part be attributed to the Revd Dr Browne, who encouraged such men as Joseph Stokes, mayor in 1875, to take the matter of slum clearance seriously, ridding the town of the nuisances highlighted in the Barnard and earlier reports. A presentation was made to the mayor for his efforts, and his portrait painted. Once the library was operating, it became a focus for cultural acivity, and in 1881 there was the first great commemoration of Shakespeare, doubtless aided by the way in which this Midland surname has survived in Dudley.

97 Advertisement for F.W. Cook, clothing warehouse, 1892.

Improvements to the eastern entrance to the town centre went ahead during the 1880s, with the demolition of houses in the extreme end of Castle Street. In 1888, a statue of the Earl of Dudley was erected here. The approach up Castle Hill was enhanced, and at the very end of the century, on 4 September 1899, a fine opera house was opened half-way up the hill. The first performance was of Gilbert and Sullivan's *Mikado*. The first public park in Dudley was opened in 1892 at the Buffery.

Brooke Robinson

In 1886 a new MP was elected, whose name became almost a legend in the town. Brooke Robinson[21] was a local man, born in Beaconsfield House, with roots deep in Dudley's bourgeois history. A Conservative, he was in constant communication with his constituents during his twenty-year tenure. He was in possession of historical documents belonging to his ancestors, and could trace his family in the Dudley area back to 1523. He also owned a family Bible belonging to his wife with entries going back to 1723. He later presented a collection of furniture and pictures to the town. He was finally defeated in 1906, the year of the Liberal landslide throughout the nation.

Education

The year 1870 saw the passing of Forster's Education Act, paving the way for setting up school boards in counties and some boroughs. These would harmonise the confusing provision of schools and oversee new building, etc. The education provided by an array of small private schools, often with unqualified teachers, church (national) schools, and schools set up by large-scale employers, such as those set up at Holly Hall by Cochrane's (1860), would now become more standardised. Schools like Kate's Hill came under the jurisdiction of the Dudley School Board, and were often known as board schools, later council schools. In Netherton, St Andrew's School was insufficient for the locality, and new schools were set up at Cinderbank (Brewery Street) in 1877, the Iron Schools (Halesowen Road) in 1882, and Northfield Road in 1891. These were added to already existing national schools at Darby End and Dudley Wood.

The logbook at St Andrew's gives evidence of some of the difficulties faced by teachers.[22] The head noted that in November 1871, the school closed for Wake Week; in January 1873 he writes that fourteen boys were admitted 'who had not previously attended any school. Consequently they know very little and cannot tell all their letters.' A small fee was paid by parents, and in 1884 a miners' strike led to default. Fees were finally abolished in an Education Bill of 1891, when national money began to be paid to local schools. During the 1870s, schools had been subsidised by subscribers, including local firms, who recognised the need for literate workers. A point noted in the school logbook for 1892 was the absence of many children whose parents took them to Herefordshire for 'hopping' in September. Large numbers of Black Country families went to collect hops throughout this season. The Bluecoat School moved to new, rather grand Gothic-style premises in Bean Road in 1879.

A report in 1871 stated that Dudley Grammar School was one of the least classical schools in the West Midlands. Dudley inhabitants had earlier pressed the case for more practical subjects such as Arithmetic, French and German.[23]

Though the School Board had representatives on the governing board, the Grammar School was still independent of it. Its current situation in King Street soon came to be regarded as inconvenient, and in 1896 new land was offered by the Earl of Dudley in St James' Road. The new premises, opened in 1899, were a marvellous improvement, including classroom accommodation for 160 boys, a gym and headmaster's house. The curriculum was somewhat extended, and governors were added from the counties of Stafford and Worcester and Mason's College, the forerunner of Birmingham University.

ten

EDWARDIAN EXPANSION

I n the new century, Dudley Market Place and High Street had become a centre for commercial activity, drawing customers and clients from a wide area, not only the Dudley parish, but Tipton, Rowley Regis, Brierley Hill, Kingswinford and Sedgley. It was a curiosity that house and shop numbers ran in a series beginning at the Castle Foot, up Castle Street on the south-east side, through Market Place, which had its own street name but no separate numbering system, and up High Street to Queen's Cross, then down the northern side to the market again and along Castle Street.

On the south side of Castle Street were three public houses, The White Swan (No. 3), The Angel (No. 9) and The Woolpack (No. 15).[1] Stanton's, piano dealers, were at No. 10, exemplifying the growth in the popularity of this instrument. The Seven Stars was at Nos 20 and 21. This old public house previously had an entrance in Hall Street, but its main door was now opposite the market stalls. The Old Bush is given no number in the 1900 directory, but was probably No. 47. On the north side of the market the Dudley and District Building Society occupied rooms in the building which had once been Maurice's printers (No. 224).The Fountain tea rooms, named after the fountain which had taken the place of the old Town Hall, were now 'refreshment rooms'; Harry Lane also ran 'dining rooms' at No. 240. On the Castle Street corner was The Hen and Chickens (No. 244) and further along the street The Castle, a hotel rather than a public house, and The Green Man at the head of Green Man Yard. This stretch of the street also harboured solicitors, as had been the case for a long while.

At the far end of High Street, beyond Stafford Street, on the north side was the High Side row, with a tunnel leading from the street probably for a defunct mineral railway. There were two public houses at the town end of the row. Opposite St Thomas' was the Bell Inn, descendant of the former Bluebell. Mrs Lett, at No. 188, and Thomas Higgs, at Beaconsfield House, were now hemmed in by small shopkeepers, their own houses soon to be converted to business premises. Apart from these, only the two ends of the High Street (including Castle Street) had room for private gentry. At the west end, beyond the church, Nos 94, 98, 99 and 100 remained private residences, as did Nos 256, 258, 259, 266 and 272 near the castle.

Castle Fetes

For many years the castle grounds had been used from time-to-time for popular fetes, the profits of which had been used for various charitable purposes, beginning with paying off the debts of the Geological Society in 1850.[2] In this way the Mechanics' Institute, Art School and Library were helped, and other money helped the Guest Hospital. In Edwardian times these gatherings were popular in the whole Black Country area, and in 1908 were combined with a great Dudley historical pageant.

The castle courtyard made a splendid arena. Some liberties may have been taken with historical events, but a huge local choir provided enthusiastic backing, and the fete that year was attended by many dignitaries, including the Earl of Dudley, Lord Cobham and Gilbert Claughton MP. Among useful services at the fetes was the presence of members of St John's Ambulance Brigade, which had been formed in 1892 and first appeared at a fete in 1899.[3]

In 1921, Halesowen author Francis Brett Young portrayed one of the castle fetes through the eyes of Abner fellows and his wife, main characters in *The Black Diamond*.

98 Remnants of a stone-built house in Upper High Street. This may be the remains of the Bluebell or 'Bell' public house.

THE
BLACK DIAMOND

by

F. BRETT YOUNG

LONDON: 48 PALL MALL
W. COLLINS SONS & CO. LTD.
GLASGOW MELBOURNE AUCKLAND

99 *The Black Diamond* title page.

After a rattling journey from 'Mawne' (Cradley Heath) 'roaring like a spent shell' through Netherton, the family are 'ejected' at the foot of Castle Hill after the tram disgorged its sweaty contents to mix with the cooler occupants of brakes and char-a-bancs.

> Through the dense foliage of the castle woods that hung limp in the heat like painted leafage in a theatre, the discordant music of competing roundabouts floated down, and beneath it one could hear the low exciting rumour of the fair, toward which a steady stream of new arrivals was setting. It was a stiff pull up the slope of the castle hill and everyone who climbed it seemed bitten with an infectious speed. At the top of it the crowds thickened beneath the construction of a narrow Norman arch and then burst and scattered into the huge central courtyard where grey ruins looked down upon this modern substitute for the tourneys of the middle ages.[4]

A New Library and Art School

From 1888, Dudley Library was dominated by the librarianship of William Southall, and on his death in 1900 he was succeeded by his daughter Miss E.J. Southall.[5] She employed her sister, E.L. Southall, as an assistant, and together they opened a reference section. E.L. Southall took over in 1913. Pressure on space was solved when Andrew Carnegie's foundation supplied a grant of £7,500 to build a new library. Building began in 1908 and was finished the following year. The location was the top end of St James' Road, and the architect was George H.Wenyon.

Under an Act of Parliament, Dudley became responsible for technical education within the boundaries from the beginning of the new century. The School of Art was part of the plan to improve technical knowledge in the borough. Once the library had transferred to its new building, space was released on the opposite side of the road for the creation of a pottery room. This later became the geological gallery.[6] The art gallery itself continued to expand through the acquisition of new paintings. Meanwhile, the Technical College remained in buildings which had once been the Lancastrian School in Stafford Street.

Dudley was beginning to wake up to its history, two important figures in this process being Arthur Rollason and Edwin Blocksidge. The first had been born in Upper Gornal in 1850, and educated at Baylies' School. He wrote many articles for the *Dudley Herald*, tracing the vicars of St Thomas' Church in the article

'Dudley Parish Church and its Vicars' (1900), the history of the Grammar School house at No. 60 High Street, and local families such as the Cardales, the Badgers and the Hawkes. Edwin Blocksidge ran the family printing firm, but was also a considerable artist, drawing views of the church and castle among others. He was particularly interested in the castle, but did not omit accounts of the priory from his historical work. He also published *A Guide to the Saltwells* in 1906.

Transport Development

Though trams were an effective means of transport for very local traffic, heavy rail was more important for greater distances. Dudley Port station, on the LNWR main line, was some way outside the borough in Tipton, but could be a useful starting point for some people at the east end of Dudley. By 1910 there was a through service to London at 7.06 a.m. and others at 8 a.m. and throughout the day. The first train to Birmingham stopping at all stations was at 5.15 a.m. In the other direction one could leave Dudley Port at 6.21 a.m. for Chester, arriving at 9.03 a.m. On the Walsall line of the same company, one could leave Dudley at 7.53 a.m. and reach Walsall at 8.13 a.m.

The branch line to Wednesbury via Princes End and Ocker Hill took ten minutes, but the service here was poor, the tram competition already being effective.[6]

Dudley station was jointly in the hands of the LNWR and the GWR. As a result there was a through service to London Paddington competing with the LNWR service from Dudley Port via Birmingham. A train left Dudley at 8.49 a.m. arriving at Paddington at 2.03 p.m. This route ran through Oxford, but it was more use for travel to Kidderminster and Worcester. This was many years before the concept of trains which ran at regular intervals, but a train left for Kidderminster almost every hour. There was also a Great Western local service to Birmingham via West Bromwich, a journey of 9 miles taking just over half an hour. The Dudley to Old Hill route via Netherton had a station

E. BLOCKSIDGE,

LAW STATIONER,

Printer & Lithographer,

20, STONE STREET,

→ DUDLEY. ←

Ornamental Addresses

Suitable for presentation to Clergy, Nobility, Schoolmasters, Superintendents of Sunday Schools, Sunday School Teachers, Tradesmen, &c., &c., carefully and tastefully designed and executed *on the premises*, at any price from Five Shillings to Twenty Guineas, as may suit Customers' requirements.

100 E. Blocksidge's advertisement, 1899.

at Blowers Green and one at Windmill End, but the 'halts' at Darby End and Baptist End were not even given firm timings. The service was run by a railcar and took about 14 minutes. Certain journeys either continued to Halesowen or connected with another railcar for that town. Dudley was an important station. with extensive buildings, an island platform and a bay for the local trains.

Tram routes were gradually converted to electric power after the Stourbridge conversion of 1899. This was followed in 1900 by the route to Cradley Heath and the Kingswinford route later the same year. There were complications for the Wolverhampton route which had terminated near the Post Office in Wolverhampton Street, because the street was too narrow. Accordingly a diversion was created to run via Stafford Street and electric trams ran down High Street through the market to Castle Hill, beginning late in 1902.

Electric traction on the Birmingham service via West Bromwich began in May 1902 and on the route via Oldbury in November 1904. By the next year the first tram left Dudley at 5.13 a.m.[8] Tipton and Ocker Hill followed in 1907. Congestion at the Dudley station terminus was severe.

Canal traffic had begun to decline over the last decades, and some damage had been caused to canals through mining subsidence. In 1894 part of the Dudley Canal at Blackbrook fell into old mine workings and had to be closed, along with part of the Two Lock cut. This short canal was subject to serious undermining from mines which had been abandoned, and in 1909 it was closed. The through route to Selly Oak via Lappal, which had to pass through the long tunnel to emerge near Weoley Castle, was also closed in 1917 when part of the roof fell in. For a while the railway companies had connected with canals, carrying bulk products such as coal, ironstone and bricks very efficiently from such places as Withymoor. Decline in both the iron and coal trades affected the profitability of these enterprises.

BIRMINGHAM, GREAT BRIDGE, and DUDLEY.—Great Western.

Miles	Down.	Week Days.													Sundays.							
	Snow Hill Station,	mrn	mrn	mrn	mrn	aft	aft	aft	aft	aft	aft	aft	aft Except Sats.	aft Sats. only	mrn	mrn	aft	aft	aft	aft		
	Birmingham ....dep.	7 0	9 0	1020	11 5	1 55	3 0	4 15	5 35	7 40	8 20	8 45	1110	1135	8 0	1030	1 55	3 25	7 10	9 15	....	....
1	Hockley................	7 4	9 4	1024	....	2 1	3 4	4 19	5 39	7 44	....	8 49	1114	1139	8 4	1034	1 59	3 29	7 14	9 19	....	....
1¾	Soho and Winson Green	7 7	9 7	1027	....	2 4	....	....	5 42	7 47	....	8 52	1117	1142	8 7	1037	2 2	3 32	7 17	9 22	....	....
2¾	Handsworth and Smeth-	7 11	9 11	1031	....	2 9	3 10	4 24	5 46	7 52	....	8 57	1122	1147	8 12	1042	2 7	3 36	7 22	9 27	....	....
4¾	West Bromwich ..[wick	7 17	9 16	1036	1114	2 14	3 15	4 29	5 51	7 57	8 32	9 2	1127	1152	8 17	1048	2 12	3 42	7 28	9 32	....	....
5¾	Swan Village............	7 21	9 20	1040	1118	2 18	3 19	4 33	5 55	8 1	8 36	9 6	1131	1156	8 21	1053	2 16	3 47	7 33	9 36	....	....
7	Great Bridge........[89	7 28	9 27	1045	1123	2 23	3 25	4 38	6 0	8 6	8 42	9 12	1137	12 2	8 26	1058	2 22	3 52	7 38	9 41	....	....
9	**Dudley** (Main) **86**, arr.	7 37	9 34	1053	1130	2 32	3 32	4 45	6 6	8 13	8 50	9 20	1145	1210	8 33	11 5	2 30	4 0	7 45	9 48	....	....

Mls	Up.	mrn	mrn	mrn	mrn	aft	aft	aft	aft	aft	aft	aft				mrn	mrn	aft	aft	aft	aft		
—	**Dudley** (Main).....dep.	8 3	9 20	1033	1122	1 10	2 44	4 10	4 58	6 35	9 10	1115	....	....	....	9 35	1135	2 42	4 30	8 20	10 5	....	....
2	Great Bridge............	8 10	9 27	1040	1129	1 17	2 51	4 17	5 5	6 42	9 17	1122	....	....	....	9 42	1142	2 49	4 37	8 27	1012	....	....
3¼	Swan Village **74**........	8 14	9 31	1044	1133	1 21	2 55	4 21	5 9	6 46	9 21	1126	....	....	....	9 46	1146	2 53	4 41	8 31	1016	....	....
4¼	West Bromwich...[wick	8 19	9 36	1050	1137	1 26	2 59	4 25	5 13	6 50	9 25	1130	....	....	....	9 51	1151	2 58	4 46	8 36	1021	....	....
6¼	Handsworth and Smeth-	8 24	9 41	1056	....	1 31	3 4	4 30	5 18	6 54	9 30	1135	....	....	....	9 56	1156	3 3	4 51	8 41	1026	....	....
7¼	Soho and Winson Green	8 27	9 44	1059	....	1 34	3 7	4 33	5 21	....	9 33	....	....	....	....	....	1159	3 6	4 54	8 44	1029	....	....
8	Hockley............[**448**	8 30	9 47	11 2	1146	1 37	3 10	4 36	5 24	....	9 36	1139	....	....	....	10 0	12 2	3 9	4 57	8 49	1033	....	....
9	**Birmingham 81,417** a	8 35	9 52	11 7	1152	1 42	3 15	4 41	5 29	7 1	9 41	1144	....	....	....	10 5	12 7	3 14	5 2	8 55	1040	....	....

101 1910 train times.

Life in Netherton

In 1984, George Baker wrote an article for the *Blackcountryman Magazine*, in which he recalled his visits to Netherton at his grandparents' house in Northfield Road.[9] He recalled going with his grandfather to help maintain the clock at Pearson's blast furnaces. He would stand on the pedestrian bridge over the branch railway line and watch molten metal from the furnace running into the mouls of sand to create pig iron. Slag was then taken away by train to be dumped near the park. Mousesweet brook was (and is) the boundary between authorities here, in those days between Staffordshire (Rowley Regis) and Worcestershire (Dudley). The patrolling policemen would meet here at midnight from each side of the boundary to confirm that all was well. Canals provided a source of danger to be faced and overcome; people, often children, collected coal from the edges and even the water itself, which sometimes proved lethal, and the collector was drowned.

Coal Mining

Dudley coal production declined after 1870, and by the early twentieth century many pits were closed, worked out or abandoned. According to Trevor Raybould's research, the quantity of coal sold by the Earl of Dudley declined from over 1 million tons in 1871 to 289,000 in 1880, then picked up to a new peak of over 916,000 tons in 1893, but declined again to 525,000 tons in 1905.[10] By this time the old Russell's Hall estate was riddled with disused shafts covering an area stretching from Springs Mire to the Himley Road. A golf course now covered some of the southern part of the estate. Mineral railways had been built across the golf course boundary, running under the old turnpike beyond Holly Hall and over it at Scott's Green. Yorkspark and parts of Parkhead collieries had been abandoned. On the west side of Netherton the relics of disused pits could be seen at Peartree Lane and Blackbrook Road, though the long-lived Yew Tree coal deposit was still being worked.[11] Near Baptist End were many old shafts scarring the wasteland round the White Lion Inn. Colliery railways ran from Bumble Hole across to Windmill End and through Gad's Green. Collieries were still in production at Dudley Wood and at Saltwells. The latter colliery would be one of the longest lasting in the area. To the north of these, the Prince of Wales pit near Dixon's Green had been worked out and there was no more coal at the pits behind Cawney Hill. Here the old mineral line tunnel beneath the Oakham Road could still be seen.

Glassmaking[12]

The manufacture of glass was always centred more in Wordsley and the Stourbridge district than in Dudley itself, and by the beginning of the twentieth century glassmaking within the town was faltering. Though a new enterprise had been started at Eve Hill in the 1880s, the older glassworks had declined. Castle Foot works, near what is now the Dudley College site, closed in 1899 and its contents were auctioned in 1900. Dudley Flint glassworks at the corner of Stone Street had long been derelict, its buildings having been used for a hide and skin market. The cone collapsed in 1886 but some of the old buildings remained to be photographed. Its ghost featured in local papers up to 1902, and more recent publications have reproduced the ancient photos. Phoenix Glassworks in Hall Street was used as a furniture sales room in 1903, its cone still surviving. It had previously been one of the most successful of all Dudley glassworks. By the close of 1903, demolition had begun, after having been advertised as 'the largest furniture establishment in the Midlands'.[13]

Education

Under the 1902 Balfour Education Act school boards were abolished and county boroughs put in charge of most education provision. This meant that many Dudley schools came, for the first time, under the direct control of the local authority. An important aim was to increase the provision for secondary education, which was achieved by the building of the Upper Standard School in Blowers Green Road. This was to become Dudley Intermediate School and later took the name of Gilbert Claughton, the mayor at the time of its foundation and the general manager for the Earl of Dudley. It was opened in 1904 and became a major educational institution in the town, serving also as a meeting place, as for instance when the Boer War memorial was opened in the neighbouring cemetery.[14] For Dudley Grammar School, the Education Act created a new environment, in which council governors became much more important than previously, and the gap between other schools and itself was narrowed.

102 Dudley Intermediate School.

In the new school buildings, the school began to find its feet under a new headmaster, Hugh Watson.[15]

In 1910 a new home for the Girls' High School was built in Priory Road and the Teachers' Training College was opened on high ground off The Parade. The High School building was designed by J. Hutchings and matched the Grammar School in educational aims. The school had been preceded by a Proprietory School for girls, which had been taken over by the council in 1904 and was also open to girls from neighbouring Staffordshire areas. The Teachers' Training College was a necessity when many new teachers were required for the expanding local authority schools. The new college had cultural aspirations, almost at once beginning a literary magazine called The Wren. New buildings were also provided for primary schools, some still partly maintained by the church authorities or charities such as Jesson's. One such church school was St Andrew's at Netherton. Its new building was constructed in 1907, and like the Upper Standard School was designed on two levels. It was much bigger than the 1836 building, and had the air of a town school instead of the village building, which had been sufficient up to that time.

The foundation stone of the new St Andrew's School was laid on 30 November 1907 (St Andrew's Day) and children moved into the new building in the cold February of 1908. While the new school was being erected they had been using temporary accommodation in the Public Hall (Netherton Arts Centre). The hall's heating was poor and the children had shivered in the wintry weather.

Money had been found to pay for the new premises through the Bluecoat Trustees and the local architect, Mr .W. Glazebrook had been the designer.[16] Meanwhile, Dudley Blue Coat School had a location at the rear of Dixon's Green Road, having moved from its previous cramped site in Fisher Street.

Public Utilities

The proliferation of electric tramways necessitated the building of electricity works capable of producing the quantities of power increasingly needed as these tramways grew. In Dudley this was supplied by the Springs Mire Electrical works, which was initiated by the town council.

103 Dudley Art Centre.

Using coal as its fuel, this power station was able to accommodate new domestic users as well as the tramway companies, but many domestic users in Dudley and Netherton continued to use gas lighting. The works had been built in 1899, but was bought by the Shropshire Worcestershire and Staffordshire Electric Supply Company in 1914.[17] Meanwhile, the long-running problem of Dudley's water supply was finally cured in 1899 by the construction of a new reservoir at Shaver's End on the Sedgley border. This was later a principal source of water for the South Staffordshire Water Company, whose area stretched as far as Smethwick. Gas was supplied from the town gas works at Cook's Tetnall, the gas holder being a prominent landmark in that part of the town.

The First World War[18]

Following the outbreak of war in July 1914 many men volunteered to join the forces. Most Dudley residents applying to fight joined the Worcestershire Regiment, which soon saw service in France. The delusion that it would all be over by Christmas soon faded, and volunteers became much harder to attract, resulting in the introduction of conscription. An important element in the fighting was the use of the versatile horse, and many were collected at Netherton to engage in supply work.

One effect of men leaving for the war was that more women were employed in factories; the National Projectile Factory at Waddams' Pool was one example. This was constructed on land near the Bean Car Factory, purchased from Messrs Harper and Bean. It was completed by 27 May 1916.[19] The factory needed workers from beyond Dudley, and to cater for them temporary accommodation was built in the shape of wooden houses at Brewery Fields in Burnt Tree.[20] These huts, erected in 1916, were extremely susceptible to fire, twenty-one being burnt between March 1920 and June 1921.

Apart from direct war work, many organisations were set up to provide comforts for the troops, especially among young women and girls who could not go in person to the front. They undertook the provison of clothing and other comforts, and also became temporary nurses for the wounded returning from the front. The war was largely fought at a distance; only rarely did Dudley see any close evidence of German forces. However, there was the famous occasion when zeppelins lost their way in an attempt to reach Liverpool and instead found the Black Country on 15 January 1915. No injuries were recorded from Dudley but the authorities became aware that blast furnaces lit-up the whole area and could provide a much more secure route to Liverpool, or indeed to the Black Country war effort in the future. As a result, early in 1916, Dudley council arranged with the volunteer arm of the Worcestershire Rgiment to act as air-raid wardens and shoot their rifles in the air if an attack from any more zeppelins should be imminent. It is not clear how far the sound of these rifle shots would carry amidst the general noise of the town and surroundings at the time.

By the end of the war about 600 Dudley men had died. Their graves lie scattered through Northern France and Belgium.

The war sometimes brought well-bred ladies into hospital to talk kindly to people of a type they had never met and never imagined previously. It is said that one particular lady visiting a severely wounded man, his face swathed in bandages and so hardly visible, sweetly asked, 'Have you been wounded, my man?' To which the soldier replied briefly, 'No, only bit by a canary.'

eleven

LOOKING BACKWARDS
AND FORWARDS

The war had changed the attitude of people in many ways. It had been suggested that when the soldiers returned there must be an effort to provide homes fit for heroes. To enable this to take place, land had to be acquired in various parts of the borough for new council housing to be sited, and in 1924 the area round the priory was identified as one likely site. This would provide homes to those living in slum clearance areas round Flood Street. Experiments were made with metal houses, like at Burnt Tree, but it was decided that conventional building was the best.[1] In 1928 an Act of Parliament gave new planning powers to Dudley council, in particular extending the boundaries to include Castle Hill and parts of Sedgley parish. Priory Fields was purchased from the Dudley Castle estate in 1924 and the planning of the housing estate could then begin. The foundations for the first two houses were laid on 16 July 1929. Council housing was also built in smaller areas at Netherton, Cawney Hill and Woodside.

Transport

The Birmingham and Midland Tramways Joint Committee had been co-ordinating services in the conurbation since 1904, but after the war there was a re-assessment.[2] New trams were ordered for the Stourbridge route and made their appearance in late summer 1919. Some new trams were actually built at Tividale works, not far outside the Dudley boundary at Burnt Tree.[3] Tracks were relaid on the Dudley to Cradley Heath route, the section in Dudley being positioned by arrangement with the borough surveyor. Mining subsidence had affected this route as it had done elsewhere. Castle Hill was always a problem for trams (and later, in snow, for buses). On 29 November 1920 there was an accident with a brand new tram, No. 77. As it approached the top of Castle Hill it slipped on greasy rails and came down the hill at about 40mph (normal tram speeds were 12mph). New brakes were applied, but without success. A supply of sand intended to retard trams in such situations did not work and the tram left the track near the Opera House, hitting a lorry. Near the station at the bottom of the hill the tram, now derailed, ran onto the footpath and came to rest partly over the railway bridge. The conductor had closed the doors to stop passengers jumping off, and no one was hurt, though the conductor suffered grazed knees. At the enquiry, his action in closing the doors was commended.

The Wolverhampton service was complicated by the fact that the Wolverhampton Corporation preferred a surface contact system and only in 1921 decided to convert to trolley poles like the rest of the Black Country and Birmingham system. However, the arrangement was provisional, renewable from year to year. At this time fares from Dudley to Sedgley Bull Ring were 3d, and from Fighting Cocks (Wolverhampton boundary) to Dudley 5d.[4] Local authorities had the power to control elements of the transport within their own areas, yet all were affected by the each other's decisions. This complicated through traffic, which was essential in the Black Country and Birmingham, where one authority ran quickly into another. In June 1923 an agreement was made between Birmingham and West Bromwich that Birmingham Corporation trams should work the route into Dudley (No. 74 service from April 1924). This route, now served by buses, is still No. 74 at the time of writing. All the tram routes in the Black Country were protected by maximum speed limits and compulsory (red plate) stops at possible danger points.

On the other side of the town, Wolverhampton remained unsatisfied with the tramway system, and as a result of a visit to Birmingham in 1923 to see trolleybuses on the Nechells route, it was decided to convert to that form of transport. This would clearly have a considerable effect on Dudley, since the main Wolverhampton route via Sedgley could not be operated without support from the Corporation. It had been possible for the Wolverhampton and Dudley company to run this since 1921, after the Wolverhampton conversion. Trolleybuses owned by the Wolverhampton Corporation took over the service from 1925.

By this time, the Midland Red bus company had expanded so that its services covered the whole Midlands, from Leicester to Hereford. As tram routes in the Black Country began to prove costly and inflexible, partly because of the proliferation of new estates, where it would have been expensive to lay tram track, the company stepped in, unless the municipality owned its own buses. Walsall,

West Bromwich and Wolverhampton, as well as Birmingham, had taken advantage of legislation which allowed this, but Dudley, although a county borough, had not. As tram routes in Dudley were abandoned, Midland Red buses therefore took over. Thus on 21 December 1925 the Dudley to Kingswinford service began to be run by Midland Red, and in March 1930 the route to Stourbridge followed. The tram route to Netherton and Old Hill had closed at the end of 1929. Midland Red built a new bus garage at the foot of Castle Hill to house the large fleet they now operated in the area.

Train services in the 1930s began to be less frequent than before, as first tram and then bus competition forced them out. However, in 1922 the service to Old Hill, still served by a railcar, was

Midland "Red" Motor Services

RIDE THE "RED" WAY.

RIDE EVERY DAY.

¶ The Midland "REDS" are a great convenience to business people who want to visit the numerous towns and villages in the Midlands. Plenty of Buses run daily from Birmingham to all parts, and where there are no Through Buses, convenient connections are arranged.

¶ Call at the Town Booking and Enquiry Office, Bull Ring—or Telephone 386 Central—if you want any information.

¶ Purchase Books of Discount Tickets and save over 3/- in the £ on your Bus Fares.

¶ Anywhere Tickets—Price 5/6—issued at Company's Offices only available on any day except Saturdays, Sundays and Mondays.

¶ Cheap Excursions to all the chief places on the system, every Tuesday, Wednesday and Friday. Ask Conductor for Return Excursion Ticket.

¶ Official Time Table and Map—Price 3d. On sale by all Conductors.

PRIVATE HIRE. Saloon Buses and Motor Coaches can be booked up for Private Parties of any size.

CHIEF TRAFFIC OFFICES :
Bearwood, Birmingham.
Tel. : 3300 Midland.

O. C. POWER,
Traffic Manager.

104 Midland Red advertisement, 1926.

as frequent as previously, with the same early morning start, and some trains not calling at the halts.[5] The service to Birmingham via Great Bridge was slightly increased, though Sunday services were withdrawn. There was a slight reduction in trains to Wolverhampton. On the LNWR line through Wednesbury to Walsall there were thirteen trains each weekday, much the same as before the war. Canals began their slow decline, hastened through strikes like that in 1926, and by the larger and more efficient lorries which could deliver direct to coal yards.

One aspect of the new era in transport was the production and ownership of private cars. In Dudley, the firm of A. Harper, Sons and Bean Ltd had been producing cars since before the war, but really came into their own in the 1920s. As well as the factory at Waddams' Pool, they made parts in Tipton and Smethwick. As one of many small/medium car manufacturers in the Midlands, they had their own ideas about design and facilities in the cars. The Dudley factory made the bodies, where a great deal of the work was done by hand, including painting and the application of beading.

When finished, the cars sold for anything between £335 and £425 according to specification, and were regarded as being reliable and pleasant to drive. They were particularly favoured in Australia for their sturdiness and craftsmanship. The company also began to produce lorries in 1927, by which time it had become part of a conglomerate and was largely operating at Tipton.[6]

Entertainment

Through the marvellously detailed research of Ned Williams we can understand how the cinema became the mainstay of popular entertainment in Dudley during the years before television was invented. The story begins in 1909, when the old Public Hall, previously the Mechanics' Institute and before that Gilbert Gillians' stone house in Wolverhampton Street, began to show films. This venue was never particularly good as a cinema, and the following year a small cinema opened next to the Opera House on Castle Hill. This was a particularly suitable site, accessible by tram and later bus, and within walking distance of the close-packed houses at Kate's Hill. This cinema started off as the Colosseum, but changed its name several times, and was enlarged. In the mid-1930s it was demolished and a larger, architect-designed cinema in the modern style opened. Sited next to the Opera House, it was to be the nucleus of an entertainment quarter, which never came to full fruition.

The most interesting cinema in Dudley architecturally was the Criterion, occupying a site which had once been that of Thomas Wood, wine and spirit merchant and later proprietor of a popular meeting place and victualler. The premises developed into a small music hall, and films were shown in a room attached to the auditorium. By 1913 this had become a cinema only.[7] After the war, with films becoming a type of entertainment much in demand, it was essential for a new cinema to be built on this site. The design was a mixture of Classsical and pre-war Renaissance styles, with a triangular pediment over a large front window which could have been Italian. The cinema was opened on 17 November 1923 with a live orchestra; upstairs was a fine café, making this one of the major attractions in Dudley town centre.

Much later, the Odeon cinema was built on Castle Hill, adding to the 'entertainment quarter' atmosphere of the area. This was opened on 28 July 1937 and soon became the town's most popular cinema, highly accessible from everywhere in the neighbourhood. It had a fine auditorium approached by

a stylish foyer, typical of the interwar years, clean-lined and giving a bright impression.Other cinemas in the town centre were the Regent, which later became the Top Rank Club, nearly opposite Top Church (St Thomas') and the Empire in Hall Street.

Dudley Opera House continued to function as a live theatre, though it was more likely to be staging pantomime than opera. Variety shows were also a mainstay until in 1936 when the building was burnt down in a spectacular fire. By this time it had added the title Hippodrome, and after the fire in the same year a cinema was opened on the site with that name. But live theatre had not been forgotten in Dudley, and in December 1938 the Hippodrome theatre took its place, a vast new building which staged variety, concerts and pantomime.

A walk in the park was a cheap and pleasant way of being entertained, and perhaps meeting potential life partners on a Sunday. Dudley parks were initiated in 1892, when the county borough bought land at the Buffery and a small section of what had been the New Park, the latter becoming Grange Park. Both areas had been ravaged by mineral extraction, but the borough now laid them out attractively, and parks were added at Netherton in 1901 and at Woodside. In 1932 the splendid park at the priory was laid out as part of the amenities for the priory estate.[8] During the interwar years, children's play equipment was added and these parks became a marvellous facility during the depressed years of the 1930s.

There were innumerable small public houses in Dudley. Dave Reeves records No. 22 in Kate's Hill, some of which had been there for many years, many opened in Victorian times.[9] One, the Freebodies, retained the old name of the district. No doubt there was far too much drinking by working men on their way home from work on a Friday night. Some pubs, such as the Shoulder of Mutton, sold beer brewed on the premises.

Dudley also had its share of larger breweries, such as that of Julia Hanson in Upper High Street. This had been the site of the Peacock inn, occupied in the 1850s by John Francis. Soon after the war Hanson's built a new brewery on this site, and ran 200 pubs in parts of the Midlands.[10] Still standing at the time of writing are the buildings of Queen's Cross brewery, the Lamp Tavern, at the top of Blowers Green Road (Bath Hill). Both alcoholic and non-alcoholic drinks were brewed here, but production stopped in 1934. Netherton also had many public houses, the most famous of which is the Old Swan, locally known as 'Ma Pardoe's', where ale was brewed under the surveillance of Frederick Pardoe during the years between the wars.

Life in the Interwar Years

At the end of the twentieth century nostalgia prevailed. The century, at any rate since the First World War, had produced so many changes that it became hard for some older people to accommodate to them. A flurry of reminiscences was published, dealing with life in the Black Country – in particular in Dudley – as it had been in the interwar years. Among these were memories from Kate's Hill, collected by Dave Reeves, and from Netherton, collected by M.H.W. Fletcher.[11] These and others provide an archive very much more emotive than memories from previous periods and give a fine picture of what it was like to live and work in one of those communities in the first half of the century. Many more memories were printed in the *Blackcountryman* and the *Black Country Bugle*. Fletcher records some pithy sayings: 'I should 'ave spoke t'thee last night but thee wast out of sight afore I sed yer'; 'Weer thee living now?' and 'Cross the cut side; ony time thee's coming by, drap in'.

It was certainly no world for feminists: wife-beating was common, and a straw handle was put on the door of men who had done it. There was hard drinking at the weekend and women would suffer black eyes, then do the washing on Monday, followed by drying and ironing.

At Kate's Hill there was very little furniture in the houses and generally no carpets. The woman of the house, with the help of daughters, would scrub stairs and tables, and Dave Reeves records that floors were kept clean by scattering brick dust and sweeping it out every week. There were still no flush toilets, and human waste was mixed with ash from the ash hole, the product of coal fires, to be taken away by 'night soil' men; the smell of disinfectant was pervasive. Fights between neighbours were rare except at election times, when yellow rosettes (for Labour) and red rosettes (for the Tories) sometimes caused clashes. Emma Rhodes, born in 1917, wrote an article for the *Blackcountryman* in which she too wrote of the life at Kate's Hill. She recalled her father, the 'soldier poet', William Horatius Harris who composed tragic verses. Her picture is of small shops, which were well kept, selling products some of which were home made, including the hand-raised pork pies and the shortcake and gingerbread made in the shop sold for a halfpenny.[12]

In the 1930s the *Dudley Herald* published a series of 'Black Country Stories', compiled by T.H. Gough, which were later reprinted and sold in book form by Hudson's, the Birmingham booksellers:

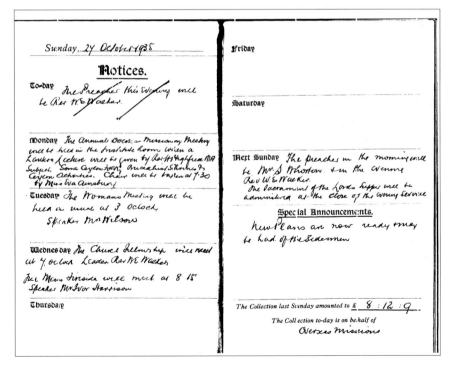

106 Extract from 1935 Wesleyan diary.

One section dealt with 'quips'; an example was:

'Weer am yer gooin', Bill?'

'I ay gooin nowere.'

'But yo must be gooin' somewere.'

'Well, I ay then, I'm a-coming back.'

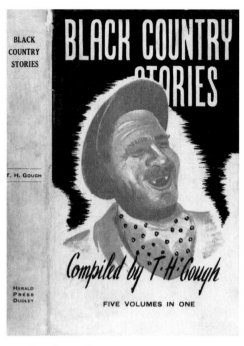

107 'Black Country Stories' from the *Dudley Herald*.

Dudley mayors were proud of the borough regalia, the mace of which was the one passed down from the court leet.[13] One of the items was a mayoral chain of office, with the borough coat of arms in the centre. It is said that a man from a neighbouring borough told his friend, 'We'm just bought our Mayer a noo chein to put round 'is neck.'

'Oh, we ay got a chein for ourn,' the friend replied, 'we lets the beggar run loose.'[14]

Darby End was famous for growing watercress, which used to be hawked by sellers in clothes baskets, particularly on Sunday afternoons, when it would be bought as a delicacy by the local inhabitants. A handful would cost a penny.[15]

An extraordinary event took place in September 1933, when the demolition of the wooden huts at Burnt Tree was accomplished by setting them all on fire. A house was first soused with petrol, and the mayor and an alderman went in with blazing torches, watched by an enthusiastic crowd. The fire brigade were in attendance, spraying nearby fencing with water to prevent the fires getting out of hand. The show took one hour, and the wooden huts were gone. So ended a very unlikely housing enterprise.[16] It was more than a tree that was burnt at Burnt Tree that day.

Churches and Chapels

Religious affiliation was always strong in Dudley, and this showed no sign of diminishing in the interwar years. The stability of the community was enhanced by the many clubs and activities run by the churches, not by any means always overtly religious but branching out into pantomimes and variety shows, parades, fashion shows and sports teams. New churches and chapels were built, for example St Francis' Church on Priory Estate, of which the foundation stone was laid shortly after the estate was built, in 1931. A mission church was consecrated at Dudley Wood: the church of St Barnabas and St John on 30 October 1930. St Peter's at Darby End continued its high church tradition under successive clergymen, though a clergy house was not purchased until 1947.

A glance at the 1935 pulpit notices for Wesley Church in Wolverhampton Street shows varied activities.[17] A women's group met every Tuesday afternoon. Outings by coach were organised, for example on Saturday 14 September, when the organiser was a Mr Victor Round. A Harvest concert was held on Monday 30 September (tickets 1s), on the day after the Harvest festival services, for which gifts of fruit, vegetables and flowers had been solicited the previous Sunday. A Church Fellowship gathered in many of the worshippers on selected Wednesdays, when Bible study took place, while a 'Fireside' followed at 8.15 p.m. We learn that Pew Rents were still charged. Christian Endeavour meetings were well attended, and there was a junior branch of this organisation. Sales and missionary meetings are also in evidence.

Dudley Baptists managed to move their church from New Street to Priory Road, finally opening in 1937, after the town council decided to widen New Street. After losing the New Street premises, and before the new church was open, the church met in the Castle cinema, High Street. The Baptists held Evangelistic meetings in the open air, in Tower Street, in the 'big yard' near Baylies' Hall.[18] Singing was a very important part of Nonconformist worship, and the Baptists went round lodging houses in King Street with a harmonium to accompany the hymns. There was, apparently, little success in an attempt to make Baptists of the new arrivals on Priory Estate, when considerable efforts

108 Building on the corner of New Street, built 1923.

109 Providence Chapel, Darby End ('Darby Hand') now at the Black Country Museum.

took place to contact the occupiers of some of the new houses. The Baptist Sunday school recruited a steady number of about 100 children regularly throughout the interwar years.

At Providence Chapel in Darby End concerts, often dominated by young people, were held, especially during the winter months. These developed into small dramatic entertainments. In the early 1920s expeditions were made on Saturdays to various Midland beauty spots, such as Kinver and Clent, and it is recorded that they 'frequently burst into hymn singing' as they walked. On Whit Monday the Providence choir would frequently go to Claverley, on one occassion being entertained by the vicar, who showed them round the old church with its Medieval wall paintings. Accounts by those who remembered these church and chapel activities suggest they were marvellous self-organised occasions, with people at all levels of society very actively engaged.[19]

These home-grown activities were supplemented by the large-scale gatherings addressed by evangelists from other parts of the Kingdom, or even overseas. One such was Edward Jeffreys, whose 'crusade' led to the establishment of newer forms of Nonconformity in Dudley, one such being Pentecostalism.

He held a crowded meeting at the Town Hall in March 1930, for which the queue stretched right down Priory Road past the library. The chuch association with day schools continued at such places as St John's and St James'. These friendly, undogmatic schools, now called faith schools, provided very standard education in an unthreatening context.

Dudley Castle and Zoo

In the search for open space which had led to the establishment of the town's parks, the council looked for the opportunity to lease the castle grounds, making more secure public access which had been established by the series of castle fetes. They were able to negotiate a lease from the Earl of Dudley in 1924 at the rate of 10s per annum. Finance to develop the park was harder to find, and when the earl (the 12th Baron Ward) died in 1932 the lease lapsed. The new earl was open to the possibility of developing a leisure facility on Castle Hill and the Dudley Zoological society was formed. Contact was made with Berthold Lubetkin, a designer with new ideas, very willing to use the contours of Castle Hill as a basis for an extensive zoo where animals could be seen in almost natural conditions: limestone workings forming caves and deep pits made excellent homes for tigers and bears.[20]

Lubetkin produced plans which conformed the new zoo to the lines of castle hill and integrated the castle itself into the design. The scheme involved terracing the hillside, providing flat surfaces from which visitors could watch the animals in pits below. One writer did notice that it was 'disconcerting to see signs within the castle walls that point the way to tropical fish, and to watch the elephants lumber round the lawn in front of the keep'.[21] The zoo was opened on 6 May 1937 by the Earl of Dudley, with 50,000 visitors being allowed inside, though many more had arrived in the hope of admission. Two years later a miniature railway was added to the attractions, carrying passengers through the woods towards the old mill area. The original line was relaid in 1946 to a 15ft gauge, having proved itself a great success.

Municipal Buildings

During the 1920s and '30s it was decided to enlarge and bring up to date the rather rickety council accommodation. Dudley was emerging as the capital of the Black Country, a large population centre with an enterprise to match, but its municipal buildings had not kept pace with this development. Messrs Harvey and Wicks were entrusted with the task of designing a new Town Hall, which was opened in 1928 and awarded an architectural prize. The Brooke Robinson Museum was opened in 1931, though the exhibits were later transferred to the main art gallery, where they remain. The Council House was built in 1935, being opened by the Duke of Kent on 2 December. In 1941 a new police station was completed despite the Second World War, and there was also a new fire station at Tower Street.

Education

As the centre of a large industrial area, Dudley needed effective technical education, which had been provided by the Mechanics' Institute and the Technical School, occupying the buildings of the former Lancastrian School in Stafford Street. After the war the council agreed with Staffordshire to build a new college, to be renamed Dudley Technical College.[22] A fine site was acquired beneath the castle at the top of Broadway. Work began in 1931 and most of the college, with assembly hall, was in a condition to be opened in 1935. The formal name was to be The Dudley and Staffordshire Technical College. The rest of the work remained incomplete and was overtaken by the outbreak of the Second World War. However, by this time the facilities at the college were good, including an electrical engineering laboratory, a junior technical and commercial section,welding, chemistry and secretarial courses.

The Upper Standard School in Blowers Green Road had become the Higher Elementary School, but once again it changed its name in 1929 to become the Intermediate School.[23] Other secondary schools were being opened as a result of the Hadow Report (1926), especially where new estates had been built to accommodate people moved out from the condemned property in the town centre. Such was, for example, Rosland School near Kate's Hill. It should probably have been called Roseland, as the name clearly echoed the old farm and had been correctly used in nearby Roseland Avenue. The Bluecoat School continued in Bean Road. Primary schools were opened at the Priory and Wren's Nest to serve new populations,while others were expanded.

At Netherton, the headmaster of St Andrew's School was S.B. Simpson, who commenced duty on 1 October 1925. He kept a detailed record of school events, among which were visits to a West Bromwich Albion football match, a school camp at Astley Burf, and the cold suffered by pupils during the coal strike of 1926. The school beat Jessons in a cricket competition in 1929. Mr Simpson also noted the school closure in late August for hop picking: this took four weeks. In 1931 the school became mixed, with junior girls and boys occupying the ground floor while the upper floor was taken by the new C of E Senior School.

At Dudley Grammar School the influential headmaster Hugh Watson retired in 1930. It would be hard to fill the shoes of a man who had lifted the school almost from the beginning of its new premises to prominence among the grammar schools of the West Midlands, but after a short period under the direction of T.W. Watson, Mr David Temple was appointed in 1934.[24] At this point, fees were still charged for entry, and the school was competing with the new range of schools, including the Intermediate School, which were under council control. David Temple was a great advocate for the wider curriculum his school could provide, including such vocational subjects as woodwork and technical drawing.

Dudley in 1936

Kelly's Post Office Directory always provides an overview of what the outsider thinks are the most important features of any place.[25] The 1936 Worcestershire edition gave a brief history describing Dudley's rail connections: 92 miles north of Bristol and 44 south-west from Derby were among the mileages given. The prominence given to these towns and their rail links shows that road transport had not yet supplanted the train in Dudley's economy. The passenger station at the foot of Castle Hill was still a major hub, and the goods sidings at Blowers Green dealt with large quantities of freight.

Public transport was still thought of as vital, as is shown by the detail given in the directory. Tram and trolley bus routes are described, connecting Dudley with Wolverhampton and Handsworth. Nothing is said about private road transport, or the roads leading to Tipton, Halesowen or Stourbridge.

The South Staffordshire coalfield still features early in the directory's article. After a short summary of the development of municipal government, the article continues with an account of the churches.

This section begins with St Thomas', clearly holding pride of place among the parish churches. By a natural progression the writer goes on to describe St Edmund's, mentioning two chairs dated 1611 which do not feature in other literature. The vicar at the time was Thomas Charles Jones, BA. Next mentioned is St James' at Eve Hill, with its redrerdos erected in 1922 to the memory of those who fell in the First World War.

The account of St John's, Kate's Hill, mentions its ten tubular bells and memorials to John Beddard of Dixon's Green and the Revd E.H.L. Noot, whose incumbency lasted from 1843 to 1905. The parish hall, dating from 1932, is also mentioned in the account. It is worth noting that Freebodies, the old name for the area, has quite disappeared by this time.

St Luke's Church in Wellington Road and St Augustine's at Holly Hall follow in the directory article, with a short section on the new church at the Priory. The directory account then moves to other denominations, moving first to the Roman Catholic church. This order represents a change from previous practice when Nonconformist churches were thought of next to those of the Church of England. After the Catholic church come the Congregational church in King Street and other Congregational churches at Hall Street, Woodside and Park; the Methodist chapel in Dixon's Green; Trinity Presbyterian church; Wolverhampton Street Methodist chapel (Wesley); the Baptist chapel (currently undergoing renovation, though the directory does not say so); the Unitarian chapel and three more Methodist churches. Altogether, nearly a page is given over to these ecclesiastical buildings, on the second page of the section on Dudley. Religion, we can deduce, was still most important as an influence in the town, and one which would be at the forefront of those reading the directory.

It then takes a tour round the municipal buildings: police station, Town Hall, public library and the Brooke Robinson Museum; the Council House also attracts attention. As well as the council chamber, Kelly's writer is interested in the committee rooms and the various officials: town clerk, borough engineeer, borough treasurer, and those in the health and housing departments. Public libraries are clearly important; the directory describes the accommodation at St James' Road, with its hall, juvenile library, newsroom, lending and reference facilities. The Geological Museum and School of Art are described, and there are references to the fountain in the market place and the Earl of Dudley statue. The baths at Blowers Green Road and the former Mechanics' Institute also merit a mention.

The priority of municipal institutions is very interesting; it is only after this that the town's industries are explored, and then not thoroughly. This may be because they are to be featured in the alphabetical section, but still the emphasis on public buildings is very much a sign of the times. Dudley has emerged from the nineteenth-century stranglehold of the richer entrepreneurs, just as that hierarchy had replaced the rule of the manorial lords. Now the expectation is that a town will be judged by its municipal provision for its citizens. The phrase 'municipal Socialism' is nowhere used, but the climate of the times is such that municipal enterprise is much valued.

The decline of the coal industry is clearly marked at this time. The directory mentions the South Staffordshire Mines Drainage Commission offices in Trindle Road. The territory of the Commission extends for 81 square miles, including Oldbury, which, like Dudley, is in Worcestershire. However, coal is still being mined in Tipton, Kingswinford and Old Hill districts. Efforts to drain these areas have proved impossible, and in 1920 'the complete abandonment of the idea of any drainage scheme for the district' had been recommended. The report concludes that 'meetings are not now fixed and are very irregular'. The end of the coal industry had occurred, though there was a good deal of coal still unmined, some quite close to the surface.

In 1936 there were seven sub-post offices in the Dudley borough, at Adshead Road, Dixon's Green, Eve Hill (Salop Street), Kate's Hill, Market Place, Upper High Street and Wellington Road. Three of them offered facilities for telephone calls and there were other phone offices, one being at Holly Hall. At this time there were seven municipal wards for the election of councillors, all multi-member 'constituencies'. Four were named after churches, as one might expect from the prominence given to them in the introduction to Kelly's article. They were St Thomas', St Edmund's, St James', and St John's. Castle, Woodside and Netherton were the names of the other three wards.

By this time, Dudley officials did not all live in the borough, or even in the area usually considered to be part of its sphere of influence: Kingswinford, Sedgley, Rowley Regis and the like. Of the borough magistrates, five lived at a distance: Percy James Hingley at Droitwich; Godfrey Muggitt at Charlton Kings in Gloucestershire; William Thompson at Harborough Hall in Blakedown; and two magistrates at Kinver. The county court district covered Tipton, Sedgley,

Coseley and Rowley Regis as well as Dudley itself. The registration district comprised Rowley Regis, Old Hill, Sedgley, Upper Gornal and Tipton as well as Dudley. A faint echo of the past lingered in the function of William Charles Camm, with offices in Wolverhampton Street, who was 'Deputy Steward of the manors of Sedgley, Kingswinford and Rowley Regis'. In time most of the areas under Dudley influence would come to be added to the borough.

The directory noted the strength of the grammar school, with a roll of 370 boys, and the Girls' High School, with its governing body composed of eight members from Staffordshire, six from Dudley and one from Birmingham University. This shows that the school was expected to serve the surrounding Staffordshire communities as well as the borough, and reflects the influence that Birmingham still had, in the shape of the local municipally inspired university. However, Dudley Training College was beginning to rise in importance, having had extensions in 1931 and wholly reporting to the Dudley borough authorities. Its future as a centre for Higher Education in the borough looked assured.

An investigation of the addresses of the main private residences of the town shows which were the favoured streets and areas. Fewer now lived in the centre of town. Wellington Road was home to a number of residents, including Joseph Plant, William Taylor, Benjamin Sidaway and Joseph Pearsall; the large Victorian terraces were obviously an attraction. A number of such residents lived in The Broadway and Priory Road, but some favoured the eastern side of town, especially Dixon's Green, home of the Mason family, Eli Bradley and John Brevitt. Beyond this, Oakham Road and Cawney Hill were desirable areas. Twenty-nine residents of this part of town were thought important enough to be included in the private residents' section of the directory. Some houses in Oakham Road and a few elsewhere were isolated or prominent enough to warrant being without street numbers, surely a cachet. Arthur Meyer lived at Greenfels, Oakham Road; Miss Dorothy Bate lived at Hybank in the same road, while Ronald Alexander lived at Apsley House, The Broadway, and Cyril Down at Glentworth, St James' Road. These new house names did not reflect the local names of those parts of the borough, though as in the case of Alfred Preedy's The Knoll, Tansley Hill Road, they did occasionally have a local reference. Vincent Powell lived in the only private farmhouse near the centre of Dudley: Tansley Hill farm on Oakham Road.

The Second World War

The transformation of Dudley town centre was completed in May 1939 at the opening of Coronation Gardens. This, with the statue of Eros, gave a new feeling of openness to this part of the town centre. But dark clouds were gathering over the nation. In the same month conscription was introduced, and few people thought a war with Germany could be avoided. Local engineering firms converted to war work: Grazebrook's and Netherton Iron Works made high explosive bombs, while incendiaries were made by Louise Marks of Upper Hall Street.[26] Some occupations came under the 'reserved' heading, in which skilled workers were included, making precision artefacts for war. Miners were also exempt, though by this time there was little mining in Dudley itself.

Those men who stayed at home in the reserved occupations, and those too old to be called up, found other forms of war work. The Dudley branch of the Local Defence Volunteers (LDV) was reconstituted as the Home Guard in 1941 and played a vital part in guarding important points in Dudley. It was organised as a military force, complete with soldiers' uniforms, and allied to the Worcestershire Regiment. The television series *Dad's Army* has somewhat parodied the organisation, which was often well-organised, having some members who were ex-soldiers now too old to feature in the front line. Women did not join the Home Guard, but were enrolled as air-raid wardens and firewatchers to protect local factories.

To prepare young men to serve in the Air Force, the Air Training Corps recruited many Dudley boys into the organisation which had been formed on 21 January 1941. Many went on to join the RAF. Meanwhile, German aircraft carried out many raids on the Midlands. Dudley was perhaps fortunate in that German attention was focused more on Birmingham and Coventry, but evidence surfaced that the Luftwaffe had maps of Dudley to help them target local factories.[27] Maps cannot always be the source of accurate bombing, as was shown by a bomb which exploded near St Thomas' Church, causing some damage to the church. This was clearly not the target.

During the war, normal activities did not disappear completely, and a landmark in our knowledge of the history of Dudley Priory was published. During 1939, C.A. Radford had carried out excavation on the site and published his findings in *The Antiquaries' Journal, Vol 20*. This was fortunate, as his actual reports were lost in the bombing of Exeter University.[28] He traced the outlines of the lost cloister and other buildings beyond the church, which had been disturbed by the later industrial buildings, and discovered many encaustic tiles. They date from the twelfth to the fourteenth centuries and many have been saved, though they are not currently on site, despite an earlier attempt to replace them. The loss of Radford's reports made exact replacement difficult, and the tiles were in any case subject to weathering and vandalism on a site which cannot be continually guarded. There has been some dispute about the patterns and illustration on the tiles, but coats of arms of the Suttons and Despensers have been recognised. Other tiles have concentric ring patterns and leaf patterns which can also be found in other Midland monasteries.

twelve

BRAVE NEW WORLD

T he Second World War was over, and throughout the land communities were looking for a new beginning. Dudley had a legacy
of industrial squalor to set to rights, with much slum property
and many industrial scars to rectify. This process began in the
1950s and '60s and eventually changed the face of Dudley radically. Sometimes
the clearing of old housing and the cleaning of old industrial scars could be
combined, as in Russell's Hall Estate, where old mines and spoil heaps ('pit
bonks') made way for attractive new houses. In other areas whole streets were
lost, with elegant Georgian houses being demolished alongside crowded, poor
quality dwellings.

The south side of Dudley town was officially designated the 'Clearance Area'.
Housing demolition was associated with the redevelopment of part of the
shopping area, the town end of Hall Street and some parts of High Street itself.
The plan was adopted in 1962 and took seven years to complete.[1] Much of
the demolition took place on what had been in Medieval times Peacock Field
and Church Field. There would have been little of ancient archaeological value
here, though some streets still followed the field divisions, allowing some reference to the past. Some of the area was further disturbed when the southern
bypass was built in the early twenty-first century.

Oakeywell Street (its name commemorating the well below the hill on which
an oak tree – or more than one oak tree – stood) almost disappeared in this process, and many more streets were denuded of their original buildings. Among
them were Bond Street (with its tall Victorian houses and square bay windows),
Bath Street, and many appalling terraces and courts. Interesting warehouses
such as that belonging to E.C. Lewis in Church Street were also demolished.
This was a three-storey building with typical late-Victorian lintels and a stone
plaque with Lewis' name and the trade, 'Tea and Provision Merchant', written
on it. The National Projectile Works was one of the industrial buildings to go

110 Dudley southern bypass from the pedestrian bridge.

in Oakeywell Street, having previously become a factory for making holloware supplied to the Co-op[2]. Chapels were also demolished. This was a closely packed area, and it is quite understandable that much of it had to be razed to the ground, but in clearing such areas for complete restructuring, interesting buildings were not spared.

The nearer to the town centre demolition took place the more one can regret the wholsesale nature of the clearance. King Street contained many pleasant, though neglected, properties dating from the very early nineteenth century. Some of these were three-storey houses erected in the period after the Napoleonic Wars, others rather older had only two storeys. On the corner of Flood Street was the well-built Green Dragon, with its first-storey bays and upper-storey sash windows. The Salvation Army citadel was another casualty. Unfortunately, King Street was not improved by this demolition, except in so far as it became easier to use for traffic. The town centre end of Hall Street gave way to Birdcage Walk and the Churchill Precinct. Some interesting sculpture was provided on the first of these, featuring stylised workers and geometric chains.

Similar exercises were promoted at Netherton, where tower blocks were erected to take families removed from their old decrepit dwellings. Many of these deserved to go; they were often well kept by the women of the house, but only by struggling with dirt and obsolete washing facilities, outside toilets and wash

houses, small irregular yards and dark entries. Some of these, and their coun-
terparts in areas such as Wolverhampton Street, were the very same described
and condemned by Ballard in 1874. Tower blocks also made their appearance in
Salop Street, where a good deal of poor-quality property was removed.

Dudley town centre had featured a long street, the name of which changed
many times, since the Middle Ages, but which surprisingly retained a single
number series throughout: Upper High Street, Market Place, Castle Street (at
times also Queen Street and Turnpike). In the early 1960s this still kept many
gracious buildings, some dating from the eighteenth century, and overall giving
the impression of a fine country town. But developers were eyeing Dudley as
a likely place to change wholesale. This fitted quite well with the council's aim
to renew the town and bring it up to post-war standards. As we have seen, this
process was sorely needed in some of the 'slum' areas built willy nilly on the old
Peacock and Church Fields. It was not quite so clear that wholesale demolition would suit the town centre. In Castle Street were elegant buildings like
the Woolpack and what had become Stanton's music shop, originally the home
of the Baddileys on the corner of Fisher Street. In the market place was the
old Dudley Arms, the glory of later eighteenth- and early nineteenth-century
Dudley, and historic meeting place of many political and philanthropic socie-
ties. During the nineteenth century this building had housed the Rating and
Excise Office, and it was from here that the Riot Act was read in 1864 during a
hotly contested election.

At the east end of the market place on the north side was the Brown Lion
and its neighbours, the shops of Collins and Tyler's. On the south side was the
half-timbered Seven Stars, which, though it had been revamped by a brewery
company earlier in the century, still retained a sixteenth- or seventeenth-century
frame. In Upper High Street were Beaconsfield House, birthplace of Brooke
Robinson, and the ancient shop of Bunce's, with its Strawberry Hill windows.
Beaconsfield House was later occupied by the furniture firm Spiers. These
and others presented an attractive and varied vista. However, the 1960s was
a radical age, with new notions about architecture and a fine self-confidence.
Steel-framed brick-faced buildings were erected to replace them, unfortunately
sometimes of cheap construction, whose feeling is that the builders and occupiers spent little time exploring the visual effect or historic appropriateness of
their work. One pleasant mid-nineteenth-century building that survived was
the shop on the scorner of High Street and Stone Street, occupied in the 1950s
by Hiltons and later by Thomas Cook.

Religion

Following the period of commonwealth immigration, which began in the later 1950s, a Muslim community has been established in Dudley. When St Edmund's School became redundant, it was purchased by this community and became Dudley's central mosque. There have been efforts during the early part of the twenty-first century to rebuild and replace these rather cramped premises, in a way which would benefit the town as a whole, providing community facilities. These efforts have met with some setbacks, but at the time of writing the plans are still in process.

Churches and chapels flourished after the Second World War, many running the pre-war activities unchanged: Sunday schools continued to flourish. However, in the later 1990s and the early twenty-first century there has been a retraction of church influence. The Church of England has concentrated on St Thomas' and to a lesser extent St Edmund's. This has sadly meant the closure of St John's at Kate's Hill. A pleasant Victorian, stone building, like its counterpart, St James' at Eve Hill, St John's has been declared unviable. The congregation has been meeting in the church hall, across the road. Nevertheless, the church has importance not only from a religious point of view, but as a historic building; Dudley has lost too many of these. A 'Save St John's' group was set up to try to preserve the church. Much useful work has been

111 St Andrew's Church choir in the 1940s.

carried out, including care of the churchyard, where the graves of Josie Darby, the Netherton canal jumper, and the education specialist Marion Robinson (famous for her handwriting reform) can be seen. Some churches, especially those of the Nonconformists, have been enhanced by new members whose heritage is the Caribbean, but this has not saved all from closure, where buildings have been severely damaged by time or deserted by other members migrating to the fringes of the Dudley area, such as Kingswinford or Sedgley. In Netherton the wild fire that raged below ground at the rear of St Andrew's churchyard finally subsided, and some chapels, such as Ebenezer Baptist, have retained good support.

Transport

The final tram routes in Dudley had been replaced by buses in 1939: the No. 74 in April and No. 87 in October. The West Bromwich route was run jointly by West Bromwich Corporation and Birmingham, while the No. 87 was more conveniently worked by the Midland Red, the company which was already running almost all the Dudley bus routes. The trams were taken to storage in Birmingham, to be kept until after the war in case they might be needed. These ex-tram routes terminated at Dudley station, making a connection with the still-vibrant railway services. Green Wolverhampton Corporation trolley buses on route 58 turned at the art gallery in front of the Saracen's Head. An excellent turning circle was provided by the square which had been The Horsepool, and much later a market. Most Midland Red services terminated at Fisher Street, though a few ran across the town and linked other Black Country communities on each side. Birmingham and the Black Country had got rid of their trams much before other cities, such as Leeds, Sheffield, Liverpool and Glasgow, partly because of the narrow

112 1976 bus timetable cover.

guage favoured in the West Midlands which meant tramcars were narrower and less comfortable.

As part of the post-war rebuilding, old property in Birmingham Street was demolished and the Fisher Street bus terminus expanded so that buses used the new stops from September 1952. The Midland Red had been overworked during the war and the company resorted to an unusual measure: they put into service a fleet of rear entrance buses produced by Guy Motors of Wolverhampton. Company policy had been to provide front entrance for passengers, and this departure was initially confusing for passengers. Birmingham Corporation had used Leylands on the 74 route from the beginning, and now bought Leyland PD2s for their Hockley garage. West Bromwich persevered with Daimlers, neatly turned out in their cream and two shades of blue, with West Bromwich coat of arms on each side. Wolverhampton trolley buses remained green and yellow, but the 58 route could not be extended to Fisher Street.

The Midland Red ran a small number of bus routes with the prefix 'D' for Dudley, mainly for buses which terminated inside the borough boundaries; the through routes had numbers within the normal series.

By the late 1960s it was clear that bus transport in the Black Country and Birmingham was so interrelated that an umbrella organisation was needed.

113 Midland Red and Birmingham Corporation buses near the bus garage.

A Passenger Transport Executive (PTE) was formed and previously Corporation-owned systems merged. In the West Midlands this meant Birmingham, Walsall, West Bromwich and Wolverhampton. A new livery was designed incorporating the colours of all the municipalities except Wolverhampton, whose green could not be fitted in with the predominant blue. (Wolverhampton got its own back later when trains were painted green.) Midland Red services were added in the following years, the buses at first retaining their red livery, but eventually being repainted in the PTE colours. Dudley and Hartshill garages were transferred to the PTE.

Soon enough, however, the political pendulum swung the other way and with it came deregulation and the end of publicly owned transport. PTE services were not broken up but transferred to a new company, the West Midlands Travel, later Travel West Midlands, now National Bus West Midlands.

There remained an integrating body, Centro, later Network West Midlands, which rebuilt Dudley bus station. The company, however, pursued a policy of closing down bus garages, including all the former Midland Red garages in the area, Dudley and Hartshill being local casualties. Dudley garage ceased operation in August 1993.

Routes 74 and 87 continue to run at the time of writing, with buses working out of West Bromwich garage. At Fisher Street the wheel has come full circle, as most of the buses are now red, as they were in Midland Red days.

Railway history in Dudley has been much less enhanced. Dudley station itself lies derelict at the time of writing, after various vicissitudes and unsubstantial promises. It was closed to passenger traffic in 1964 and in 1967, before being converted into a freight terminus. This opened on 6 November 1967, with a train to Glasgow. Freight traffic in the Black Country languished, and the terminal closed in 1986. Many regret this loss of an apparently viable facility. Freight trains continued to work through Dudley until 1993, but the South Staffordshire freight route linking Dudley with Walsall and Derby, potentially a most useful line for development, now has trees growing on the track.

114 Bus timetable from 1993.

115 Leyland TD6c awaiting return to Hockley garage after working the number 74 route.

The 1989 Metro (tram) bill envisaged a light rail link between Dudley and Walsall, which has not materialised despite constant attempts to revive the project. It has never been clear why the West Midland Metro system has languished while other industrial areas have been awarded national finance to develop their tramways. Dudley sorely needs an alternative to the bus to connect commuters with Birmingham and Wolverhampton.

Meanwhile the branch line originally connecting Dudley with Halesowen also closed, after an earlier closure of the Withymoor branch. Passenger sevices to Old Hill were ended in 1964, the Withymoor branch in 1965, and the whole line in 1969. The southern portion of the line through Round Oak to Stourbridge is still in use for freight at the time of writing, retaining a double track for use with several industrial sites. However, this railway barely fringes the old Dudley parish boundary. The 1973 British Rail timetable cheerfully calls our attention to West Midlands PTE routes to Birmingham and Wolverhampton and does not mention Walsall.

After the Second World War, traffic on the local canal system became sporadic or non-existent. The extraordinary Dudley tunnel, running through the limestone caverns deep below the castle grounds, was closed at Parkhead in 1962. Like the railways, canals were seen as an ancient method of transport

116 Dudley station in 1956.

117 Canal near Windmill End.

118 New Road (A4123) Bridge near Tipton Cross Roads.

now firmly outdated. It was the age of the car, and few people imagined the way in which cars would block roads and create the need for demolition of roadside properties. A number of stalwarts joined the campaign to reopen the Dudley tunnel, culminating in its return on 21 April 1973. The more modern Netherton tunnel did not suffer in the same way and reached its 150th birthday in 2008. Boat building flourished at Bumble Hole, and the Windmill End wharf on the far southern edge of Dudley began to be used again by pleasure boats.

The greatest transport change has been the proliferation of the private car, though days of the Dudley Bean are long past. This has meant widening existing roads and cutting new ones. The A4123 between Birmingham and Wolverhampton touches only the fringe of the old parish, but its junction with the Dudley to Birmingham roads via West Bromwich and Oldbury has necessitated major reshaping at Burnt Tree, which has now become a huge and slightly confusing junction. Previously, a north–south route was constructed, called the Southern Bypass, which opened in 2001. Road alterations just south of the town centre have changed the face of the junction of Hall Street with King Street. Beyond Scotts Green there have been major alterations near Russell's Hall Hospital. Pedmore Road (A4036) has undergone a number of modifications, especially since the opening of Merry Hill. Much of the widened route is outside the old Dudley boundary.

Education

There may be something symbolic about the contrasting fortunes of two Dudley educational institutions. While Dudley and Staffordshire Technical College (later just Dudley College) flourished, Dudley College of Education (the former Teachers' Training Institution) moved, after the 1970s, towards extinction. The Tech widened its remit by combining with the School of Arts and Crafts as early as 1947. The Staffordshire element took a back seat when Wednesbury College and Cannock Mining Technical College lost their statutory input in 1953. In 1966 the role of Staffordshire was extinguished as Dudley boundaries changed. Meanwhile there was further building on the Broadway site, to include motor vehicle and electrical engineering. As part of the boundary extensions, Brierley Hill had become part of Greater Dudley and Brierley Hill School of Art and was added to the Holly Hall annexe of Dudley College. Later still the the functions of Holly Hall annexe were transferred to the main site.[3]

After the demise of Dudley College of Education, local authority functions such as the language and literacy centre were moved to the forever expanding Dudley College of Technology, which also acquired a role in computer training. By the turn of the twenty-first century, the college was the undisputed further education centre in Dudley, though other institutions had been added to the borough at the time of the boundary expansion. Dudley College, as it finally became known, was well situated in pleasant grounds and serviceable buildings. It was able to host such institutions as the Open University, which had previously used the College of Education buildings, and had a special management suite. The college also had links for a while with MG Rover at Longbridge in Birmingham.[4]

Dudley Training College, at its site in Castle View off The Parade, had catered for teachers in training for many years. During the 1960s a new science block was built, incorporating excellent laboratories at a time when science was being promoted nationally. The college formed part of Birmingham University's consortium of colleges, with representatives from the University School of Education on the governing body.[5] The notion of 'training' had been replaced by 'education', and intending teachers were to be given a full university-style curriculum with specialist subjects including sciences, maths and sociology. They would take students with two or more A-levels intending to teach in infants', junior and secondary schools. Part of their education was

DUDLEY COLLEGE OF EDUCATION

D. BROADHURST,
    M.A., M.Ed., J.P.

Principal

OUR REF.

YOUR REF.

CASTLE VIEW

DUDLEY

WORCS.

TEL. 53451/2/3

119 Dudley College of Education letterhead.

professional, with subjects such as education history, psychology and classroom management being important components. Part of the students' time would be spent in subject areas, developing their knowledge from A-level towards university standards. Cambridge-educated Dennis Broadhurst was determined to make the college one of the first of its kind in the country. Students were enrolled from the whole of the United Kingdom. The educational aspect was further enhanced when the course designation became degree level (BEd) instead of certification. The three-year couse was suitable for specialists in primary schools (though secondary work was not neglected) at a time when the government had decided that knowledge of subjects and classroom techniques were equally important. At this time entry qualifications in English and maths were vital, and even those who held O-levels in these subjects were tested before entry.

The existence of colleges of education, which had been turning into mini-universities, was questioned in the mid-1970s, and it became clear that the work of Dudley College of Education, with West Midland rivals both in and out of Birmingham University's remit, would be threatened. Within the Black Country there were colleges at Walsall and Wolverhampton, and nearby in north Worcestershire as well as within Birmingham boundaries. At the same time polytechnics, of which there was a strong example at Wolverhampton, were becoming a favoured method of vocational education. It was argued that teaching was a vocation that could be catered for in such an institution better than at one linked to a university, though the arguments for this were not made clear. The tripartite system of higher education – colleges of education, polytechnics and universities – seemed unnecessarily divisive.

Dudley Borough, and the college authorities, were thus faced with a dilemma. The college could be linked with another West Midland college, or try to form a partnership with Wolverhampton Polytechnic. There was some urgency involved, since by this time other West Midland colleges were also trying to form links, and Saltley, a venerable college in Birmingham, was to be closed. Negotiations with Wolverhampton began, with Dudley borough seeking a joint institution, perhaps to be called Dudley and Wolverhampton Polytechnic. However, it may appear that Dudley, which had in a sense won a victory with Staffordshire over the Technical College, lost to Wolverhampton over the College of Education. It was absorbed into Wolverhampton Polytechnic along with other colleges in the Black Country, without any recognition of Dudley in the title. The campus became known as The Faculty of Education for a while.

120 Children at Russell's Hall Primary School, 1960.

Inevitably, later centralisation caused the campus to be abandoned, leaving Dudley with no higher education provision. Hegemony in higher education naturally transferred to the Technical College.

At school level the post-war years were years of expansion and new building. Under the 1944 Education Act the grammar school became a 'controlled' school, run by the local authority, with Staffordshire represented. Reorganisation of the school system was needed, with specialisation for boys, and a competitive house spirit introduced.

The new Act specified that children should be educated according to age, ability and aptitude, and though it demanded knowledge of English and maths, otherwise the curriculum was not

121 Russell's Hall children perform the traditional game, green peas and barley.

specified. Sports were diversified at Dudley when a new swimming pool was opened and hard tennis courts were built. In the early 1960s all politicians were in favour of the expanded grammar schools, including Dudley; there was also a move to expand boundaries to include areas such as Brierley Hill where new grammar schools had been set up by the South Staffordshire authority.

However, by this time the new notion of comprehensive schools had become a major political issue.Purpose-built comprehensives in the West Midlands had been pioneered in Coventry. Recognising that these new institutions would have to be very large, their organisation was broken down into houses, where children could be treated on an individual level and would not feel lost in the vast numbers involved. Neighbouring Staffordshire built a comprehensive school at Tividale, its catchment area ring-fenced so that Tividale children all went to the same school whatever their ability level. By 1966 this issue had to be faced in Dudley, with various forms of amalgamation suggested. The situation was not comparable with Tividale, where there was no previous school in existence other than an all-age Victorian building. Dudley could not start from scratch.

122 Students from the 1976 rag.

A possible scheme to amalgamate the Girls' High School with Dudley Grammar School fell through, and a Sixth Form College was proposed, as was to happen with King Edward's at Stourbridge. The future of Dudley eduation became highly contentious, as in other areas, with two rival parties seeking opposing solutions. The nub of the argument was whether, in the comprehensive age, to settle for all-through schools with sixth forms or for the sixth form college model. All-through schools would be too large, while the sixth form college model would leave 11–16 schools without academically trained staff. There was no satisfactory solution, and for eight years, arguments raged.[6] Finally it was decided to merge Dudley Grammar School, Dudley Girls' High School and Park

123 Flyer for Diploma in Musicianship at Castle View, 1984.

Boys' and Girls' Schools. Further amalgamation took place in 1989 when the Bluecoat School was added to the mix. As with the decisions over the College of Education one effect was to empty students from the centre of Dudley, this time to Stourbridge or further.

In Netherton, a newly designed secondary modern school was built at Hillcrest, and was later followed in other parts of the borough by Holly Hall and Wrens' Nest. All these became comprehensive under the reorganisation. Their architecture was severely 'sixties', with flat roofs and large windows, which made teaching in them on a hot summer's day difficult. There was little external decoration other than some brick patterns of geometric character. When opened the schools seemed airy and light, but over time they lost their freshness and seemed unimaginative. Wrens' Nest, later called Mons Hill, became part of the Technical College, later Dudley College. Catholic children were catered for at secondary level by the new Bishop Milner Secondary School, which opened in 1960. The headmaster, Mr Newton, was highly skilled and very determined, and produced an excellent school with exemplary discipline.

The primary sector also had new schools after the war. Prominent among new buildings was that at Kate's Hill, where the original stone buildings became offices.

The character of the Kate's Hill area was radically altered in the 1970s, with a new school building appearing to be one of the least of the changes. The old 'villagey' feel of Kate's Hill was completely changed, with roads being diverted and many shops demolished. At Netherton the replacement two-storey St Andrew's was abandoned, though the building itself remained in use as a warehouse. New premises for the school were opened on Yew Tree Hill.

Entertainment

Just as the opera house had lost popularity and Dudley entertainment had been led by the cinema, so in turn the cinema was to fade at the development of television. Once again Ned Williams has charted this process. For visitors coming in from Birmingham or Oldbury, their first sight of Dudley town centre was Castle Hill, the entertainment quarter, with the zoo a central feature flanked by the Hippodrome, home of the Christmas pantomime, then the Plaza next to it, and on the other side of the road, the Odeon. Visitors must have thought this a very considerable cluster for a moderate sized town. The Odeon outlasted many Black Country cinemas but eventually closed in 1975, while opposite, the Plaza continued.

In the market place the Criterion operated until 1956 and further up High Street the Gaumont closed in 1961, becoming, as was often the case with Black Country cinemas, a bingo hall. Its fine Wurlitzer organ was sold to a gentleman from Peterborough.[7] Amateur dramatics were often staged by church groups, and Netherton Arts Centre continued to have its stage plays and variety shows. On the whole, the trend towards private viewing at home was unstoppable, and this concern for individual entertainment eventually spread to public houses. The loss of such places as the Brown Lion in the market place was not enormously significant, and just round the corner in Stone Street the Saracen's Head and Albion kept going.

Dudley has no large professional football club of its own, and supporters are mainly divided between Wolverhampton Wanderers, West Bromwich Albion and Aston Villa. But one of the town's greatest heroes is footballer Duncan Edwards. He attended Priory Junior School and began his career with Wolverhampton, but was soon picked up by talent spotters for Manchester United. He played his first serious professional match for United against Cardiff City in 1953, and was becoming a nationally recognised star when the

Manchester team was involved in the fatal Munich air crash of 1958.[8] A statue was erected in the market place to Duncan Edwards on 14 October 1999; there is currently debate about whether its location should be changed. However, it is certain that many more Dudley inhabitants will recognise him, wherever his statue is, than the old gentleman at the other end of Castle Street, Lord Dudley.

Worcestershire County cricket team played a number of their matches each year on the cricket ground north of Birmingham Road which was created over the coal and limestone workings at what was once the Old Park. The ground was set up as long ago as 1865, possibly earlier, but was subject to frequent collapses of the limestone pillars beneath, hardly suspected by the visiting teams at county or club level. Dudley Cricket Club played in the Birmingham League, but the highlights of the season were always the county matches, during which in later days the redoubtable Worcestershire player Don Kenyon could be seen scoring well against such local rivals as Warwickshire. Kenyon was born in Wordsley, then in South Staffordshire, but now part of Dudley. Meanwhile, below the ground the limestone pillars were eroding, and on 25 May 1985 a large hole appeared in the centre of the pitch. The ground became unusable and was closed. No more county matches were played in Dudley. Since then a hotel and other buildings have been erected in this part of the town. Netherton Cricket Club was formed in 1867, with a ground at Lodge Farm. Some thirteen years later the club moved to new premises near St Andrew's Church, where it still remains.

Despite its name, Cradley Heath Speedway had a home ground in Dudley Wood. The club was formed in the late 1940s and competed for five years, when finance forced a closure for six years. The team was famous throughout the Black Country and scored many successes against local and distant rivals. However, the ground was sold in the early 1990s and houses built on the site. A further rather unusual form of entertainment was the annual hop picking, during which local families would leave Dudley for the far side of Worcestershire, or Herefordshire, to help gather in the hop harvest. On the face of it, this was not entertainment, and was indeed hard work, but it was the only holiday many people were able to afford. They travelled to the hop fields in neighbourly groups, in mid-century days from Dudley or Blowers Green stations. Worcetershire and Herefordshire farmers eventually bought machines to do the job, and hop picking died out some time after the Second World War.

Culture and Tourism

The Black Country Museum

Dudley clearly had great potential for tourism, with the castle and zoo being prominent features. This was much enhanced by the development of the Black Country Living Museum, an enormously ambitious project, which depended for its existence on hard work by many people, both before and since its opening. Regional pride in the Black Country was stirred during the decades after the Second World War, as the mining industry finally ended, and as larger local authorities took the place of the small town councils which had been close to people. Though the two halves of the West Midland conurbation, Birmingham and the Black Country, clearly depend vitally on each other, there arose a strong sense that the two should not be blurred together. This movement found expression in the foundation of the Black Country Society, and the newly formed county and later Metropolitan Boroughs, after some encouragement from enthusiasts, decided to support the development of a new museum to preserve the vanishing ethos of the Black Country. A central site was chosen, convenient to all the authorities, at the edge of Dudley, near to the boundary with Tipton, which came under a different local authority. The initial stages of the museum project were supported by the then Director of Libraries and Arts, Alex Wilson. A major impetus was given by the work of Richard Traves, the Dudley Museum Curator. The Musuem Director for many years was Ian Walden.[9]

The site had been worked over many times. It was bounded by the Dudley Canal at its entrance to the limestone caverns, by Tipton Road and the woods of Castle Hill. This had originally been farmland, then a coal mining area, an industrial site, a sewage treatment plant and was now virtually derelict. It covered 26 acres of slightly sloping land with indifferent soil. Into this area were transported buildings about to be demolished all over the Black Country, creating a typical local village with shops, small gardens and 'fodes' (fold-yards originally, then back yards), pubs, a canal bridge and its own transport system with trams running once again on the West Midland narrow gauge, and trolley buses from Walsall and Wolverhampton. This collection and operation took years to develop, and could not have been done without the support of an army of volunteers, some of them members of the Friends of the Black Country Museum, inaugurated in 1970. Over the years, the friends organised fundraising events, researched and lobbied, wrote for the magazine *Contact*, and

124 The Black Country Living Museum attracts many visitors.

made endless suggestions to the professional management. The Earl of Dudley became president, and many of the volunteers were from Dudley, though the membership of the friends included people from throughout the Black Country and Birmingham, as well as far away countries.

Dudley buildings relocated to the museum include St James' School, where children can experience school life as it was in late Victorian times, Emile Doo's the chemist from Netherton, where traditional pharmacy had been retained until after the Second World War, and Darby End Methodist Chapel, where Sunday school anniversaries and Christmas services are still to be encountered. The canal wharf is the original, from which boat trips can be taken into the Dudley hillside. This was the site of Shirt's Mill and the two Dudley pools.

Mushroom Green Chain Shop

The Black Country Society has been instrumental in saving some most valuable features of Black Country history and tradition. One of the most impressive was the rescue of Mushroom Green Chain Shop.[10] The matter was highlighted in 1972, when the Dudley Planning Department raised questions about the future of the then deserted building, which had been in use until 1965. A number of members of the society's Industrial Archaeology Group were determined to save the old workshop, and were informed that the cost of repairs would be £18,000. Preservation was considered to be important, as the chain shop had six hearths, making it an interesting example of a transition from the single-hearth one-family backyard building to the later factory type. It was agreed that voluntary labour might be used to fulfil the project, and this would reduce the cost greatly. The site was bought and careful dismantling took place, revealing the surprising fact that the chain shop had a brick floor, when it had been thought that the floor was earth. By 1977 the restoration of the chain shop was complete, and it came under the aegis of the Black Country Museum.

This splendid effort may indicate ways in which other Dudley features may be retained.

Municipal Expansion

This book has confined content to events within the old Dudley parish, Dudley manor, including the Castle Hill, and a reputed manor at Netherton. These later became Dudley Borough, maintaining the same territorial area as had existed in the Middle Ages. In 1948 a large survey was published, covering the whole of the Birmingham/Black Country district, under the title Conurbation. It listed six county boroughs, eight non-county boroughs and ten urban districts. These authorities were inter-dependent, with roads and rail communication shared, industrial plants woked by a population which did not always live in the area controlling the firms. Administration was inevitably confused and petty arguments among the towns could make the situation chaotic. During the 1960s, central government decided to group such authorities, not ony in the Black Country, but also in other areas of Britain, providing each with an umbrella 'county'. The West Midlands would also add Coventry.

It is beyond the scope of this work to discuss how the new authority worked, but the effect on Dudley was to extend its territory and rebrand it as a metropolitan borough. To the original borough were added Halesowen and Stourbridge boroughs, and, by a two-stage process, Amblecote, Brierley Hill, most of Coseley, and Sedgley. This enormously increased the size of the borough, but not the town centre, since the location of Dudley old town was much to the north of the centres of population. Stourbridge and Halesowen had always had links with Dudley, but their inhabitants did not necessarily consider it their local shopping centre. A most difficult situation for the town centre was the development of the Merry Hill area, taking in land on which Round Oak steelworks had been situated. The effect of this, with the geographical expansion in the borough, was to move the commercial centre of gravity south along the canal to Merry Hill. The full implications of this may not yet have been experienced.

It is difficult to forecast the future of Dudley. Consultation is taking place at the time of writing prior to renewing the market area. The market place no longer hosts a fine hotel or prestigious shops like Marks & Spencers, and commerce in the town centre will probably not return to its previous importance. Nevertheless, most of the borough administration is still in the central area, despite this being far away from the geographical centre. Institutions such as Dudley College bring many students into the centre, and the zoo has its regular visitors. It is not clear that they, or the large number of visitors to the Black Country Living Museum, spend much time or money in Dudley town centre. Efforts have been made to encourage tourism; there is a great deal to see in the enlarged Dudley, with helpful guidance provided on pamphlets available from the art gallery, library and archives, as well as the satellite towns.

In the inevitable re-planning and rebuilding to come during this century, it will surely be important to conserve and enhance the splendid heritage that Dudley has sometimes neglected in the past.

DUDLEY BURGAGES

When this study began, I had high hopes of being able to identify present sites in Dudley town centre with medieval burgage sites. It would, I thought, be theoretically possible to trace the history of each site from at least the sixteenth century to the present day. This could be facilitated by the prolific documentation held at Dudley Archives in the form of lists prepared for the lords of the manor. I also expected to find site-related burgage lists in the borough records.

As I shall explain, there are records of both kinds, some appearing to provide clues to the solutions I was hoping to find. Nevertheless, there appear to be two difficulties: one is that these lists are not quite accurately ordered in the same order that the properties lie within the streets; the other problem is that burgages were sold out of the possession of their previous owner, so that names can change without a surviving record to show what has happened.

As suggested in the text, it is possible that the original burgages were allocated on the site of previously existing furlongs and field strips. This cannot be proved, but the placing of burgages in Market Place opposite each other suggests that this is a tenable theory. In R. Bearman's *The History of an English Borough* (Stroud, 1997) reconstructed plans of the medieval fields at Stratford-on-Avon seem to suggest something similar. This book also traces the changes and developments of the original burgage plots. Another local example dealing briefly with the development of burgage plots is S. Buteux, *Beneath the Bull Ring* (Studley, 2003), which explains how Birmingham plots have been combined and divided over the years.

The earliest mention of a Dudley burgage I have found is in Roper's transcript of a deed of 1446, granting '*uno burgagio et uno curtilagio*' by the lord to John Holyns of Bewdley. A possibly sure foundation is in the Roper transcript of the 1541 list, but this may be a rent roll rather than a burgage list.

(Many plots are specifically called 'burgages', but Jon. Mason pays three half-pence for 'a cottage' and John Combe a penny for 'a house and garden-place late Wintes'.) There are other entries which are clearly not burgages. Part of the original document was missing at transcription.

There seem to be about sixty-five burgages, depending on how we interpret the missing portion and any burgages combined. Hardly any are given a location, though Sir George Throckmorton has one 'at Peselane end' (which end?).

Subsequent lists do try to identify properties which are burgages by adding the letter 'B' or other methods. Perhaps an alternative place to begin is the fragmentary 1686 list which helpfully claims to be a catalogue of the burgages in Dudley. This starts with a property of Mr Tandy, late Mr Bendy (stewards of Lord Dudley) 'by the Lower Church'[St Edmund's] and one 'late Mr Foley's being now a stable at the Over Church'. One of them may be the same as the house which 'standes voide' belonging to Mr Bendy in the 1649 survey. This could be the one at 'Lower Church', where we know there was much destruction in the Civil War. What does 'at' mean? St Edmund's was surrounded by a churchyard which remained clear for many years. Perhaps the burgage was on the opposite side of the road from the church. In the absence of maps, even this location is dubious.

The 1686 list at Dudley Archives suggests that even a 'croft' may be a burgage; George Clement has one 'by ye vicar[age]'. Likewise, John Jenkins has a 'toft'. Perhaps these open spaces once had burgage houses on them. There is what appears to be a useful heading, 'In the High Street', but there are no more headings and the list drifts off to Castle Street at its fragmentary end, without apparently signalling this. (Possibly it did so in a missing piece.) John Smith has 'ye Corner house' and another occupier; Hampton, according to Roper, has a house in Middle Row. Does this mean that Middle Row was part of the original burgage dispensation? Surely not, these properties must have been erected later on the site of temporary stalls.

We can compare the 1686 list with the survey of 1701, a well-organised list. Its properties are numbered and the letter 'B' appears by burgages. There appear to be about sixty-three of them, though some houses are combined, and it is not clear whether these are several burgages or just one. The numbers in the corresponding survey from 1702 given in Hemingway, *An Illustrated Chronicle of Dudley Town* (pp. 146), is assumed by the author to indicate a continuous run similar to modern numbering.

However, it is not certain that this is the case. The surveyor seems to cross over the street at times. For example, in a deed, Robert Senley occupies the house at the corner of Stone Street/High Street (north side of Market Place) at No. 133, but John Bate or Sylvanus Wordsley is known to occupy The Swan (south side) at No. 139. Richard Attwood appears to occupy premises which later became the Barley Mow at No. 149, suggesting that the surveyor has returned to the north side. Francis Gough, at No. 152, is at 'X'[The Cross] according to a court roll, the cross being at the west end of the market. All or part of it may well have remained in front of the Town Hall; something like a pillar seems to be visible in the 1760 drawing. While we can reasonably say that this 1701 and the subsequent 1702 survey locate the properties sequentially, we can't be sure how the surveyor moves from side to side of the street. The same is unfortunately true of later residents' lists.

The document of 1703/04 labelled 'A List of Burgages in Dudley as appeareth from the court rolls there' uses the same numbers as the 1701 and 1702 surveys, though a few proprietors have changed. A feature of the list which does not occur in the others is that a small number of burgages have fractions attached which seem to imply that in some cases not all of the property in question is regarded as a burgage. Thus Mrs Willetts of Hall Street has the fraction 'five sixths' by the side of her number '4', and John Winshurst of Castle Street has 'four fifths'. John Shaw of the Cock has 'five sixths' and John Payton of Hall Street 'three quarters'. This feature may be due to division of inheritance, per- haps, or – more interestingly – division or extension of the property.

These surveys are quite good at labelling the streets. In 1701, High Street includes Queen's Cross and The Farthings at the west end, then moves along High Street to modern Stafford Street, diverting to the north for John Wordley's windmill. There are other properties in the fields here. One house is known to stretch to Back Lane (King Street?), and the division created by the houses in Middle Row is not observed, so that some properties may be in Queen Street. However, there is separate entry in 1701 for Back Lane, this time apparently meaning Queen Street (Middle Row only, not the north side). Four of these houses are marked as burgages. Castle Street harbours a number of burgages, and there are also some in Hall Street, Hampton Lane, New Street (one only) and Stoney Lane, but there are no burgages in Vicaridge Lane (Birmingham Street), Sheep Fair (Priory Street) or Fisher's Lane. This emphasises the prob- ability that most or all burgages were initially on High Street, Hall Street and Wolverhampton Street.

It is hardly necessary to say that there were no burgages in the outlying areas such as Netherton or Woodside. The aim was to solidify and enrich the town, and this is what happened. Throughout the years until 1791 there were borough courts and manor courts, but it is clear that not all who lived in the borough were burgesses, though it seems that only burgesses could serve on the borough court. Deeds show that burgages were sold. The 1722 residents' list gives only nine burgages in High Street, two in Hampton Lane, and one each in Stoney Lane and Hall Street, though it is defective. In 1763 there are twenty-two, one being added in pencil. Possibly the manor had lost count of what the borough administration was doing. A list ascribed to Mr Bate, dated around 1780 in the archives, but possibly from about 1770, gives forty burgesses (DE 3; 3?3, box 24, bundle 1) of whom fifteen can be securely located in High Street (confusingly called Queen Street in some documents) or Castle Street. But one, Richard Timmins, is located at Skirts Mill (the castle mill on the site of the Black Country Museum). One burgess can be traced to Stoney Lane and one, Benjamin Pickrill, in Hall Street. This last is interesting, as Richard Pickrell was the only burgess in Hall Street in the 1722 list. The 'suit roll' of 1784 gives the number of burgesses in High Street/Queen Street as thirty-four. Hall Street contained three, but there do not seem to be any more.

Another source of information about burgesses is the series of court rolls. Burgesses did not pay such heavy fines (equal to taxes) for their notional infringements on borough regulations. It is possible that borough juries may have been made up of burgesses only, but more research would be needed to assert this. Burgesses paid 'black bills' when they died; these are mentioned in the rolls, but I have not come across any copies. The 1784 suit roll seems to be the last, continuing to 1789 before presumably the town commissioners superseded this distinction. Locating the burgages has proved a slippery exercise, but these medieval parcels of land still exert their influence on the shape of holdings in High Street and Castle Street.

ABBREVIATIONS AND REFERENCES

BCM   *Blackcountryman* magazine
BRL   Birmingham Reference Library
C & H   Chandler and Hannah, *Dudley, as it was and as it is*
DA   Dudley Archives
SRO   Staffordshire Record Office
WHC   Worcester History Centre
WRO   Worcester Record Office
WSL   William Salt Library, Stafford
Full details of abbreviated titles can be found in the Bibliography.

Chapter 1

1. Plot, *Natural History of Staffordshire*, Chapter 5
2. Roper, Transcripts (1960) p. 5
3. Hemingway, *Barony*, p. 16
4. Hemingway, *Barony*, p. 120; C & H, Chapter 2
5. Sandwell Priory was dissolved in 1526. The Sandwell land has proved impossible to locate, though Monks' Field in Netherton is a possible candidate.
6. C & H, p. 59
7. The most important archaeological work on the priory was carried out by C.A.R. Radford in 1939 and an account appeared in *The Antiquaries Journal Vol XX*
   Radford's notes were destroyed in the Second World War
   See also Hemingway, *Priory*, p. 56, and Appendix, pp. 71–8 for details of the encaustic tiles

Chapter 2

1. Mander & Tildesley, *Wolverhampton*, p. 29
2. Barrow, W., 'Birmingham Markets and Fairs' in cited journal, copy in BRL; C & H, pp. 130–1
3. Burman, *Stratford-on-Avon*, Chapter 3

4   Hemingway, *Town and Manor*, p. 63

5   Hackwood, *Sedgley Researches*; Guttery, *Pensnett Chase*, p. 8

6   Hemingway, *Town and Manor*, pp. 51–3

7   Hemingway, *Priory*, Chapter 6

8   Hemingway, *Castle*, pp. 41ff

9   Worcestershire Historical Society, transcribed F.J. Eld, 1895; WSL, 'Records of Dudley' transcript of Lay Subsidies in National Archive E 179/200/137

10 Razi, *Life and Death*, based on Halesowen court rolls, BRL

11 *Sedgley Resources*, p. 17

12 WSL, 'Records of Dudley' vol. 3, p. 65

13 C & H, Plate 90

14 Deeds, transcribed Roper, p. 3, 1 April 1441

15 Deeds, transcribed Roper, p. 6, December 1473

16 Tilley, St Edmund's

17 Hemingway, Priory, p. 46

18 *See* Illustration 16 – an unusual tile from the priory. Hemingway, *Priory*, pp. 71–8, has an excellent section on these tiles, incorporating material from the 1982 archaeological project

Chapter 3

1   Mander, G.P. and Tildesley, *A History of Wolverhampon* (Wolverhampton, 1960), p. 28

2   Copy in BRL

3   *See* Appendix

4   Hemingway, *Town and Manor*, pp. 63–4

5   Extent quoted Hemingway, *Town and Manor*, pp. 42–3, 51; Hackwood, *Sedgley Researches*, p. 10

6   Hemingway, *Town and Manor*, pp. 51–3, 64

7   Hemingway, *Priory*, p. 36

8   C & H, pp. 21–4; Hemingway, *Castle*, pp. 41–5

9   Razi, Z, *Life, Marriage and Death in a Medieval Parish* (Cambridge, 1980).

10 Hackwood, *Sedgley Researches*, p. 17

11 'Records of Dudley', vol. 3, p. 65

12 C & H, Plate 90 facing p. 132

13 Deeds transcribed Roper WRO 5/08 (5949), p. 3

14 Deeds transcribed Roper, p. 4

15 Deeds transcribed Roper, p. 6

16 Tilley, *St Edmund's*, p. 4

17 Hemingway, *Priory*, p. 46

18 Hemingway, *Priory*, p. 47

19 Most of Netherton was part of Pensnett Chase, but Records of Dudley, vol. 2, p.70 is an inquisitio post-mortem from 1532 which mentions a messuage 'called Newerton'

20 Will of John Robinson, WHC
21 Lease 6 April 1592, transcribed by Roper DA 18/12
22 DA 6/5 transcribed by Roper

Chapter 4

1 Deeds transcribed Roper WRO 5/08 (5949) p. 73, 10 June 1613; C & H, p. 42
2 Deeds transcribed Roper, p. 74, 23 May 1614
3 Peacock, *The Seventeenth Century Foleys*, p. 11
4 Deeds transcribed Roper, pp. 154–160
5 Watson & Temple, *Dudley Grammar School*, Chapter 2
6 Churchwardens' Book, transcribed Roper
7 Manor court roll, 1640. Typescript copy at Dudley Archives
8 C & H, p. 42; Guttery, *Civil War*, Chapter 31; Hemingway, *Castle*, pp. 95ff
9 Guttery, *Civil War*, pp. 123–4
10 Shepherd, revised Roper, Parish Church of St Thomas, p. 9
11 Transcribed Roper, DA 19/36
12 Roper, *The Seventeenth Century Town*, p. 17, ascribing the date to a lost parish book quoted by Blocksidge
13 Roper (transcribed) Churchwardens' Book
14 *Ibid.*, p. 102
15 Register of Messiah Baptist Church, Netherton
16 Microfilm copies at Worcester History Centre, Reel 3 etc., Hemingway prints Michaelmas 1664, pp. 130ff; Lady Day 1671 is in WSL Records of Dudley
17 Deeds transcribed Roper, p. 126
18 Churchwardens' Presentments at Bishop's Visitation 1674, WRO BA 2289/7, 807
19 *Ibid.*, 1676
20 *Ibid.*, 1682
21 Deeds transcribed Roper, p. 126
22 *Ibid.*, p. 130
23 *Ibid.*, p. 132
24 *Ibid.*, p. 135
25 *Ibid.*, p. 135
26 Plot, pp. 141–2
27 Court, pp. 154–5
28 *Ibid.*, pp. 155-8
29 *Ibid.*, pp. 156-8
30 Plot, p. 408
31 *Ibid.*, pp. 39ff
32 Churchwarden's Presentments, WRO, 1682 no day or month
33 *Ibid.*, 19 July 1687

34 *Ibid.*, 5 November 1699
35 Accounts of Dudley Horse Fair, 1702–8, DA
36 WSL, 'Records of Dudley', transcript of National Archives C5/553/6, 12 January 1683

Chapter 5

1 WRO Foley Scrapbook, vol. 4, p. 293; DA, DE 3. Hemingway prints the 1702 list in town, pp. 145ff
2 The Back Lane, later Queen Street, begins about No. 144. Richard Attwood's house (No. 149) probably occupies the site of the public house known in the 1960s as The Barley Mow
3 WRO BA 75, 705 – 18/7
4 WRO Confirmation Candidates
5 DA, DE 3 1/26ff
6 DA , DE 3, borough court, 1702
7 DA, DE 3, borough court, 4 October 1703
8 Will of Hugh Dixon, microfilm, 4 August 1721, WHC
9 Will of Christopher Braznell, 8 March 1705, WHC
10 Will of Catherine Bond, 24 June 1709, WHC
11 Will of Edward Blunn als Wright, 22 August 1720, WHC
12 Will of Oliver Shaw the Elder, DA, Town Clerk's Deeds, I 22
13 Dudley Suit roll 1726–32, DA, DE 3
14 WRO Parochial Box (by permission of Worcester Diocesan Registry)
15 National Archive, Wills, 21 May 1733
16 C & H, p. 138
17 WRO Ref. 3449
18 BRL Holte manuscripts, 190
19 The so-called Court Map
20 DA, DE Cottage Rents and court roll 1710
21 Whiffen, M., *Stuart and Georgian Churches*, p. 37
22 Tilley, *St Edmund's*
23 DA, Court Map, 329C
24 Ellis, *Glassmakers*, pp. 286–7
25 Ellis, *Glassmakers*, p. 288
26 Additional information and plan in Hemingway, *Town and Manor*, pp. 177–9
27 DA, court roll, Foreign June 1711
28 WRO, Foley Scrapbook, with cutting of *Worcester Journal*, 3 November 1742 and list of Dudley residents
29 Hemingway, *Castle*, pp. 146–7
30 C & H, pp. 46, 51

Chapter 6

1   *See* illustration No. 39
2   Original in Dudley Art Gallery
3   WRO BA 73 705.15
4   DA, DE 4 1/1/3
5   DA, DE 3 3/1/28
6   DA, DE 4 5, spine marked ED 7240
7   DA, 892A
8   Hadfield, *Canals of the West Midlands*, pp. 75ff
9   *Ibid.*, p. 77
10 *Ibid.*, p. 78
11 C & H, p. 138
12 DA, DE 4 1/7
13 DA, Town Commissioners' Minute Book; C & H, Chapter 13
14 C & H, p. 153
15 DA, Town Commissioners' Minute Book
16 Prudence Caddick had been offending since at least 1782 (court rolls)
17 DA, Town Commissioners' Minute Book, 7 September 1797
18 SRO D 695 11/12/78
19 Priory illustrations in Hemingway, *Priory*, pp. 83–7
20 Hemingway, *Priory*, pp. 83–7
21 *Ibid.*, pp. 83–7
22 DA, 892
23 Wesley Chapel Centenery Souvenir, pp. 6–7
24 *Our Goodly Heritage*, p. 1
25 *Ibid.*, p. 3
26 *Old Non-Parochial Registers of Dudley*, Copy in BRL
27 *Ibid.*
28 Hemingway, *Town and Manor*, p. 165
29 DA , Residents' list 1763ff
30 *Old Non-Parochial Registers of Dudley*, p. 35
31 BRL 356370, Rollason, A., Proofs for articles in the *Dudley Herald*, p. 30

Chapter 7

1   WRO, St Thomas' Parochial Box
2   DA, St Thomas' Vestry Minute book, Accession 6750
3   This was probably in his role as Free School Master
4   DA St Thomas' Vestry Minute Book gives 22 October as a date for payment,
    but Shepherd (revised Roper) says 25 October
5   Shepherd, p. 12; Whiffen, *Stuart and Georgian Churches*, p. 81
6   Whiffen, *Stuart and Georgian Churches*, p. 81

7 WHC, Land Tax microfilm reel 11, pp. 18ff
8 DA , Dudley Estate revised Valuations 1800–01, old number 620, Box 20
9 WHC, 1807 Land Tax
10 St Thomas' Parish Order Book, copy Dudley Public Library
11 *See* illustrations Nos 53 to 55
12 DA, Town Clerk's Deeds, I 21
13 DA, DE 4, 'Survey Parish of Dudley 1840'
14 *Ibid.*
15 Quoted in Register of the Messiah Baptist Chapel, Netherton
16 St Thomas' Parish Order Book
17 *A Brief History of Netherton*, p. 35
18 St Thomas' Parish Order Book
19 C & H, p. 77
20 Elwell, *Black Country Essays and Reviews*, p. 32
21 C & H, p. 109
22 C & H, p. 110
23 Lewis' *Topographical Dictionary*, pp. 77–8
24 C & H, pp. 166–7
25 Homer, *The Story of Netherton*
26 C & H, p. 170
27 *Ibid.*, p. 152
28 Copies of Treasure's Map in DA and BRL
29 DA Inclosure Map
30 *Our Goodly Heritage*, pp. 7ff
31 *Wesley Chapel, Dudley,* pp. 8, 11
32 *Wesley Chapel, Dudley*, p. 17
33 Ellis, Glassmakers, Chapter 32
34 WHC, 1807 Land Tax. Badger memorial tablet, St Edmund's
35 WHC, 1807 Land Tax
36 *BCM*, vol. 42
37 *BCM*, vol. 42, no. 2
38 Compare 1787 survey with Land Tax 1807
39 Details of No. 60 High Street in Rollason, 'Printers Proofs'
40 Rollason, 'Printers Proofs'
41 Croft and Lewis, p. 3

Chapter 8

1 Barnsby, p. 32
2 Hemingway, *Town and Manor*, p. 209
3 Census available on CD Rom or on microfilm at DA and WRO
4 For more detail about the nail trade see Davies and Hyde, Chapter 6
5 Hemingway, *Town and Manor*, p. 244; Barnsby, pp. 35ff

6   C & H, pp. 71, 73, 77–80
7   Hemingway, *Town and Manor*, p. 272; *Parish Church of St Thomas*, p. 13
8   *Alpha to Omega*, pp. 8–9
9   *Ibid.*, p. 10
10 Parish Register transcribed by Margaret Bates
11 Christiansen, Chapter 4
12 Christiansen, pp. 122ff
13 Printed copies of Lees' report are in DA and Dudley Library
14 C & H., pp. 167, 183
15 Kingswinford, however, was in Stourbridge Union
16 Davies and Hyde, pp. 77–8
17 Hemingway, *Town and Manor*, p. 215
18 *Ibid.*, p. 301

Chapter 9

1   C & H., Chapter 14
2   Kelly's Directory 1869
3   Ellis, G., *Glassmakers*, pp. 354, 355, 357
4   Elwell, *Black Country Essays and Reviews*, pp. 58ff
5   *BCM*, vol. 18, no. 2, p. 15
6   This section based on Dr Ballard's Report of 1874
7   *Kelly's Directory* 1878
8   A.T.C. and E.M. Lavender in *BCM*, vol.19, no. 3, pp. 54ff
9   This section is mainly based on Webb, J.S., *Black Country Tramways*
10 Webb, vol. 1, p. 109
11 *Contact* magazine, no. 72, p. 7
12 Hadfield, *Canals of the West Midlands*, p. 260
13 *Ibid.*, p. 263
14 A Brief Intimate Story of Netherton, p. 45
15 *Wesley Chapel, Dudley*, p. 23
16 *Ibid.*, p. 43
17 *Our Goodly Heritage*, p. 10
18 *Alpha to Omega*, Chapter 2
19 *Netherton, Edward I to Edward VIII*, p. 29
20 *Centenary of Dudley Art Gallery*, etc. p. 2
21 C & H, pp. 113–4, 188
22 *History of Netherton C of E School*, pp. 8–9
23 Raybould, Dudley Grammar School, *BCM*, vol. 42, no. 4, p. 6

Chapter 10

1   *Kelly's Directory* 1900

2 Hemingway, *Town and Manor*, p. 303
3 *BCM*, vol. 16, no. 1, p. 14
4 Brett Young, *The Black Diamond*
5 Radmore, *Dudley Art Gallery*, p. 8
6 *Ibid.*, p. 13
7 Bradshaw's Railway Guide, 1910
8 Webb, vol. 1, p. 188
9 *BCM*, vol. 17, no. 2
10 Raybould, *Economic Emergence of the Black Country*, Chapter 6
11 OS Map, 1902
12 Detail in this section is based on Ellis, *Glassmakers*
13 Postcard unknown provenance, copy in Dudley Archives
14 Clare, Dudley, p. 104
15 Watson, revised Temple, *Dudley Grammar School*
16 *History of Netherton C of E School*, p. 12
17 Hemingway, *Town and Manor*, p. 320
18 *Ibid.*, pp. 346ff
19 *BCM*, vol. 21, no. 3, p. 50
20 *BCM*, vol. 17, no. 4, p. 12

Chapter 11

1 An example of the iron houses is at the Black Country Living Museum
2 Webb, vol. 2, p. 43
3 *Ibid.*, p. 44
4 *Ibid.*, p. 51
5 Bradshaw's Railway Timetable, 1922
6 *BCM*, vol. 18, no. 3, pp. 16ff
7 Williams, *Cinemas*, p. 143
8 Hemingway, *Town and Manor*, p. 328
9 Reeves (no page numbers) who also gives many other fascinating details
10 Hemingway, *Town and Manor*, p. 289
11 Fletcher, *Netherton*
12 *BCM*, vol. 17, no. 2, p. 18
13 C & H, plates 95–7
14 Gough, *Black Country Stories*
15 *BCM*, vol. 19, no. 4, p. 24
16 *BCM*, vol. 17, no. 4, p. 18
17 Wesley Church Diary, 1935
18 *Our Goodly Heritage*, p. 18
19 *Alpha to Omega*, p. 26
20 Hemingway, *Town and Manor*, p. 344
21 W. Allen, *The Black Country*, p. 22

22 *Golden Years of Dudley*, pp. 80ff
23 Williams, *Dudley and Netherton Remembered*, p. 60
24 Raybould in *BCM*, vol. 43, no. 1, p. 9
25 Kelly's 1936 *Directory of Worcestershire*, from which the ensuing details are taken
26 Hemingway, *Town and Manor*, p. 351
27 *Ibid.*, p. 347
28 Hemingway, *Priory*, p. 72

Chapter 12

1 *Dudley Living Memories*, p. 58
2 *Ibid.*, p. 64
3 Details of the progress of the Technical College are from *Golden Years of Dudley*, pp. 80ff
4 *Golden Years of Dudley*, pp. 80ff
5 Details concerning Dudley College of Education and The Polytechnic, Wolverhampton are from the author's memory
6 *BCM*, vol. 43, no. 3, pp. 6ff
7 Williams, *Dudley Rediscovered*, p. 144
8 Hemingway, *Town and Manor*, pp. 373–4
9 *Contact* magazine
10 This paragraph is based on Moss, *Mushroom Green Chain Shop*, especially pp. 8ff

BIBLIOGRAPHY

Manuscript and Other Archive Material

Court Map of Dudley, DA 329C (date discussed in text)

Churchwardens' Presentments, 1669ff, WRO 807; 2289/7

Deeds, The Level etc., SRO D 695/1/12/78 and 83

Deeds, mainly Payton and Badley, WRO 705 BA 72

Deeds, BRL Lee Crowder 813,815B, Holte 190, Homer 124 (Birmingham Archives)

Deeds, Russell's Hall etc., WRO 705.122

Dudley Burgess Lists; 1541 transcribed by J.S. Roper; October 1686 (damaged, MS); 1703–4 (MS); 'Mr Bates' list (c.1772?) DA DE 3

Dudley Castle Archaeological Project 1983–5 (typescript) (Dudley Library)

Dudley court rolls, various dates, MS DA DE 3

Dudley Deeds, transcribed by J.S. Roper (typescript), WRO 5949

Dudley Estate Rentals: 1704–6, 1720/3 (cottage rents),1768 (cottages), 1779 etc., DA DE 4 1/1/14 etc.

Dudley Land Tax, various years (MS; microfilm at Worcs History Centre)

Dudley Parish Map, catalogued as c.1787 (however, this plan was made before the Pensnett Chase enclosure, and may be about 1782–1784. It is inaccurate, being based on the earlier Court Map), DA 892A

Dudley Parish Order Book, 1821–1856, transcribed by A.J. Ware (Dudley Library)

Dudley Parish Survey for Poor Relief, c. 1787 (later than the foregoing map, since this includes Inclosure entries), DA 892

Dudley Probate Inventories, 1544–1603, transcribed J.S. Roper, typescript (1965)

Dudley St Thomas' and St Edmund's Parish Registers, microfilm at DA and WHC, transcribed printed copy to seventeenth century, copies at DA, BRL (Staffs Register Society)

Dudley Suit Rolls (lists of 'resiants' made for the manor stewards; 1699 is not in place order; later lists, 1726 etc., are approximately street by street), DA DE 3

Dudley Town Clerk's Deeds (mainly collected as a result of town centre redevelopment), DA

Dudley Town Commissioners' Minute Book, 1791ff (no accession number), DA

[Dudley Transcriptions] Dudley Burgage List, etc., transcribed by J.S. Roper (typescript, 1960), copies at Dudley Library

Dudley Wood Enclosure Award, large bound volume; spine ED 7240, DA DE 4/5

Foley Scrapbook vol. 4, p. 393, includes a survey of the town of Dudley 1701, WRO 3762. (A copy of the manor survey may exist, and appears to be mentioned in *Register of Messiah Baptist Church, Netherton* (copy in BRL), without reference. Unsuccessful search has been made at WRO, but the survey may still be there.)

Hearth Taxes, 1662 etc., microfilm WHC

Home Office Censuses, 1841, 1851 ff, available on microfilm and CD

Map of the Parish of Dudley surveyed by Brettell 1824–5 (presumably this is the Poor Rate map agreed in the Parish Order Book on 15 July 1824), DA 901A

Parochial Box (permission acquired from Worcs Diocesan Registry), WRO 3015

Records of Dudley (3 vols), transcribed J.S. Roper, William Salt Library, Stafford, 193/1/81 (National Archives)

Rollason, A.A., Articles in the *Dudley Herald*, in 'Printers' Proofs and MS for A.A. Rollason's articles, BRL 356370

St Thomas' Churchwardens' Book, transcribed J.S. Roper, 1981, DA

Survey Parish of Dudley 1840 (accompanying DA 901A – it is very unlikely that 1840 is the correct date, though pencil additions may be much later than the original), DA DE 4

Wills, WRO and microfilm at WHC

Vestry Minute Book, 1804– *c.* 1817, bound MS volume, DA 6750

Printed Books and Pamphlets

Allen, W., *The Black Country* (London, 1947)

Barnsby, G.J., *The Dudley Working Class Movement, 1750 to 1860* (Dudley, 1967)

Blockside, E., *An Illustrated Guide to Dudley Castle and Priory* (Dudley, 1898)

Chandler, G., and Hannah, I.C., *Dudley as it was and as it is Today* (London, 1949)

Christiansen, R., *A Regional History of the Railways of Great Britain*, vol. 7, The West Midlands (Newton Abbot, 1973)

Clare, D., *Images of England: Dudley* (Stroud, 2005)

Collins, P., *Dudley, Living Memories* (Salisbury, 2005)

Crofts, P.H. and Lewis, D.C., *The History of Netherton C of E Middle School, 1836– 1986* (Dudley, ND)

Crossley Book Publishing, *Nostalgic Dudley,*(Halifax, 1998)

Davies, S.J., Wesley Chapel, *Dudley: A Centenary Souvenir* (Dudley, 1929).

Davies, V.L. and Hyde, H., *Dudley and the Black Country, 1760 to 1860* (Dudley, 1970)

Dent, R.K. and Hill, J., *Historic Staffordshire* (Birmingham, 1896)

Elliott, D., *Our Goodly Heritage; Dudley Baptist Church 1772–1972* (no publisher given, printed Wolverhampton)

Ellis, J., *Glassmakers of Stourbridge and Dudley, 1612–2002* (Harrogate, 2002)

Elwell, C.J.L., *Black Country Essays and Reviews* (Kingswinford, 1998)

Fletcher, M.W.H., *Netherton, Edward I to Edward VIII* (Dudley, 1949)

Guttery, D.R., *From Domesday to Doomsday: Some Chapters from the History of Kingswinford* (Brierley Hill, 1947)
_____ *The Story of Pensnett Chase* (Brierley Hill, 1950)
Hackwood, F.W., *Sedgley Researches* (Dudley, 1898)
Hadfield, C., *Canals of the West Midlands* (New York, 1966)
Harris,W., *Rambles around Dudley Castle* (Halesowen, 1845)
Hemingway, J., *An Illustrated Chronicle of Dudley Town and Manor* (Dudley, 2009)
_____ *An Illustrated Chronicle of the Castle and Barony of Dudley* (Dudley, 2006)
_____ *An Illustrated Chronicle of the Cluniac Priory of St James, Dudley* (Dudley, 2005)
Homer, L.E., *A Brief Intimate Story of Netherton* (Netherton, 1948)
Moss, R., *Mushroom Green Chain Shop* (Kingswinford, 2001)
Nash, T., *Collections for the History of Worcestershire* (Oxford, 1798)
Parsons, H., *Murder and Mystery in the Black Country* (London, 1989)
Peacock, R., *The 17th Century Foleys* (Kingswinford, 2011)
Pigot & Co., *Commmercial Directory, Staffordshire* (London, 1835)
Plot, R., *The Natural History of Staffordshire* (Oxford, 1686)
Radmore, D., *Dudley as it was…* (Lancashire, 1977)
Raybould, T.J., *The Economic Emergence of the Black Country* (Newton Abbot, 1973)
Reeves, D., *The' was onny one an' th' w' be another* (Dudley, 1990)
Roper, J.S., *Dudley, the Medieval Town* (Dudley, 1962)
_____ *Dudley: The 17th Century Town* (Dudley, 1965)
_____ *The Story of the Parish Church of St Thomas, Dudley* (Cheltenham, 1979)
_____ *A History of Russell's Hall*, Dudley (Dudley, 1973)
School of Art & Free Library, *Dudley Art Gallery* (Dudley, 1984)
Shepherd, A.P. revised Roper, J.S., *The Story of the Parish Church of St Thomas, Dudley* (Cheltenham, 1929)
Smith, H.G. and J. Greaves, *Alpha to Omega* (Dudley, 1978)
Stenson, J.R., 'Under Boots Clock' (Sedgley, 1996)
Stokes, G., ed., *Dud Dudley's Metallum Martis* (Dudley, 2004, reprinting 1854 ed.)
Tilley, R., *St Edmund's Church, Dudley* (?Dudley, 1983)
True North Books Ltd.,*Golden Years of Dudley* (Halifax, 2002)
Twamley, C., *History of Dudley Castle and Priory* (London, 1857)
West Midland Group, *Conurbation* (London, 1948)
Whiffen, M., *Stuart and Georgian Churches Outside London* (London, 1947–8)
Williams, N., *Cinemas of The Black Country* (Wolverhampton, 1982)
_____ *Dudley and Netherton Remembered* (Stroud, 2010)
_____ *Dudley Rediscovered* (Wolverhampton, 2008)
Directories: Holden 1816–7; Lewis, S., *Worcestershire General and Commercial Directory*, 1820; Pigot 1835; Kelly 1860; Kelly 1869; Kelly 1900: Kelly

(Worcestershire) 1936

Illustration Sourcing

Blocksidge, E., *Illustrated Guide to Dudley Castle*: 11, 14, 15, 17–20, 95
Braun, *The English Castle* (1936), photo ascribed to Midland Air Services: 21
Dent, R.K. and J. Hill: 67, 68
Eagle magazine: 122, 123
Kelly's Directories: 97, 100
Nash, T., *Worcestershire*: 49, 50
Newman College Resouces: 31, 60
Plot, R., *History of Staffordshire*: 26
Welsey Church Memorial Souvenir: 64, 65, 88, 89, 90
Young, F.B., *Black Diamond* (title page): 91

All other illustrations submitted by author. Any acknowledgement omitted or copyright inadvertently infringed will be duly remedied in any future edition.

INDEX